Living
without EW

The Crash of the
Post-Ewing Knicks

Marc Berman

ALBION PRESS
Tampa, Florida

A Cataloging-in-Publication record is available from the Library of Congress.

ISBN 09709170-8-2

Photos by Charles Wenzelberg.

Interior design and typesetting by Sue Knopf, Graffolio

Published by Albion Press, Tampa, Florida.

Printed in Canada.

To my lovely wife and editor, Linda,
my beautiful kids, Matthew and Stephanie,
and the families who lost loved ones
in the World Trade Center.

Contents

Acknowledgments

This book wouldn't have been possible without Greg Gallo, sports editor of *The New York Post*. In 1999, Gallo pried me from my beloved New York Islanders beat and challenged me to cover the Knicks because he wanted my words in a more prominent spot in the newspaper.

Most reporters/authors cite their bosses in these silly things to thank them for the time off they provided to do a book project. Not so here. Gallo never gave me a day off to work on this book nor would I ask him for one. My contributions to the next day's *Post* and our faithful Knick readers were as important as any book. Gallo is why *The Post* has the most aggressive sports section in the country.

Thanks to everyone from the Knicks during this bizarre season: the players, management, PR staff, training staff, coaching staff and especially Jeff Van Gundy, who doesn't realize how fascinating a character he is and gives us journalists plenty to work with. I was given no special access for this book and some of the recreated behind-the-scenes dialogue in this book was pieced together through interviews with members of the Knicks family.

The help I got from executives from around the league was invaluable. A special thank you to Seattle president Wally Walker, Orlando GM John Gabriel, Raptors GM Glen Grunwald, Atlanta GM Pete Babcock, Bucks GM Ernie Grunfeld, Bucks assistant GM Ed Tapscott, Dallas GM/coach Don Nelson, Mavericks assistant Donn Nelson, Pistons president Joe Dumars, Spurs coach/president Gregg Popovich, Grizzlies president Dick Versace, Jazz GM Kevin O'Connor and Jazz director of player personnel, Dave Fredman. Sonic publicists Robyn Jamilosa and Marc Moquin were vital all season.

Kudos to publicists around the league: Toronto's Jim LaBumbard, the Rockets' Tim Frank, the Heat's Rob Wilson and Tim Donovan, the Nets' Gary Sussman and Aaron Harris, the Warriors' Raymond Ridder, the Blazers' Sue Carpenter and the Magic's Joel Glass. Agents Robert Gist and George Bass and business manager Rick Kaplan were always there to help.

ACKNOWLEDGMENTS

There is no nicer group of guys than the six other writers who were on the Knicks' beat last season. Their insights and friendship through this turbulent season will always be cherished. The roll call includes Newsday's Damon Hack, *The Star-Ledger's* Dave D'Alessandro, *The Daily News'* Frank Isola, *The New York Times'* Chris Broussard, the *Westchester Journal-News'* Mike Dougherty, and the *Bergen Record's* John Brennan. Chris Sheridan, the AP's national basketball writer, and MSG Network producer Howie Singer were also invaluable.

Thanks for the help from my *Post* writing brethren: Peter Vecsey, who has more sources in the industry than should be allowed; Kevin Kernan, who writes the toughest column on the Knicks in New York; and Fred Kerber, Brian Lewis and Paul Schwartz, who helped me cover the locker rooms like a blanket. And kudos to *The Post's* assistant sports editor Dick Klayman, whose relaxed demeanor is the perfect complement to Gallo's fire, and *The Post's* night desk, ruled by Pat Hannigan and Dave Blezow, whose back page creations are still one of the best things going in sports journalism. Also, thanks to *Post* librarian Laura Harris for access to my clips.

And, finally, thanks to the book's editor, Dave Rosenbaum of Albion Press. Remembering my work in another lifetime in the Albany-Troy area, he recommended me for this project to publisher Lonnie Herman. Rosenbaum, who wrote a must-read hard-hitter about the championship Marlins a few years back, took great care in ensuring the quality of the narrative.

Oh, and thanks to Patrick Ewing for being Patrick Ewing.

Prologue

Troy Crooms climbed through the kitchen window of the big, beige house at 141 Miller Road. All of the other entrances were shut. He opened a drawer and took out a kitchen knife. It was 3:30 in the morning.

Crooms, a 28-year-old who grew up inside the hardscrabble Hartford, Connecticut, projects, had never been able to end his relationships with women gracefully. As a child, he lived with one relative after another. As a teenager, crack cocaine was his companion. He was in and out of jail. While attending high school sporadically, Crooms drove his then-girlfriend to a Motel Six after she broke up with him. Crooms beat her up and used scissors to cut her shoulder-length hair into a short Afro.

"No other boys will like you if I cut your hair," Crooms told her. He was arrested and received one year in prison for his crime.

That was 10 years ago. Now it was the morning of April 23, 2001. Crooms had been released from prison on December 29 after spending five months for passing counterfeit bills in Bristol, Connecticut. He had been dating Monica Camby since February. She was a real catch, 21 years old with a rich, famous brother. Monica, like Crooms, had grown up in the Hartford projects at Bellevue Square in the dangerous North End.

"She liked the bad boys," Crooms' cousin told the *Hartford Courant.*

Monica's brother, Marcus Camby, was a star center for the New York Knicks. The night before, in Game 1 of the playoffs at Madison Square Garden, Marcus had played heroically, coming back from a 10-day lay-off after injuring his hip to grab 18 rebounds in a victory over the Toronto Raptors. Monica had watched the game with her mother, Janice, and her older sister, Mia, in their five-bedroom, four-bath Colonial in upscale South Windsor, 20 minutes from the Bellevue Projects. Marcus had spent $462,000 to buy the place for his mother in 1996 after he joined the NBA as the second pick overall in the draft and signed a three-year, $8.6 million contract, rescuing his family from the drug-torn projects.

After the game, Monica and Crooms had argued on the telephone for two hours. She had been trying to break up with him for a week. Finally, Monica told Crooms she wanted to stop seeing him completely.

"You act like you can't get it," Crooms shouted. It was a threat, but Monica didn't pick it up at the time. She ended the argument by hanging up on Crooms at about midnight.

Three hours later, Crooms, clutching a knife, walked up the stairs of the house to Monica's bedroom on the second floor. He walked in, jumped onto her bed, wrapped his hands around her throat, and started choking her in the dark. He placed the knife flat against her cheek and put his fingers into her mouth.

"I have a gun and a knife," he threatened. "I'll kill you."

Each time Monica tried to break free, she slit her hands on the knife. She cut her forehead on the blade when she broke free to run to the bathroom. Crooms followed and tackled her to the floor. Monica reached out, grabbed a lamp and tried to strike Crooms, but he muscled it out of her grip.

The house alarm went off. In the next room, Mia quietly dialed 911 on a cell phone. Shortly afterward, Crooms looked out the window and saw two police cruisers.

Officer John Bond of the South Windsor Police Department entered through the garage door, using a code provided by Mia during her phone call. Officer Bond heard a scream coming from the second floor. He climbed the stairs and moved toward the bedroom door. It was slightly ajar. Looking inside, he faintly made out that the bed sheets were soaked in blood. He took out his gun, raised it to the ready position and pushed the door open with his foot. Crooms was standing behind Monica with both arms wrapped around her upper torso and a knife pointed at her throat.

■ ■ ■

At 4:15 that morning, a ringing phone shook Marcus Camby out of his sleep at his home in Westchester.

"You need to put on clothes and come to the house right now, Marcus," said Chooey, Mia's boyfriend. "Right now."

CHAPTER 1

Summer of Ewing

Scott Layden leaned against the red brick building facing the sun-splashed parking lot outside the Purchase College gym. A dozen journalists surrounded the low-key Layden, all eager to hear what the Knicks' bespectacled general manager had in store for Patrick Ewing and the Knicks.

It was June 4, 2000, and this get-together was known in the NBA as Trash-Bag Day. Players came to the Knicks' practice facility in rural Westchester, New York, cleaned out their lockers, met for the final time with the coaches and said good-bye to the season.

Two days earlier at Madison Square Garden, the Knicks' bid to return to the NBA Finals had ended against the Indiana Pacers in the Eastern Conference Finals. Reggie Miller, the long-time Knicks-killer, put them in their grave with 17 points in the fourth quarter. Hitting a multitude of sky ball jumpers in the closing minutes, Miller secured the 93-80 victory in Game 6, ensuring that Ewing went another year without an NBA championship. After the game, Ewing walked through the hallway connecting the locker rooms on his way to his car parked beneath the Garden. Two EMT workers offered consoling words.

"You're still the man," one of the men said to Ewing.

"Not anymore," Ewing responded in a barely audible voice.

The other man said to Patrick, "You'll still get your ring." Ewing looked up and said, "I hope so." Then he continued on to his car, not knowing if he'd ever again make this walk from the Knicks locker room.

A couple of weeks earlier, during the Knicks' second-round series against the Miami Heat, Ewing had decided he was through in New York. A Garden fan had screamed at him, "You're a bum," after the Knicks lost Game 3 of the series in overtime. The taunt, a familiar one at the Garden, hurt him far more than it should have. At that point, Ewing decided he would attempt to break free of New York when the playoffs ended.

In the Indiana series, Ewing missed two games with a sprained foot. The Knicks won both games. The Knicks lost all four games Ewing played in the series. Ewing's critics in the media and radio talk-show callers were calling him old, slow and vulnerable. The Knicks scored an above-average 94.5-points-per game with Ewing sidelined, invigorated by a transition offense that had rarely been seen at the Garden during the season. With Ewing as the focal point in the four games he played, the Knicks averaged 83.2 points.

Wallace Matthews, the hard-hitting columnist of *The New York Post,* wrote a front-page column during the Pacers' series pleading for coach Jeff Van Gundy to bench "The Big Fella." Even Latrell Sprewell, the coach-attacking forward who had turned into a politically-correct gentleman since changing coasts before the 1999 lockout season, offered up a slice of brutal honesty before Game 6. Asked if the Knicks were better without Ewing, Sprewell said, "The numbers definitely say that."

Moments after the series-clinching loss to the Pacers, a beaten Van Gundy, Ewing's No. 1 public supporter, acknowledged the Knicks had to get more durable next season. If that wasn't a direct shot at Ewing, it sounded like a sideswipe. Ewing's availability had been a question mark on the eve of several playoff games.

Now, on Trash-Bag Day, Ewing exited the brick building, loping into the Purchase College parking lot. He had very little to say. Surrounded by television cameras and radio guys with microphones, Ewing was asked if he'd be back next season for his sixteenth year in New York.

"Last year, I said something and you guys blew it out of proportion," Ewing responded. "I'm not going to do the same thing this year."

The previous season, after the Knicks marched to the 1999 Finals with Ewing sidelined by an Achilles tendon tear, the Knicks center was asked on break-up day if he'd be willing to reduce his role in the team's offense to better complement emerging stars Allan Houston and Sprewell.

"I'm not changing," he muttered. The words were splashed on the tabloids' back pages, as if they had been uttered defiantly.

With a loud screech, Ewing backed his sleek Porsche convertible out of his parking space and blew out of the lot, wondering if he was doing so for the last time.

With the rest of Ewing's teammates having completed their parking-lot interviews and taken off for summer, Layden held court. The topic quickly turned to Ewing's future. He had one year left on his four-year, $68 million contract and was reportedly seeking a two-year contract extension. Several times during the season, Ewing had said he thought he had a few good years left in him. Knicks brass, however, was not prepared to give Ewing another two years, considering his long list of injuries and his advancing age. Ewing would turn 38 in August. They privately wished the issue would somehow go away.

Layden was not given to bold proclamations. He was the antithesis of his garrulous, eccentric Brooklyn-born father, Frank Layden, the former president and coach of the Utah Jazz. The glibness gene had not been passed along. The son had seen his father put foot into mouth too many times. Scott took the opposite approach: the less said the better. "Scott thinks before he speaks," Frank Layden once said. Scott goes off the record with reporters to utter the most innocuous statements, such as "No comment." A player agent can finish a 20-minute phone conversation with Scott Layden and be left without the slightest indication of whether the Knicks were interested in his client.

"I love him," Van Gundy has said of Layden. "That's the guy we need as our Secretary of Defense. He's giving nothing up. He's the best. He does it with such sincerity, you still like him. I try that, I'm an insincere bastard."

Those who had worked with Scott Layden for more than a decade in Utah knew so little about his dreams and passions that they were sure he was going to turn down Garden president Dave Checketts' offer to become the Knicks' general manager. That was in August 1999. Jazz employees were stunned to learn that Scott was accepting his dream job. It was also once the dream of his father, who grew up in Bay Ridge, Brooklyn. Frank Layden urged Scott to take the position. He told his son that if he didn't take it, he'd be in Utah forever.

"I'm hoping this will be the final break from him being called Frank Layden's son," Frank said after Scott took the job. "He's been Frank Layden's son for too long."

On this sunny June day, Scott Layden was ready to cut the "Frank's son" tag forever. He was ready to let it rip on the hot-button topic in New York sports.

"We need to find a way to get back to the Finals," Layden said, showing a fervor for the first time since he had taken the job a year earlier. "I believe in order to get back to the Finals, he has to be part of this team. That's very important. Patrick, being our captain, is a critical part of our team. Being here for a year, I appreciate what he brings night in and night out. Patrick is a Knick, an example of what this organization is all about."

And so it was settled, at least in Layden's mind: Ewing was coming back to complete the final year of his contract at $14 million. He was coming back to take one more shot at bringing New York City an NBA championship.

■ ■ ■

The NBA's free-agent sweepstakes began July 1, and the Knicks had their eyes on two players: Grant Hill, the star small forward from the Detroit Pistons, and Portland power forward Brian Grant, who would give the Knicks a rebounding force they had lacked during the 1999-2000 season.

The Knicks' starting power forward was Larry Johnson, a former Hall of Fame candidate whose Converse commercials featured him dressing up as "Grandmamma." Those spots were all the rage when Johnson played for the Charlotte Hornets. But at six-foot-six and with a chronic disk problem, the running joke was that Johnson could no longer jump as high as "Grandmamma."

Hill's glamorous star power and Wheaties image was as important to Garden management as his ability to penetrate the lane. Signing Hill was all about making a splash, adding another superstar to the Garden marquee, making a Knicks game the place to be for celebrities and super models visiting town. The Knicks had two standout players in Houston and Sprewell, who played Hill's swingman position. Because the Knicks were over the salary cap, they could only obtain Hill in a sign-and-trade with the Pistons. Either Houston or Sprewell likely would have to go.

In mid-June, before the courting period began, Hill visited Manhattan for a promotional appearance at Tourneau Watch Store on Madison Avenue. Stuck in midtown traffic, Hill arrived 25 minutes late and hobbled into the elegant watch palace on crutches. He was rehabbing from a fractured left ankle that had forced him to miss part of the season.

Hill downplayed his traffic misadventure and said it would not curtail his desire to consider the Knicks. Knicks management, though, wished his first smell of New York was not the fumes of midtown traffic. They envisioned driving him through the rolling hills of Westchester and Connecticut, where the players lived, rather than immersing him in the bustle of Manhattan.

"It's busy. There's no place like it," Hill said of New York. "But I hear they have some nice suburbs. I haven't seen that. The idea of trying to help Patrick win the championship is appealing. I grew up a Patrick Ewing fan, watching him at Georgetown, wearing 33."

It was the politically correct thing to say, but the scuttlebutt had Hill leaning toward Orlando. Five days earlier, Hill had been spotted in Orlando with his wife and brothers, reportedly house-hunting.

Orlando was the first city Hill visited on his recruiting tour. He arrived in Orlando the night before July 1, stirring whispers of tampering by executives around the league. Teams were not allowed to have contact with a free-agent-to-be until July 1. How would Hill know Orlando management was ready to whisk him around Orlando the next morning if there had been no contact?

Tim Duncan, the superstar power forward from San Antonio, joined Hill on the three-day visit. It was a smashing success. The highlights were visits to Isleworth, the exclusive community where former Magic center Shaquille O'Neal still owns a mansion, and Disney World's Magic Kingdom. They visited a private golf course and were introduced to Tiger Woods, who took time out from practicing to greet the two recruits. The Orlando contingent gained a backdoor pass to Magic Kingdom so that they could avoid the lines. Hill rode Space Mountain four successive times, and Magic GM John Gabriel told him he had set an NBA record.

The Magic put together a 15-minute Chamber-of-Commerce-type video that spread the gospel on the benefits of living in central Florida, complete with endorsements from resident Greg Gumbel and NFL wide receiver Andre Reed. Magic owner Bob Dandelion hosted a barbecue lunch for Duncan and Hill at his Isleworth mansion. They took Hill and Duncan on a Sea-Doo watercraft in the channel that served as Dandelion's backyard. The two stars were put up in posh suites at the Disney World Hotel. On their drive to the Magic facility, they passed billboards with pictures of themselves in Magic uniforms.

Hill was overwhelmed. Quoting unnamed sources, the *Orlando Sentinel* reported that Hill had told Magic brass, before taking a flight to Detroit, that he would sign with them. Nothing could become official yet because teams couldn't sign free agents until August 1. Duncan, too, seemed to be in the Magic's bag. The balance of power in the East was about to tilt to Central Florida.

■ ■ ■

The Knicks would not surrender. Hill's agent, Lon Babby, had told Layden that Hill would likely visit New York following the Orlando trip. But Hill was so enamored by what the up-and-coming Magic had to offer that he decided against coming.

Desperate, the Knicks took their elaborate show on the road in hopes of convincing Hill to make a recruiting visit to New York. They pulled out all the stops. Checketts, Layden, vice-president of franchise operations Steve Mills, and Van Gundy took a Cablevision charter flight to Detroit. To add some pop to their presentation, the Knicks brought along celebrity-row regulars Star Jones, Matthew Modine, *The Sopranos* star Michael Imperioli, Peter Boyle and Chazz Palmintieri.

This was where giving away freebie $1,500 courtside seats to the rich and famous paid off, although it was not why the Knicks made it a priority to entertain stars at the Garden. Attaching movie actors and super models to the courtside seats gave Knicks games a status no other NBA team could attain, even the Los Angeles Lakers. The Knicks' celebrity season-ticket holders are staples at home games. They include Woody Allen, New York Jets owner Woody Johnson, Spike Lee, Ed Bradley, Lorne Michaels, Tom Brokaw, Kevin Kline and his wife Phoebe Cates and the McEnroe family. They are joined occasionally by Chris Rock, Penny Marshall, Ben Stiller, Adam Sandler,

Jerry Seinfeld, any of the Baldwin brothers, Samuel L. Jackson, Modine, Jones and Boyle. And, when their teams are doing well, any member of the Mets, Yankees, Giants or Jets, has a front-row seat available to him with a single phone call.

One of director of public relations Dan Schoenberg's duties is finding out which actors, actresses and supermodels are in town and extending them invitations to a game. During the upcoming season, celebrity row would host Meg Ryan, Brecken Meyer, Paul McCartney, Drew Barrymore, Tom Green, Gretchen Mol, Kid Rock, Sheryl Crow, Keith Richards, David Spade, David Hasselhoff, Henry Winkler, Magic Johnson, reigning Miss USA Candace Krueger, Lorraine Bracco, John Leguizimo, Dan Marino, Derek Jeter and his date Miss Universe Lara Dutte, Wyclef Jean, Liz Hurley and supermodels Rachel Hunter, Carmen Kass and Kylie Bax, among others. Their appearances would be duly noted—often with a picture—by *Daily News* gossip guru Mitchell Fink or in *The Post*'s popular Page Six section.

One afternoon, Schoenberg got a phone call from Monica Lewinsky. She had her own tickets but wanted someone from the Knicks to meet her at the employees' entrance and escort her inside. She explained that whenever she got recognized, she got hassled. Schoenberg obliged, although Lewinsky was hardly recognizable when he saw her. She was incognito in sunglasses and a Knicks' baseball cap.

The Knicks' management team and celebrity contingent arrived at Hill's office in suburban Detroit thirty minutes early at 2:30 p.m. so they'd have time to set up their presentation. They assembled an array of doctored pictures of Hill in a Knicks' uniform.

Hill and his wife, Grammy-nominated recording artist Tamia Washington, had no idea whom the Knicks were sending to meet him. When they walked into his office, he reacted like a birthday boy stumbling onto his own surprise party. Glancing at Star and the coterie of celebrities in his office, Hill's eyes bulged.

"Oh my god! Wow!" Hill exclaimed.

Now he knew how badly the Knicks wanted him, even though his mind had been all but made up to sign with Orlando. After schmoozing with Hill for close to an hour, Jones, Modine, Imperioli, Boyle and Palmintieri left the office so the Knicks management team could get down to the real business of the day. Hill spoke to Van Gundy for half an hour. Van Gundy hinted that Hill would run the offense and play sort of a point-guard role with Sprewell and Houston on the wings.

Checketts said to Hill, "If you're impressed with Disney World, wait 'til you see Broadway." Hill was shown a video featuring Knick celebrities, including Seinfeld, making their pitch. It was a thorough presentation. Barry Watkins, the top Garden publicist, came in and talked to Hill about the community programs the Garden was involved in.

Throughout the sales pitch, no mention was made of Ewing. When Hill asked about him, the response was vague. Hill suspected the Knicks were trying to deal Ewing, but he didn't express his feeling. Playing with Ewing had been the chief reason for his interest in the Knicks. But Ewing hadn't called him to lobby on behalf of the club. That seemed strange. Ewing had played a huge role in the recruitment of Hill's former teammate, Allan Houston, in 1996, taking a charter down to Detroit to retrieve Houston and sitting next to him on the way back.

As the Knicks' management team talked to Hill, the celebrities went off to play cards. When the contingent left Detroit, they felt they had done everything they could to convince Hill to visit New York, but no one knew if they had succeeded. They had no idea that Hill had been turned off the moment Knicks management shrugged off his question about Ewing.

Hill made his decision official two days later. He was signing with the Magic. That left Duncan's decision as the most vital of the summer regarding the balance of power in the East. After returning from Orlando, Duncan spoke on the phone with Spurs center David Robinson. Robinson, who was vacationing in Hawaii, would have all of his leadership skills, learned at the Naval Academy in Annapolis, Maryland, as an officer-in-training, put to the test as he tried to save a key crewman from abandoning ship.

"The future is now," Robinson told Duncan. "People can talk about the future forever. You look at what we've got."

Robinson cut short his vacation to meet with Duncan in San Antonio. Rumors circulated that Robinson had convinced Duncan to stay. Although spirits lifted in the depressed climate of the Spurs' offices, the Spurs still had not heard officially from Duncan.

A meeting was arranged involving Duncan, agent Lon Babby and Spurs coach/director of operations Gregg Popovich.

"I'm going to Orlando," Duncan told Popovich. The Spurs coach looked stunned and stared blankly. Duncan let a few seconds pass before saying, "Just kidding."

Popovich breathed a sigh of relief. "I need a drink," he said.

Duncan's decision to stay in San Antonio triggered sighs of relief in the Knicks' offices at 2 Penn Plaza in midtown Manhattan. With Hill and Duncan, the Magic would have had the makings of a dynasty. With only Hill, they'd be tough, but by no means unstoppable.

■ ■ ■

The quotes rushed out of the Bahamas like a Caribbean summer storm. The National Basketball Players Association, also known as the players' union, was holding their annual meetings at the Atlantis Resort on Paradise Island in the Bahamas the week of July 26. Current and retired players were invited to frolic in the sun, gamble and play golf. The players paid their airfares, but the union put them up for four days at the posh Atlantis.

Ewing still manned the title of union president, even though his leadership during the 1999 lockout had been questioned. Chris Sheridan, the aggressive national basketball writer for the Associated Press, was the lone reporter covering the meetings. Sheridan lobbied with Ewing's agent, David Falk, to set up a lunch meeting to interview Ewing about his future. Ewing, private to a fault, backed out. But when most of the players went golfing, Ewing, who doesn't play, stayed in his hotel room. Sheridan called him and again invited him to lunch.

"Just ask me your questions, man," Ewing said. So that's what Sheridan did. "I'd probably like to play two more years after next year," Ewing told Sheridan. "If it's New York, it's New York. If not, it's somewhere else. I'm prepared to do whatever. I'll let Falk and the powers-that-be on the Knicks handle it and I won't worry myself with it."

When the quotes hit the AP wire that night, I called Layden on his cell phone and asked whether he still intended to have Ewing retire as a Knick. There was a long pause on the other end, then the sound of a crash, as if the cell phone had been dropped to the floor. Then the phone call was cut off. Layden called back a few minutes later to apologize. The question had clearly struck a nerve.

"You know how we feel about Patrick," Layden said unconvincingly.

The next day's back page of *The New York Post* blared "33, Skidoo?" The Summer of Ewing had begun in full gale.

■ ■ ■

The other Knicks player in the Bahamas for the union meetings was point guard Charlie Ward, the club's player representative. The devoutly religious Ward, known around the league for being a staunch Bible worshipper, was one of the few players who brought along his family: wife Tonia and infant son Caleb. On the flight home to New York, Ward sat next to Ron Klempner, one of the attorneys for the players' union. Klempner's job is to win back hundreds of thousands of dollars for players who appeal fines and suspensions.

For two hours, they talked about Ward's favorite pastime outside of basketball: religion. Ward explained to Klempner the story of his son's name, Caleb, a biblical figure who was part of the exodus Moses led out of Egypt. Ward also explained to Klempner about Jonah, the biblical figure after whom the attorney had named his son. Ward told Klempner things he didn't know about Jonah.

The conversation turned to Christ, and Klempner asked Ward about the myth of the Jews killing Jesus. Ward told him he believed the Jews were conspirators in Christ's crucifixion.

"Does that mean I have to move my seat?" Klempner asked Ward. "Do you have something against me?"

"Absolutely not," Ward said. "If it didn't happen, all the great things that followed would never have happened. It was meant to be. I don't blame the Jews."

Ward explained his biblical interpretation about the crucifixion. He asked Klempner about the Jewish holidays and customs. He took Klempner's address and promised to send him some books on the crucifixion and family prayer. Klempner came away thinking that Ward, often criticized for his religious rantings, had his act together.

■ ■ ■

Ewing didn't let his in-limbo status affect his good time in the Bahamas. That night, he bounded on stage, holding a microphone, and joined Boyz2Men in song, displaying a playfulness he rarely showed. What Ewing did not tell Sheridan was that two weeks earlier, he had spoken to Checketts on the phone and formally requested a trade.

In early July, Falk had called Checketts and said, "Patrick still wants to be traded."

"I want to hear it from his mouth," Checketts responded.

Checketts and Ewing had met for dinner at the 21 Club restaurant in Manhattan in January, one month after he had returned from his

Achilles tendinitis rehab that forced him to miss the first 20 games of the 1999-2000 season. During dinner, Ewing asked Checketts to trade him before the deadline. He wasn't getting the playing time he felt he deserved (Van Gundy had kept him in the low 30-minute range) and wasn't getting the ball enough down low. During his many injury-related absences, Ewing had said he understood that the team had shifted its focus to a perimeter style to take advantage of Sprewell and Houston and felt he didn't fit in any longer.

Checketts firmly told Ewing he was not going to shop him because the Knicks didn't have another starting center. Checketts said he felt the club could still win a championship with Ewing in the pivot and wasn't ready to break up the team.

"I'm not going to discuss it further," Checketts told Ewing during dinner. "You've been here a long time. I've surrounded you with guys that could help you win. I have a right to expect you to play your heart out. You're not going to be traded. I have a right to tell you to shut up and play. You owe me that." Then he added, "If you're still unhappy at the end of the year, we'll talk then."

This time, Ewing didn't need to have dinner with Checketts at a fancy restaurant. The day after Falk's conversation with Checketts, Ewing called Checketts and said, "I haven't changed where I was."

Checketts and Layden weren't going to fight the matter. Neither was Van Gundy. In fact, Ewing coming to them rather than the Knicks having to go to Ewing about a divorce was a blessing in disguise. After all, he had missed 88 games during the past three seasons. But to shop Ewing openly would be viewed as disloyalty to a franchise player, a public relations disaster. It would look much better to tell everyone Ewing had requested a trade. Even before Ewing's request, they had spoken to the Blazers about trading Ewing for free-agent Brian Grant and Jermaine O'Neal.

After back spasms and peroneal tendinitis in his foot troubled Ewing during the 2000 playoffs, the Knicks' decision makers figured any contribution he made to the Knicks for the rest of his career was gravy. Ewing's contract would expire after the 2000-01 season and he was already making too much noise about wanting to play two more years. Another contract negotiation with Falk had the makings of a battle royale that Checketts dreaded. Blessing in disguise. Yes, the Knicks planned to see what The Big Fella could fetch.

The problem was, Ewing had a no-trade clause. He gave the Knicks a list of seven teams he'd be willing to go to: Seattle, Portland, New Jersey, Miami, Orlando, Phoenix and Toronto. Ewing seemed obsessed with Seattle, which in late July got permission from Checketts to speak with Ewing. In August, at a restaurant in Georgetown, Sonics' management met with Ewing, Falk, Ewing's father, Carl, and Ewing's former college coach, John Thompson. The Sonics were represented by coach Paul Westphal, assistant general manager Billy McKinney and general manager Wally Walker.

For two hours, Ewing belted the Sonics with an avalanche of questions, including ones about the lifestyle in the Pacific Northwest and whether their star point guard, Gary Payton, supported having him in Seattle.

"He's appreciating the chance of playing with a true center," Walker told Ewing.

Ewing also asked about their younger players: Rashard Lewis, Ruben Patterson and Shammond Williams.

"The West is very tough," Walker said. "But we feel we're a center short of being very competitive where we can beat anyone anywhere."

Two days later, Falk called Walker and told him Ewing liked what he had heard.

The Knicks began talking trade with the Sonics and Lakers. Falk was trying to have the Lakers ship another one of his clients, unhappy free agent Glen Rice, who had warred with L.A. coach Phil Jackson during their championship run, in a sign-and-trade. The Knicks were interested in Rice. The Sonics, meanwhile, were shopping overpaid, overweight power forward Vin Baker.

The Knicks were unable to work out a deal with the Blazers, who were also on Ewing's list. Brian Grant visited the Knicks on a recruiting trip and was wined and dined on Cablevision magnate James Dolan's yacht on the Hudson River. But after meeting with Sonics' officials, Ewing's list of preferred teams had been pared to one: Seattle.

As the Knicks tried to work out a deal with the Sonics, they also made plays for free-agent power forward Danny Fortson, offering Boston Chris Childs, and Aaron Williams, but lost out on both. They were shot down on their offer of oft-injured Marcus Camby and Chris Childs to Portland for the coveted Grant, who wound up with archrival Miami in early August.

If the Knicks didn't trade Ewing, they'd be standing pat for the summer while the hated Heat added Eddie Jones, Anthony Mason and Grant, With a front line of Alonzo Mourning, Grant and Mason, the Heat had become overwhelming favorites to win the East.

■ ■ ■

The Post reported in late July that the Knicks had talked to the Blazers about a Ewing for Grant and O'Neal trade and that the organization had internal discussions about whether to shop him around the league. But other than those scant details, the Knicks kept a lid on the ongoing Ewing trade discussions. That is, until August 19, when *Daily News* columnist Mike Lupica, a friend of Westphal's, broke the story about Ewing's desire to be dealt to the Sonics. A media flurry ensued.

■ ■ ■

On Sunday night, August 20, the Sonics, Knicks, Lakers and Pistons held a conference call to agree on a four-team deal. The Knicks would get Rice from the Lakers and Vin Baker from the Sonics. Ewing would go to Seattle and the Pistons would trade Christian Laettner to the Lakers. An NBA-record 13 players were included in the blockbuster to make the salary transfers equal for all sides.

Three of the throw-ins were Greg Foster, Lazaro Borrell and Vernon Maxwell, who would be going to the Pistons. Detroit president Joe Dumars was trying to get his team under the salary cap so the Pistons could sign a prominent free agent such as Chris Webber the following summer. Hence, Dumars was attempting to acquire players whose contracts were expiring after the 2000-2001 season. The Sonics had told Dumars Maxwell's 2001-02 contract year was not guaranteed. During the four-team conference call, Dumars specified the trade was contingent on three matters: investigating Maxwell's contract to determine if Detroit could terminate it after the 2000-2001 season and the extent of back injuries to Borrell and Foster.

The next afternoon, NBATalk.com reported that the trade was a done deal. The Associated Press picked up the story, which was subsequently reported by radio and TV stations everywhere. Checketts and Van Gundy were so confident the deal was complete that they called Ewing on the phone.

"I want to thank you for a great run," Checketts said. "I want you to know that as soon as possible after you retire, we want to retire your jersey."

Van Gundy told Ewing, "If it wasn't for you, I wouldn't be a head coach. You made my career."

Meanwhile, Dumars was getting cold feet. The Pistons' president was not satisfied with either Maxwell's contract issue or Foster's health. To this day, he believes one of the teams leaked the trade to the Internet to put pressure on him to consent. The conference call with the league to make the deal official kept getting pushed back.

Late Monday afternoon, Dumars called Walker and said, "We can't move forward with what's on the table." Dumars had a better offer for Laettner from Dallas. Scrambling, the teams tried to sweeten the pot for the Pistons with draft choices. Everyone involved that night figured the deal would somehow get done by the next day.

■ ■ ■

Meanwhile, in *The New York Post* offices in midtown Manhattan, copy editor Dave Blezow was crafting a back page for the ages. Playing off a scathing column by Kevin Kernan saluting Ewing's expected departure, the headline read, "Good Riddance." Kernan had covered much of Ewing's career in New York. So had *The Post's* longtime basketball writer, Fred Kerber. Illustrating Ewing's inattentive nature when it came to the reporters covering him in New York, Ewing recently had told a confidant, "That Kevin Kerber has been on my back ever since I got to New York."

The New York media would not miss Ewing, and the "Good Riddance" headline got national attention for expressing the anti-Ewing sentiment. Not everyone appreciated the headline. Knicks vice president of public relations Lori Hamamoto, who had grown close to Ewing, said to me that morning, "That was classless. Why can't you let him leave in peace?"

Ewing's love-hate relationship with the New York fans went way back, perhaps even stemming from his college days, when he was the leader of the hated Georgetown Hoyas team that battled on many occasions with local St. John's University. As a Knicks rookie, Ewing had a poor game on Patrick Ewing Poster Night. After the game, some fans ripped up their souvenirs and threw the shreds onto the court. In 1996, Ewing criticized the fans after the Knicks barely defeated the Clippers, saying, "Yeah, they're annoying me. If they're going to act the way they're reacting, they might as well stay home. You go other places and when the team is playing bad, the fans still support the team. Here they cheer you one minute and then something goes wrong and they jump off the bandwagon. I'm just fed up with it."

Dave D'Alessandro, the beat writer for the Newark *Star-Ledger,* put together a list of post-game sayings by Ewing that any media member who had dealt with Ewing's banal post-game news conferences would fast recognize:

1. "Turn that camera light off, please."
2. "Watch my toes."
3. "I still think we're the better team.
4. "We just didn't get the job done for whatever reason."
5. "I'm done, fellas."
6. And, after a reporter persists: "I said I'm done, thank you."

For three days, the Knicks, Pistons, Sonics and Lakers scrambled to make the deal work. On Thursday, August 24, the teams held separate press conferences to announce the deal was off. Several of the executives were heading off to vacations. They agreed to come back in three weeks with fresh minds and try to put the deal back together.

In a conference call, Layden said, "Right now, Patrick Ewing is a Knick and if nothing else develops, he'll be a Knick. We feel with a healthy Patrick, we have a very good basketball team, one of the best basketball teams in the East. Whatever awkward feelings there may be, I expect him to have a great season. I know one thing: when he runs through that tunnel at Madison Square Garden, there's going to be a standing ovation."

The Knicks knew, though, that they'd have to trade Ewing. Falk and Ewing remained persistent in their demands. The Knicks began talking to the Washington Wizards, but Ewing rejected the idea of playing for a losing club. He wanted to be a Sonic. Falk even promised Checketts and Layden that he would try to force the Hawks to trade another of his clients, Atlanta Hawks center Dikembe Mutombo, to the Knicks to fill Ewing's spot. Layden had begun talking to Hawks officials in July about Mutombo, offering Camby and Larry Johnson.

Van Gundy had no contact with Ewing throughout the summer until the night the trade appeared to be a go. If another trade did not develop, Van Gundy knew he needed to mend fences with his center. Although the public perceived that Van Gundy was against trading Ewing, he was, in fact, very supportive of the deal. At the very least, Rice and Baker gave the Knicks more durability.

Van Gundy drove down to Ewing's off-season home in Potomac, Maryland. Checketts thought the trip was fruitless, that Ewing had lost his heart to be a Knick and nothing could change his mind. But Van Gundy had to go because of reports that Ewing was angry that his coach hadn't lobbied for a contract extension for him. In 1996, Ewing had pleaded with management to promote Van Gundy from interim coach to permanent coach.

When they met, Ewing assured Van Gundy that his desire to leave had nothing to do with him. "If I was mad at you, I would've told you," Ewing said.

Van Gundy warned Ewing, "I'm not sure we're going to be able to trade you. You have to prepare yourself for being a Knick again. I want you to think in those terms now."

Van Gundy's words made little impact. Ewing still wanted a trade. And, on September 20, he got it. The Suns replaced Detroit as the fourth team in what amounted to a league-record 12-player deal.

The Knicks didn't get Baker, but they got Rice and Suns center Luc Longley, who was playing for Australia in the Olympics. As throw-ins to make the mathematics work under the salary cap, the Knicks also obtained Maxwell, Lakers backup center Travis Knight, Seattle's young Russian center Vlad Stepania, and Seattle's Lazaro Borrell, a Cuban defector. The Knicks shipped center Chris Dudley to Phoenix and the Lakers wound up with Horace Grant and Foster from Seattle.

This time, Checketts made no sentimental phone calls to Ewing. It was a cold business deal. Ewing had received a phone call from team-mate Chris Childs after the first trade fell through, but got no calls from any of his teammates when the second trade became official. This was no surprise. In his final season in New York, his best friend on the team was rookie Mirsad Turckan from the Turkey League. Turckan got released in midseason.

Ewing walked around his house for two days, stunned he was no longer a Knick. Even though he had requested this trade all summer, his mind was too clogged to get the energy to leave the house and go to the gym. He was scared. The Pacific Northwest represented a vast unknown.

At the Knicks' press conference to introduce Rice, Knicks superfan Spike Lee walked around in disbelief, blaming the media for driving Ewing to Seattle.

"'Good riddance' in the tabloids, that's one of the reasons he said 'F.U. guys, I'm out,'" Lee said. "We're going to be the ones up the creek when the playoffs come. Luc Longley? He had Michael Jordan with him. Michael made everyone look better. Sad, sad day."

On the back of a press release, Lee had scribbled the Knicks' starting lineup and left a blank at center for anyone who cared to look.

A couple of days later, Ewing, appearing on former college coach John Thompson's radio show in Washington, D.C., admitted, "I did want to leave. I thought it was time for me to go. I felt they were going in a different direction and I don't feel as wanted as I felt before."

■ ■ ■

Ewing arrived in Seattle four days after the trade and had dinner with Sonics officials downtown. Fans yelled out his name as he walked the street. They came up to him and wished him well. In the first week after the trade, the Sonics sold 1,200 season-ticket packages.

At a cheery press conference the next day in Seattle, Ewing wore a double-breasted gray suit and a smile he couldn't erase. He looked nothing like the grumpy old man who had snarled at the media during the playoffs the previous spring when he didn't want to talk.

Ewing sat on the dais and spoke about being in a championship parade. "My best-case scenario is us winning the championship and me finally getting to ride in that float. Only it won't be Fifth Avenue in New York with all the confetti coming down." Ewing turned to Sonics owner Barry Ackerley.

"Where will you have the parade when we win it all?" he asked. Ackerley told Ewing that downtown Seattle had a Fourth Avenue that would be appropriate for a parade. "Then it will be Fourth Avenue," Ewing said.

The press conference continued. "They told me I'm old and that I'm ancient, but I think I left my wheelchair back in New York," Ewing said.

When a reporter introduced herself as Laura Vecsey from the *Seattle Post-Intelligencer,* Ewing stopped her.

"You're not related to Pete, are you?" Ewing asked, referring to the acerbic *Post* NBA columnist.

"No, I'm not," she said. Actually, she is his niece, but maybe she didn't want to scare off Ewing right away.

On a video screen, Payton and Baker sent messages to Ewing from the Olympics. Payton said, "He better get a lot of ice because we're going to want him to run a little bit. Get ice for the knees, buddy." Baker said, "It's going to be great. He's one of the best centers to ever play the game and it's going to be exciting for me to play with a true center for the first time in my career."

Ewing was asked about whether he'd be willing to lessen his role to fit in with the Sonics, something he blanched at with the Knicks.

"This is Vince's team, this is Gary's team, this is Barry Ackerley's team," Ewing said. "I've had enough of that in New York."

Later, in a quiet moment, Ewing was asked if any of the Knicks players had called to wish him luck.

"No," he said, shaking his head. "No one."

CHAPTER 2

Charleston Revisited

October 2

The Knicks normally open training camp in the quaint seaport town of Charleston, South Carolina. Pat Riley initiated the tradition when he became Knicks coach in 1991. But with Allan Houston having just arrived from a 14-hour plane flight from Australia, where he played in the Olympics, the Knicks decided to spend the first three days at Purchase College before heading south.

On Monday morning, Van Gundy held the first team meeting of the season. Their first practice would not be until the following day. In this pivotal address, he hoped to set a tone and mind-set for the season. Van Gundy asked his players not to allow the specter of Ewing to hang over their heads.

"I don't want us to use his absence as a crutch or an excuse," Van Gundy told the players inside the college gym. "It's too easy that way. That goes for me, too." He also warned them not to expect a change in the team's philosophy: rebounding and defense still wins championships.

Van Gundy then met with the beat writers. He came down from his second-floor office to the atrium adjacent to the Purchase gym, where he conducted all of his post-practice meetings with the beat writers. Van Gundy wore blue sweatpants, a Charleston basketball sweatshirt and, as usual, wasn't wearing sneakers, just white athletic socks, as if he was walking around his college dorm room.

Of all the layers of Van Gundy's complex persona, the sock thing is his most endearing quality. It demonstrated his lack of pretensions, despite a million-dollar bank account. He was in the second season of a four-year, $14-million deal earned on the basis of the Knicks' 1999 run to the NBA Finals. No matter how taken aback some members of the media remained over his corporate-shark ways that flourished during his lockout-season power struggle with former general manager Ernie Grunfeld, even they got a kick out of Shoeless Jeff. Nobody in New York could have imagined the ostentatious Pat Riley sauntering down in his socks to meet the press.

Van Gundy made his message clear to Knicks fans eager for the exciting possibilities of a post-Patrick club that spotlighted the dynamic Sprewell-Houston-Camby trio. It wasn't what they wanted to hear. Van Gundy warned that although Ewing was gone, the Knicks were not about to turn into a high-speed, high-octane Los Angeles Lakers "Showtime" facsimile. There would be a different cast of players but the same old Jeff and his plodding, post-up, half-court offense.

"When you get a little smaller as a team, the natural inclination is, 'Let's run and shoot and have some fun,'" Van Gundy said. "Winning is fun regardless of the style and losing is boring regardless of the style. We have been as boring an outfit as you can possibly be and that's why we sell out, because it's exciting as hell to win."

Van Gundy had statistical data to further his point. He often liked to support his statements with statistical evidence, and reporters who covered him appreciated his preparedness. Beyond his six a.m. daily arrivals at Purchase, this was a sure sign of how hard Van Gundy worked, whether getting his team ready for that night's game or getting himself ready for that day's chat with the media.

Van Gundy's stats: several of the teams that led the league in fast-break points last season were either in the draft lottery or lost in the first round. Meanwhile, the top seven teams in least points allowed were playoff stalwarts: San Antonio, the Knicks, Miami, Phoenix, Utah, the Lakers and Portland.

"If you want a predictor of success in this league, you base it on defense and rebounding," Van Gundy lectured the writers. "If you want a predictor of mediocrity, you base it on scoring and running."

Van Gundy also fired off this caution: "This year, we have more challenges and more questions than in years past because we had more change. But you talk about challenges, this is a great challenge."

■ ■ ■

In the Pacific Northwest, at Media Day on the eve of the Sonics's first practice, Ewing wore Seattle's green and white uniform for the first time.

"It looks good on me," Ewing said. "I haven't worn green since I was in high school. I'm ready to rock 'n' roll."

October 3
Before the Knicks climbed the stairs to Purchase's basketball gym for Day One of practice, Van Gundy wanted to get one more thing out of the way. He gave a brief talk to the players in the locker room, telling them he wasn't the general manager and couldn't control the bevy of trade rumors that had festered in the tabloids over the summer.

"Forget about the feeling, 'I may not be here,'" Van Gundy told his troops. "Only one guy in this league is untradeable and that's Shaquille O'Neal. And two coaches are unfireable, Phil Jackson and Pat Riley. Everyone else is tradeable. This is the profession we chose and this is the way it is."

Day One of practice featured 20 players. They were vying for 15 spots (12 on the regular roster and three on the injured list). Van Gundy didn't need long to get ticked off at his team's conditioning. And it didn't take long for the first player to say how much the club was looking forward to being freed of Ewing.

The most outspoken player was Larry Johnson, who had scored 25 points in each of the two playoff games against Indiana that Ewing missed. "Some players, myself included, probably would've wanted to see our team at times without Patrick on the floor to see if we could get some good run and gun," Johnson said. "That's not to say we didn't want Patrick on the team. But we wanted to see how we could play against Indiana in that last game with a quicker team, especially if Patrick wasn't 100 percent."

Houston also didn't hide from the issue. Asked if he was excited about this chance to see how the Knicks might fare without Ewing, Houston said, "Definitely. It's not so much, 'Uh-oh, what are we going to do now?' We all thought about how it would be sometime. Here it is. Everyone's going to be asked for more responsibility and everyone's looking forward to it."

Van Gundy was in a surly mood. He had conducted a routine timed sprinting drill to kick things off. Camby bailed out before finishing it. The coach was fuming, disgusted that Camby could be so out of shape and that he hadn't seen more of him over the summer at Purchase. He was concerned Camby was angry at Knicks' brass for all of the trade rumors that mentioned his name.

Only later did Van Gundy learn that Camby's failure to finish the running drill was related to the pain in his right knee that dogged him all summer, the after-effects of surgery he had undergone in February. Either way, it was a disturbing development. Camby had been told by team doctors Norman Scott and Fred Cushner to refrain from running on the knee all summer. Despite the rest, Camby's right knee was still sore. If Camby was not shipped to Atlanta in a trade for Mutombo, Van Gundy knew that he was a leading candidate to be the starting center, especially with Longley out for another three to six weeks with a knee bruise suffered at the Olympics.

Not only Camby's performance had Van Gundy upset. The whole running drill repulsed Van Gundy, with several guys huffing and puffing as if they had just run the New York Marathon. One player had 19 percent body fat, which Van Gundy deemed dangerous because of the rigorous training that lay ahead. He didn't name the player, but it was later learned to be 330-pound newcomer Felton Spencer, a center. At least Spencer had an excuse. Layden, who knew the seven-footer as an exemplary character player when they were both with the Jazz, had signed the free agent as an insurance pivot the day before. Spencer wasn't there last June when Van Gundy pleaded with the players to work out over the summer and invited them all to have free reign over the Purchase weight room.

Few players took him up on his offer, and Van Gundy couldn't fathom how these athletes, whose bodies were their careers, let themselves go during the off-season. It was one of Van Gundy's pet peeves regarding the modern NBA player. Van Gundy believed they were being paid obscene amounts of money not to work just from training camp to the playoffs. They were salaried for the entire year, and the four months of off-season shouldn't be wasted.

"We have a team that is woefully out of shape, heavy, and, frankly, fat," Van Gundy said. "There is no way to put it nice, unfortunately. Most of these guys are not in what I call Knick shape. I can't see a team using its summer any less productively than us. I thought I would've seen more from them. I'll tell you what it stems from: trade rumors. In this town, if you're easily distracted, you're going to be distracted. Because there have been 71 trade rumors since June 5."

Camby was in a sour mood, too, partly because of the knee pain and partly because of the slew of trade reports involving his name. One afternoon during the summer, he had bumped into a life-sized cutout poster of Grant in the locker room when he came in to work out.

"It remains to be seen whether I'm here for the long haul," Camby said after the first practice. "No one's coming up to me and saying, 'You're going to be here' or 'Don't worry about the rumors.' It's definitely tough. I was supposed to be getting traded every day since June. I mean, to come in here one day and see Brian Grant's poster down there and to read the next day about Mutombo coming here. All I could worry about is working hard, getting my knee right and having a successful season."

In another corner of the gym, Sprewell admitted he expected another trade. He pointed out the structural imbalance of having himself, Houston and Rice playing essentially the same position. He also noted the point-guard glut involving Charlie Ward, Chris Childs and newcomer Erick Strickland, whom the Knicks obtained from Dallas on Draft Day.

"I'd be lying if I said I didn't think we'll make another deal," Sprewell said. "It's kind of odd to see a team with three two-guards and three point guards." Asked if this group could win the title, Sprewell responded, "Anything is possible. You never know. You might put us out there and we'll be unstoppable. Or you could put us out there and we could get crushed on the boards. It could go either way."

October 4

Sprewell launched his Chris Webber campaign on Day Two of training camp, and he began it in *The New York Post*. The two of us were talking about the possibility of Joe Smith, his old friend from Golden State, coming to the Knicks as a free agent if his contract was voided by NBA commissioner David Stern. Sprewell changed the subject. He wanted to talk about his other Golden State buddy.

Webber played with Sprewell in 1993-94, and the two got along famously. They were teammates just one year. A feud between Webber and then-Warriors coach Don Nelson led to Webber being traded to Washington. Webber, who had a renaissance with the Sacramento Kings, was to be a free agent next summer. Sprewell had been on the phone with Webber recently and talked about the possibility of being reunited in New York.

For all of Mutombo's shot-blocking and rebounding prowess, Sprewell didn't believe the Hawks' center was the missing piece to the championship puzzle. He felt Mutombo's lack of skills as an offensive post-up threat was a problem. Sprewell felt the Knicks should not give up any of their major trading pawns to get Mutombo. If anything, they should save them for Webber, either now or next summer, when he'd be available in a sign-and-trade.

"I'm waiting for Chris," Sprewell told me. "I'm lobbying right now. If I stay here, I'm letting it be known early. I know he loves New York. And I love him and he loves me. We've wanted to get back together for a long time. We felt robbed about the whole situation [in Golden State]. It's a good chance it could happen. And I'm putting it out there early."

■ ■ ■

The day marked the two-week anniversary of Ewing's trade, and still not one Knicks player had spoken on the phone with Ewing.

"I don't think it's something he should take personally," Houston said.

The other topic of the day concerned the notorious "Big Back-court," an alignment that featured no point guard and created ill will among some players. The idea was to play to the team's strengths. Point guard had not been considered a team strength since the days when Mark Jackson was the Knicks' floor leader in the late 1980s and early 1990s.

The big-guard unit had Sprewell, their starting small forward, move to his natural position of shooting guard while Houston played point guard. The Knicks had used the alignment sporadically during the 1999-2000 season, but it never stuck. Childs, one of the point guards with Ward, once said of the configuration, "It offends me."

But with Rice, a small forward, on the team, it made more sense for Van Gundy to experiment and get his three most-prolific scorers—former All-Stars Houston, Rice and Sprewell—on the court at the same time. The other way was to have Rice play power forward, something he had never done as a pro.

Before practice, Van Gundy told the team that he would try the point guard-less lineup at times during the pre-season. Houston found the lineup distasteful, too. He felt the point-guard role hampered his ability as one of the game's premier perimeter jump shooters.

Both Van Gundy and Sprewell knew Houston's concerns. Van Gundy asked Sprewell privately if he'd be willing to handle the ball in those situations. Sprewell told him he'd gladly give point guard a try if Van Gundy felt the big backcourt was the best way to go.

Again, Van Gundy was impressed with Sprewell's selflessness. He sounded eager to go from one out-of-position slot to another for the good of the team. *Was this the same guy who choked his friend P.J.?* Van Gundy couldn't help but wonder again.

"I'm a likely candidate and I don't have a problem with that," Sprewell said. "Allan doesn't like to handle the ball as much because he feels it takes away from his game. So I felt like it was a responsibility I'd rather take on."

October 5

On the third day of camp, the Knicks planned a morning practice, then a flight to their fortress in Charleston for three days. Checketts decided to go to Charleston for the first two days. He wanted to see up close the unorthodox mix he had helped assemble. Wearing a yellow short-sleeved polo shirt, a departure from his customary dark suit-jacket-and-tie corporate gear, he watched the Knicks' three-and-a-half hour workout.

Since Layden was hired in August, 1999, Checketts had been careful to not step on the GM's toes. Checketts wanted to give the appearance that he was in the background while Layden called the shots. But, in truth, Cablevision honcho James Dolan wanted Checketts to be less visible. Dolan felt Checketts was too open with reporters.

Dolan hated the media and felt its only purpose was to be hurtful. But the tall, handsome, blond, 45-year-old Checketts presented a strong, corporate-friendly image. It made no sense to Checketts to limit his access. His charm was one of his strengths. Layden, on the other hand, was uneasy and unsure in the spotlight.

So, upon under orders from high above, the Garden president's interviews with the media on Knicks matters were scarce the past year, keeping the public from hearing the team's most charismatic official. Checketts couldn't avoid the media ambush this time. He was surrounded with no escape route. The beat writers knew that Checketts' candidness on a topic far surpassed Layden's.

"It makes all of us uncomfortable," the Garden president said of the pivotless, imbalanced, post-Patrick roster. "But I am comfortable with the discomfort because we all have to work harder to figure it out. I don't mind the organization being a little on edge about that because we're committed to winning. We're going to have to figure it out."

Checketts was asked about the chance of another blockbuster trade. "We have shown a history, whether you agree with it or not, that we'll make adjustments if it's not working," he said. "And there's no way of telling if it will work or not. That's where we are."

When the topic turned to Camby's edginess, Checketts said coldly, "The best thing for Marcus would be to average 15 points and 12 rebounds and he won't have to worry about those things."

So there it was. The Knicks were under Checketts' microscope, Camby in particular. The Garden president had put Van Gundy's team on alert.

■ ■ ■

"When you're in the NBA and you roll into a city, there's a hundred girls waiting down in that lobby. And there's 20 who make it past security onto your floor. And the boldest one? She's right there on your front door. After a while, man, it just becomes part of the game."
— Former L.A. Clippers guard Zeke McCall to his teenaged son
Quincy in Spike Lee's fictional movie *Love and Basketball*

The Knicks had kept coming back to Charleston because of Ewing. One of the most reluctant autograph signers in sports, Ewing liked the Charleston setting because of the respectful Southern hospitality. The citizens and tourists left him alone while he strolled among the shops, eateries and rainbow-colored Victorian houses built in the 1700s and 1800s. The hotel was two blocks from the College of Charleston gym, so players had the convenience of walking to practice.

Perhaps the Knicks enjoyed the former Naval fortress for more pleasurable reasons, too. Back in the 1600s and 1700s, the seaport village was reputed for its dangerous red-light district, with pirates and prostitutes herding the streets near the busy seaport. Charleston was also known as the slave trade capital of the South. Thirty percent of all African-Americans can trace their roots to Charleston's slave trade.

Prostitution didn't become illegal in Charleston until 1947. According to the FBI, the naughty Knicks brought Charleston back to its risqué past when they prepared there for the 1997 playoffs. The FBI called the Knicks offices in the summer of 1999, only a month after they had made the Finals. Interim general manager Ed Tapscott received the call.

"Patrick Ewing, Larry Johnson and John Wallace might be asked to testify in a trial about the owner of the Gold Club in Atlanta and we may have to talk to them," the FBI official told Tapscott. "They're not being accused of any criminal wrongdoing, but we might have to talk to them."

The high jinks became public in November 1999 after Steven Kaplan, owner of the Atlanta strip joint The Gold Club, was indicted on charges ranging from money laundering and extortion to running a prostitution racket. The Gold Club was linked to the mob, including the notorious New York Gambino crime family and John Gotti.

Among the FBI documents was a report that Kaplan had sent exotic dancers to Charleston in April 1997 while an NBA basketball team was training. It didn't take Bob Woodward to deduce the team in question was the Knicks. The dancers, documents alleged, performed a live lesbian sex act for a group of players at the Frances Marion Hotel, then had sex with the players.

When the story broke, the Knicks were on a West Coast trip. Ewing wouldn't comment, but subsequent court papers and grand-jury testimony fingered Ewing as a regular at the posh Atlanta strip club. Ewing and former Knick John Starks appeared on comp lists for the Gold Room, a VIP lounge where the strippers allegedly performed oral sex on celebrity customers. Kaplan's former girlfriend testified on audio tape that was played on CNN, catching Ewing with a smoking gun, so to speak.

"I actually walked into that big Gold Room and Patrick Ewing and all those basketball players were in there," she said. "Patrick was getting a blow job. I got in so much trouble for that, for walking into that room."

In other testimony, some of Ewing's teammates were said to be standing around the Gold Room watching Ewing have oral sex performed upon him. Ewing's sexcapades weren't shocking. In his native Jamaica, strip clubs normally allowed the dancers to have sex with the patrons in private rooms. A noted skirtchaser, he had reportedly been linked to an affair with a Knicks City Dancer two years before. Perhaps the more stunning testimony was that ex-Knick Mark Jackson allegedly told one of the Gold Club strippers who had offered sex, "Thank you very much, but I'm happily married." There were indeed faithful husbands in the NBA.

The specter of the mob trial in the summer of 2001, with Ewing as its centerpiece, was certainly not pleasing to Knicks officials, although no Garden official ever confirmed it was a factor in deciding to go along with Ewing's trade request. Subsequent testimony at the mob trial revealed Ewing wasn't at the Charleston sex fiesta. The players involved, according to testimony, were Larry Johnson, Starks, Dontae Jones, Walter McCarty and John Wallace. Three of the strippers were allegedly paid $1,000 apiece to have sex with rookies Jones, McCarty and Wallace. There would have been more, except one of the dancers freaked out the players, telling them she was writing a book about all the famous people she had been with, according to sources.

Johnson had also been linked to the Gold Club. According to testimony by the former club manager, Thomas "Ziggy" Sicignano, Johnson once entered the club "begging" to take one of the dancers back to his hotel suite. Sicignano told Johnson it was not that kind of place. After Johnson left the club in despair, Kaplan, who saw the byplay, ordered "Ziggy" to supply Johnson with a girl next time.

As the Knicks descended on Charleston for the first time since those tawdry revelations, only Johnson was still part of the team.

■ ■ ■

The Knicks' arrival broke the NAACP boycott of South Carolina they had supported last spring. The Knicks had refused to train in Charleston before the 2000 playoffs because the state's confederate flag, viewed as a symbol of slavery, hung on the capitol building.

Houston, who majored in African-American Studies at Tennessee, had been the most ardent supporter of the boycott. "Do I feel strongly about it?" Houston said then. "Yeah, I do. What the flag represents to me is something we've grown from. To hold on to it, obviously you have your choice. I don't agree with that choice. I vote to go else-where. To me, it says something about the mentality. At some point, you have to think about where you come from."

When Houston saw me wearing a Charleston College souvenir T-shirt at Purchase during the boycott, he remarked, "Don't wear that shirt around here." He said it with a playful smile, but I shelved the shirt until the Knicks lifted the boycott.

The NAACP boycott continued, even though the South Carolina state legislature had passed a bill to move the flag to a memorial. The compromise was good enough for the Knicks, who had looked for an alternate training campsite and found none suitable.

"Unfortunately, the Knicks bought into the propaganda the governor and the tourist board is selling the nation," NAACP executive director Dwight James told the *Daily News* as the Knicks arrived in town. "The issue is far from being resolved." James threatened to stage a protest at the Knicks' practices.

October 6

After the Knicks' first morning practice in Charleston, Checketts ducked into a limo bound for the airport. He was supposed to have taken the beat writers to lunch that afternoon, but he had to leave early to attend the Hartford Wolf Pack's Calder Cup championship ceremony at the Hartford Civic Center, home of the New York Rangers' American Hockey League affiliate.

During the ride to the Charleston airport, the hired driver asked Checketts when the Knicks were going to trade for Mutombo. Checketts smiled while perusing a stack of the day's newspaper clips from New York. His impromptu chat with the writers was given big headlines, including *The Post*'s "Checketts: Win or Be Gone."

The lunch date was still on, though. Layden, vice president of franchise operations Steve Mills and Garden's publicist, Barry Watkins, took the writers out to a seafood restaurant. Van Gundy wasn't joining the group for lunch, but walked with us from the College of Charleston gym. Van Gundy, who generally views the media as adversaries because of their penchant to accentuate the negative, was generally opposed to the Knicks PR staff taking out the writers to curry favor. He was not bashful about letting us know it.

"Marc, how much money will it take for you to write positively about us?" Van Gundy asked loud enough for the group to hear.

"I don't know, Jeff, I'll consult with my lawyer and get back to you," I answered, trying to make a joke out of an awkward moment.

"See, that's what we should do," Van Gundy said. "Forget about buying them lunch. Just cut them all a check for what they want. A $20 lunch is not going to do it. A lunch is not going to change how you write about us."

Watkins winced, knowing how Checketts would have felt about this exchange.

"We're here for the company," one of the writers said.

"No you're not," Van Gundy shot back. "You're just here for the free lunch."

Van Gundy turned toward his hotel and continued on alone rather than breaking bread with the enemy.

October 7

Vladimir Stepania, one of the half-dozen players the Knicks obtained in the Ewing blockbuster, was viewed around the league as a seven-foot project. A skilled big man from Russia, Stepania faced long odds of making the team. Van Gundy didn't take to young players and had a growing reputation as a coach who didn't like coaching Europeans.

Stepania had not impressed Van Gundy with his conditioning the first few days. But on this Saturday morning, he was at his worst. Stepania was constantly out of position during defensive sets and Van Gundy rode him badly. Finally, Van Gundy yanked him off the court during a scrimmage and made him sit out the rest of the practice.

The jetlagged Houston missed the last 30 minutes of the session, too, in his first camp outing. During a three-on-three drill, he dribbled into the lane as rookie Lavor Postell shifted over, trying to draw a charge. Houston stepped on Postell's foot and twisted his left ankle. It was the same ankle that had nagged him from February on, hampering him in the playoffs. The setback again prevented Van Gundy from getting Rice, Sprewell and Houston onto the court together. Houston was expected to miss the pre-season opener against the Bulls.

Van Gundy looked worse than ever as he came off the court, having not shaved for several days. He appeared as if he had just come off a three-day drinking bender. His facial growth was denser than ever. And he was grumpy.

"Growing a beard?" I asked, trying to break the ice as he came over to meet with the writers.

"Yeah," Van Gundy growled. "I want to look like shit, like you."

Van Gundy's news of the day was that Camby would be the starting center for the pre-season opener in three days at the Garden. He also said he expected Camby to be the starting center on opening night of the regular season. It was a curious pronouncement considering his utter disgust a few days ago when Camby quit the running drill because of knee pain. Now he had suddenly become Ewing's heir to the throne. Several of the writers did a double-take. Van Gundy's words sometimes were hard to take at face value. Was this sudden promotion a way of lifting Camby's sliding trade value? Were the Knicks trying to lift Camby's spirits? Or was Van Gundy genuinely impressed?

"Marcus has developed into a very good practice player," Van Gundy said. "I only judge guys from what I see on the floor and he's been very good. I'd think he's starting off the bat. Whether he starts all year, I don't know. But I think he's going to have a big-time year. Our goal is to have him play 82 games."

Camby, who hadn't played more than 63 games in a season because of various injuries, seemed nonplused by the news. His mistrust of Van Gundy ran deep since his rocky first year with the club in 1999, when his playing time was minimal. Van Gundy had never wanted him on the team and objected strongly when he learned from Grunfeld that the team was about to trade Oakley for Camby.

"I know what I have in Charles," he told Grunfeld. "I don't know what I have in this kid. He hasn't played enough games."

The Knicks pulled the trigger anyway. Disappointed with Camby's work habits during the first few days of practice that season, Van Gundy maligned him in the press. Grunfeld was horrified. It served Van Gundy no purpose to bad-mouth Camby publicly. Demeaning Camby would only hurt his trade value. Grunfeld told Van Gundy to stop berating the Knicks' new young big man. So, instead of publicly ridiculing Camby, Van Gundy did it privately. "He's fool's gold," Van Gundy said.

Van Gundy keeps his one-on-one conversations with players to a minimum. Camby couldn't recall more than one or two conversations he'd had with him during his troubled first season. The players jokingly call Van Gundy "Hitler," not for anything else but the way he stiffly raises his arm like a salute instead of saying hello when he passes a player in a hallway. Camby was still unsure what to make of the news that Van Gundy had named him a starter. And he admitted he still felt pain in his knee.

"I don't worry about starting," Camby said. "I just want to contribute and play."

■ ■ ■

The news from Florida rolled into Charleston like a tidal wave. The Sunday papers reported that Miami's superstar center Alonzo Mourning was undergoing tests to determine the extent of a kidney disorder. There was speculation Mourning would have to miss the season. His career also was feared to be in jeopardy.

Other than Indiana's Reggie Miller, Mourning—the pugnacious center at the heart of Pat Riley's rugged crew—was the most hated basketball opponent at the Garden. He had fought numerous battles against the Knicks in the playoffs, and the Heat's addition of Grant and ex-Knick Anthony Mason over the summer had made Miami the heavy favorite in the East. Suddenly, that had all changed because of a bad kidney. The Knicks players were in shock. None of them wanted to talk about the basketball implications of Mourning's illness.

"Scary stuff," Van Gundy said to the writers. "I hope for his sake and ours we have to deal with him."

Houston had grown close to Mourning during the Olympics in Australia. They played golf together in a threesome with billionaire Bill Gates during an off day in Sydney.

"People ask me if there was one person who was a better person than I thought," Houston said. "He was definitely one of them." Then he added, "People talk about when he's going to be back. Let's hope he can be back, period."

■ ■ ■

Included in the stack of clips the Knicks' PR staff handed out to the beat writers was a lengthy ode to Ewing. By then, most fans had grown tired of reading Ewing's obituary as a Knick, but this one was different. It was written by Woody Allen and appeared in *The New York Times*.

Allen has been a long-time Knicks season-ticket holder, but he doesn't sit in the area known as Celebrity Row. He sits on the opposite sideline, in the first row behind the scorer's table at midcourt, where the players emerge from the tunnel. He attended games with his wife, Sun-Yi Previn. Quiet and to himself, Allen was rarely bothered by autograph seekers.

Allen's 1,200-word poetic treatise to Ewing was more poignant in its simplicity than the reams of good-bye columns produced by the New York and national sportswriters. Allen wrote, in part:

Patrick became the Franchise from the day they signed him. Not only was he seven-feet, he also had a lovely shot, his wrist snapping downward as he scored from inside or out. His game instincts were great and, like Reggie Miller, he had a willingness in the clutch to take the shot and the heat if it didn't go in. For years, the Knicks simply played to get the ball into Patrick and for years he did not disappoint. He was the whole show, and only Ewing's play kept the team from languishing near the bottom of the league season after season.

When No. 33 finally did look up after a decade and found that at last there were some truly special players alongside him who might form the critical mass needed to win it all, age had eroded his brilliance and he had sustained too many bad injuries . . . And so, the years passed without a championship season and New York's impatience grew and as Ewing was the franchise, disproportionate blame went to him. I also felt, like many fans, the team was more fun to watch when he was injured than when he was in the lineup. But exciting as it was, it was not better without Patrick.

If he had been surrounded by the current personnel in his great days rather than by the pugnacious brawlers who often made up the New York roster, it might have been a very different story. Many fans felt when Ewing came off the injured list it was like going from a word processor to an old Underwood. Everything slowed down as he clogged the middle, cramping the torrid style of Latrell Sprewell, who had ignited the Knicks and turned the public on with his wicked charisma.

There's a deeper value in teams keeping certain players for life despite the inevitable diminution of their skills. One thing I'm sure of, though, is that players the caliber of Patrick Ewing don't come along too often in any game. When you see Dave DeBusschere in reruns of the old draft lottery, when New York won the privilege of having Patrick play for us, DeBusschere was right in smiling and raising his arms in triumph.

Certainly, Allen had a future in another career if he wanted. His rumpled appearance made him look more like a sportswriter than an actor/filmmaker, anyway.

■ ■ ■

The Knicks broke their abbreviated Charleston training camp with a short walk-through to prepare for the Bulls' game the next night. The players headed for the bus, parked on the narrow street outside the College of Charleston gym. A cluster of autograph seekers, mostly young teenagers, mauled the players as they tried to get onto the bus that would take them to the Charleston airport. Many of the kids carried loose-leaf binders with laminated basketball cards, hoping to get them signed. The veteran Charleston autograph hounds hadn't bothered wasting their time with Ewing the last few years. He normally would walk by them, shaking his head, saying something like, "Not today," without breaking stride.

The most notorious Ewing autograph snub had occurred the prior Thanksgiving. Ewing was rehabbing his Achilles tendinitis that forced him to miss the first 20 games of the season. He hosted a Thanksgiving party at a Garden club lounge for a few dozen terminally ill children. At the end of the party, several of the kids asked Ewing for his autograph. Ewing refused, saying it was his policy not to sign on game days. Of course, Ewing wasn't playing that night.

He had also refused to talk to a handful of the beat writers who were at the function. Selena Roberts of *The Times* wrote a sentence about the autograph incident in the notes section of her game story. The Knicks were embarrassed and, to control the damage, had Ewing appear on MSG Network a few days later. Ewing said it was a superstition not to sign on game days.

With their former franchise player no longer setting the tone, these Knicks were extremely giving with the pen. A mob scene ensued around the bus. Sprewell signed his nickname, "Spree," for a dozen kids before getting on the bus, although he was more anxious than anyone to get back to Westchester.

"Give me a choice, I'd rather stay home," Sprewell said. "But if you're going to go somewhere, this is a nice place."

If the Charleston camp proved anything, it was that Sprewell had become the team leader. He was by far the most enthusiastic, animated player on the court. If he wasn't pounding his chest, he was clapping his hands, barking encouragement, slapping a teammate's behind or high-fiving somebody. And these were just scrimmages in October.

Ewing, never one to give a locker room talk, was one of the tri-captains last season along with the ever-quiet Houston and the vocal

Larry Johnson. A tri-captaincy vacancy existed, but Van Gundy was not prepared to fill it, even if Sprewell was the obvious choice. Van Gundy probably still didn't completely trust Sprewell, despite his public statements to the contrary. After all, they were only a season removed from Sprewell's first year in New York, when he often questioned Van Gundy's logic of making him the sixth man when he returned from a stress fracture during the lockout shortened campaign.

Van Gundy wanted his captains to be fully on his side. He believed it was coaching suicide for the captains to not fully support the coach. The first long losing streak would surely bring a mutiny.

Even after the Knicks made it to the 1999 Finals, Sprewell had told confidants he still hoped Van Gundy would get fired. Instead, Van Gundy got a four-year, $14-million contract extension and made Sprewell a starter for the 1999-2000 season. One of the sharpest guys in the league, Sprewell knew going to war with another coach was not in his best interests, so he began aligning himself with Van Gundy, keeping most negative thoughts to himself.

Meanwhile, Johnson and Houston (a coach's son, like Van Gundy) never wavered from his support of Van Gundy. Van Gundy could not imagine those two ever turning against him. So Sprewell remained the team's captain in spirit only.

Because of ankle injuries suffered by Houston and Rice, the perimeter trio nicknamed "The Gotham Guns" in *The Post* had yet to get on the floor together. Van Gundy took a long look at Sprewell at point guard during the Charleston scrimmages. Sprewell remained willing to sacrifice.

"I'm not going to be the greatest ballhandler, but if it's going to get Glen more minutes and keep Allan on the floor and make him happy, I'll get it done," Sprewell said. "Allan really doesn't want to handle the ball. He felt it took away from his offense. If I could make those guys happy, I will. I'll find ways to score. I don't know if Allan feels that way."

Sprewell's dominance and selflessness at the Charleston camp was just another chapter in his transformation. One year ago, he never made it to the six-day Charleston boot camp. His civil court case in Martinez, California, had lasted longer than expected. He had been charged with running a Toyota Corolla off an Oakland highway and injuring an elderly couple while driving 97 miles per hour.

When the trial ended with Sprewell paying minor damages, Sprewell drove his customized Mercedes cross-country instead of taking an immediate flight to Charleston to join the club. Sprewell failed to notify his agent or Knicks officials during his three-day journey through middle America. He gassed the speedometer up to 90, turned off his cell phone and listened to CDs the whole trip, oblivious to the fact that he was making headlines every day in the New York tabloids for his tardiness. Knicks brass was furious.

Sprewell is a car freak. He owns eight vehicles and an Internet business called Sprewell Racing that sells customized race-car accessories. However, he has since quit excessive speeding, and it didn't take the civil trial in California to bring him to his senses. He came around during the 1999-2000 season after staring at Bobby Phills' corpse in an open casket at a Charlotte church. The Hornets' small forward was killed while drag-racing Porches at 109 miles per hour with teammate David Wesley on a road outside Charlotte Coliseum. The league ordered the Hornets to play their ensuing game against the Knicks two days after the tragedy. The Knicks flew into town the night before, but after constant pleas from the Hornets, the league canceled the game.

The Knicks stuck around for the memorial service. Each player approached the casket separately to pay his respects. Sprewell lingered the longest. He stared at Phills' dead body. A folded Hornets' jersey was by Phills' stomach. Sprewell's body trembled. He cried. Sprewell knew the person in the casket could have been him. He thanked God for being alive.

Now, as Sprewell signed autographs for the kids on the sidewalk in front of the bus after playing the Charleston scrimmages as if they were Game 7 of the Finals, he was far removed from being labeled sports' most reviled villain.

CHAPTER 3

Starting over without Ew

October 10-14

Three minutes into their pre-season opener against the Bulls, the Knicks were down 9-0. At one point during the first quarter, they trailed the worst team in basketball by 13 points. One fan yelled, "We want Pat." Another one held up a sign urging the Knicks to trade Checketts and Layden. The Garden was half-empty. Celebrity Row was vacant, even though this meaningless exhibition game carried an air of importance: the first organized game for the Knicks in 16 years without Ewing as part of the franchise.

During the gruesome first quarter, Knicks public relations director Lori Hamamoto, sitting at courtside, received an unexpected call on her cell phone. The caller was Ewing, who had been watching the game via satellite in Seattle. Ewing had made his Seattle debut the night before at the Tacoma Dome and received a very warm reception from the crowd. He had four points and seven rebounds in 20 minutes.

Ewing had called Hamamoto to tease her about how bad the Knicks looked. Ewing had become a close friend with Hamamoto, who put up with his lack of cooperation with the media. A reserved sort herself, she seemed to relate to Ewing better than anyone.

The Knicks righted themselves in time to win the game, gaining their first lead with a minute left in the third quarter. Houston did not play because of his sore ankle, but the unfortunate fans who attended the game got their first look at Rice in a Knicks uniform. Starting because of Houston's absence, he scored 20 points only because he made all 16 of his free throws. Rice appeared too anxious, rushing shots and looking awkward on post-up attempts. Van Gundy hoped to get Rice those chances because the team's former primary post option was now on the other side of the country. With Rice shooting bricks from the field and Camby (three points, two rebounds, 25 minutes) not asserting himself on the glass, the 96-91 victory had a hollow feel.

Van Gundy blamed Rice's errant shooting performance on him not being in game shape. "I don't think he had good legs under him offensively," Van Gundy said.

Rice banged his knee on the floor in the second quarter after a hard foul by Elton Brand. He needed treatment for 30 minutes after the game and limped noticeably in the locker room. But he was all smiles. He had been the most affable Knick since training camp began, a stark contrast to the scowling Ewing. Rice surprised the beat writers who had heard about his poor relationship with the Lakers' reporters last season. But he no longer felt unappreciated and no longer was playing for a coach he hated.

"It's like a tattoo," Rice said after he put on his new Knicks uniform before the game. "I don't want to take it off."

■ ■ ■

At practice the next day, rookie defensive specialist Pete Mickeal, whom the Knicks selected with the last pick in the NBA Draft, revealed that his former coach at Cincinnati, Bob Huggins, had called to tell him some good news. "The assistant coaches said you put yourself in great position to make the team," Huggins told Mickeal on the phone.

Mickeal and Postell, both second-round picks, were battling for roster spots on a team with a surplus of shooting guards and small forwards. Both were extremely cocky. They didn't take guff from anyone, and Van Gundy liked them for it.

"My chances of making the team?" Mickeal said. "Obviously, they're great."

Obviously. When asked how he enjoyed going up against Sprewell, Rice and Houston in practice—all guys who play his position—Mickeal said, "No big deal. It's just like any other competition with any other players."

"Neither is afraid," Van Gundy said. "They have toughness. It's hard to find toughness." Problem was, Mickeal, as gritty as he was, did not possess an NBA-caliber jump shot.

Emboldened by an impressive performance in a summer league in Boston, Postell almost held out of training camp because he was offered the minimum salary of $317,000. His agent, Dan Fegan, a David Falk in the making, tried to force the Knicks into trading him.

"I'm not playing to make the team," Postell said after the first week of camp. "I'm playing for playing time."

■ ■ ■

With the Sixers in town for the Knicks' second exhibition game, Allen Iverson received most of the pre-game attention. He had visited the league offices to meet with David Stern about his soon-to-be-released gangsta rap CD, tentatively titled *Non-Fiction.* Portions of the lyrics for the track "40 Bars" were released by Universal Music. The lyrics were viewed as degrading women and gays while promoting the use of handguns, and included such lines as, "Get murdered in the second and first degree/Come in me with faggot tendencies/You be sleeping where the maggots be" and "Everybody stay fly/Get money kill and fuck bitches/I'm hittin' anything/And planning on using my riches."

Ward, the Bible-studying point guard, matched up against Iverson that night. He had not heard the CD or seen the lyrics. But of gangsta rap in general, Ward said, "I refuse to listen to stuff like that. I call it garbage. That's where it needs to be. I listen to gospel. If they're not talking positive about anything, then it's garbage to me. It poisons the soul."

■ ■ ■

Ninety minutes before every game at the Garden, Van Gundy meets with the beat writers in a utility room down the hall from the locker room. Often, serious issues are discussed, sidebar material used for early editions of *The Post, The Times* and *The Daily News,* whose deadlines are too early to include an account of the game. Occasionally, his meeting with the beat writers is just a bull-rap session in which he goes off on tangents unrelated to the game. This was one of those times. The topic was clothing. I had dressed in an olive suit with matching tie that night. Van Gundy, used to seeing me dressed in Oscar Madison attire, was stunned.

Van Gundy was intrigued by clothes only because his own unstylish appearance had become overanalyzed. Van Gundy had the fashion misfortune of following the GQ-ish Riley, whose Armani suits became a fabric of Knicks' culture. When Van Gundy was his assistant, Riley once told him, "You can be a head coach in this league, but you've got to start dressing better."

The inquisitive Van Gundy wanted to know what the occasion was for the suit and tie. "It's early in the season and I still have the energy to dress up," I answered sheepishly. "Soon I'll be beaten down by the grind of the travel and it gets harder and harder to find the energy or time to dress up."

"Energy?" Van Gundy said. "Wow. Never heard that."

The topic turned to Van Gundy's wardrobe. A recent *Sports Illustrated* feature had described him as "looking like he's wearing his father's suit." Van Gundy would just as soon wear a sweatshirt and sweatpants on the bench, but league rules required a jacket. Two years ago, Van Gundy was invited to the U.S. Open Tennis Tournament in nearby Queens to sit in the United States Tennis Association president's box. He was thrilled by the invite until he found out he had to wear a suit. Although he attended the tournament all gussied up, he certainly would've rather been in the last row wearing shorts and sneakers.

Someone asked Van Gundy why he doesn't dress more casually for games, like his counterpart that night, Sixers coach Larry Brown, who often wears black turtlenecks with a sports coat.

"Larry always looks good whatever he wears," Van Gundy said. "If I did that, people would just say I'm trying too hard."

■ ■ ■

A healed Houston returned to the lineup against the Sixers and made his pre-season debut. The first look at the Gotham Guns troika lasted all of three minutes, 43 seconds. Sprewell turned his ankle on Iverson's shoe with 1:11 left in the first half. Houston, Rice and Sprewell had all sprained their ankles in the first eight days of pre-season.

But the Knicks prevailed over the Sixers as Camby, in the pivot, outplayed the stout Theo Ratliff with a 12-point, 11-rebound showing, jamming in a Larry Johnson miss to punctuate the night.

"I'll see Theo on the 31st," Camby said, referring to the season opener on Halloween Night. "I definitely want to set the tone. I wanted to let those guys know on the 31st, it's going to be the same thing."

Camby's performance didn't erase the specter of Mutombo that was hanging over the Knicks. Hawks' GM Pete Babcock responded to recent statements by Mutombo that he wouldn't sign a contract extension. Regarding trade talks with the Knicks and others, Babcock said from Atlanta, "There's nothing out there that will make us better for today or the future. There is nothing on the horizon we would consider saying yes to, but that could change tomorrow."

October 15

After the Knicks practiced and headed for Hartford, Sprewell said he wouldn't campaign for the team captaincy but would still campaign to bring in Webber, whom he had just spoken to on the phone the day before.

"We're trying to make it happen, man, as soon as possible," Sprewell said. "We're working on it." Sprewell would not elaborate, but when asked if he had spoken to Layden about Webber, he said, "They know what I'm thinking."

Sprewell claimed he was not insulted about not being named a captain. "These guys know if I have something to say, I'm going to say it," he said. "You don't have to be named captain to be a leader. You don't need more than two captains. Allan and LJ have been here longer than I have."

October 16

Van Gundy watched the press conference from his Hartford hotel room with tears in his eyes. There was Mourning and Riley on television telling the world that his kidney disorder would force him to miss the season. It sounded like his career was in doubt, too.

Van Gundy made sure the players knew about Mourning before they got to the Hartford Civic Center for their game against Washington. He told them they'd be asked about Mourning by the media and hoped they would refrain from talking about him from a basketball standpoint. He felt that would be in poor taste. The facts were the facts, though. Losing Mourning meant the Heat were no longer favorites to win the East.

In a somber locker room, the players were in no mood to discuss their suddenly enhanced position in the Eastern Conference. "I feel so badly for Alonzo and I'm just really thinking right now about his health and recovery," Van Gundy said. "Right now is not a time to discuss how his absence affects basketball when there are so many greater issues out there."

Houston said, "It's unfair to talk about basketball, the NBA and how it has changed at the expense of somebody's life."

Only Camby, who always speaks his mind, came closest to acknowledging what Mourning's illness meant to the Knicks. "It was wide open even before he was sick," Camby said.

That night against the Wizards' 285-pound center Jahidi White, Camby posted solid numbers: 16 points, 11 rebounds. But he was pushed around severely by the bullish Wizards center. On one play, White, who outweighed Camby by 60 pounds, backed him into the lane, turned and dunked over him as if he wasn't there.

A native of Hartford, Camby was unhappy with his performance. As part of his Cambyland Foundation, he had bought 600 tickets for school children from Hartford elementary schools. He had recently been criticized by a Hartford school official for relocating his "March with Marcus" from Hartford to Harlem. Camby, who does more community service work than any Knick other than Ward, walked a group of Harlem children to their first day of school. Imagine getting criticized for such a benevolent act.

After the game, when he was asked about White's inside dominance, Camby became protective. "I'm not a center. I'm not a center," he said. "Let's get that in print. I'm playing out of position."

The remarks surely didn't go down well with Van Gundy's morning coffee the next day. At the following practice, Van Gundy said, "Let me clarify it. He is a center. For us." Van Gundy absolved Camby of blame in the White matchup. He felt Camby's teammates left him out to dry. "We backed away as much as we could," Van Gundy said. "We have to be willing to have our noses bloodied."

Van Gundy also criticized the "Big Backcourt" cameo, mostly for its defense. Continuing to hint the experiment was about finished, he said, "I'll tell you, our point guards have been our best players so far." Van Gundy hadn't said those words before.

■ ■ ■

The hype for the upcoming Subway Series between the Yankees and Mets had swept through the city and grabbed most of the media attention from the post-Patrick Knicks. Long-time trainer Mike Saunders was a diehard Yankees fan and assistant trainer Said Hamdan, a Long Island resident, bled Mets' orange and blue. Saunders and Hamdan each campaigned the players to join their sides.

"I'm Jewish and he's Arab and we see eye to eye on that stuff," Saunders said. "But when it comes to Mets and Yankees, that's where we draw the line."

Travis Knight, who played at UConn but hails from Utah, wore a Mets cap around the locker room throughout the Subway Series. "I don't really like the Mets," Knight said. "I just hate the Yankees."

Van Gundy, an astute follower of New York sports, was interested in his fellow New York coaches and managers. He liked to see how they got treated in the tabloids. And he liked to read their quotes, how they publicly handled the tricky, controversial, in-house issues. Van Gundy professed to admire Mets manager Bobby Valentine and Yankees skipper Joe Torre.

"I think they've both done it with totally different personalities," Van Gundy said. "It just proves it's not about personality. It's about getting them to believe. They've both done that. I like reading the articles about them every day. Joe had a great line the other day: You have to be intense without being tense. I pick up things like that from both of them."

October 18

The Knicks faced the Bucks at the Garden in their third exhibition game, which gave Van Gundy and Milwaukee general manager Ernie Grunfeld another chance to ignore each other in the hallway.

Grunfeld, a New York native who was selling his house in New Jersey, had close ties to New York. He had worked for the Knicks for 18 years as a player and administrator, working his way up the corporate ladder. Checketts fired him over dessert in an Italian restaurant in Westchester during the 1999 lockout season. Grunfeld had lost a bitter power struggle with Van Gundy, who led Grunfeld's players to the Finals and earned a four-year, $14-million contract extension.

Despite Van Gundy's opposition, Grunfeld had traded for Camby because he knew the Knicks had to get younger at some point. Camby shone during the playoff surge. Now, as he took his seat a few rows behind the Bucks' bench, Grunfeld was still in shock that his successors had traded Ewing.

"It was never discussed when I was here," Grunfeld said in his thick Brooklyn accent. "Patrick was a franchise player. To see him in a Seattle uniform was strange. I spoke to him and he's happy and I'm pleased for him. But the Knicks are still a team to be reckoned with."

Grunfeld was in the process of hiring former Knicks interim general manager Ed Tapscott as his right-hand man. At the time of Layden's hiring in August, 1999, some reporters were outraged that Checketts did not name Tapscott as GM instead. An African-American with a law degree and nine years with the Knicks, Tapscott was shocked he didn't get the job after spending three months as the interim GM. But he was extremely close with Grunfeld, which hurt his bid. Checketts was worried that Van Gundy and Tapscott would have trouble working together. Van Gundy did not offer his support for Tapscott either, feeling it was best to bring in fresh blood.

Tapscott felt he had been hung out to dry six weeks before on the drafting of seven-foot-two French center Frederic Weis. The Knicks passed on popular New York swingman Ron Artest of St. John's. Weis, clearly a project lacking strength, was such a bust at the summer league in July that *The Post* ran the front-page headline, "French Toast."

Tapscott had his reasons for passing on Artest. When Artest came in for a pre-draft workout at Purchase in front of the scouts and coaching staff, he begged off with a stomach ache and didn't participate. Shawn Marion was also in that day. The Knicks had planned for them to work out against each other. The super-talented Marion, now a star with the Phoenix Suns, had badly outplayed Artest in a prior workout with another organization. With Artest desperately wanting to be drafted by his hometown team, some members of the Knicks' staff thought he was faking his illness to avoid looking bad against Marion. The Knicks' front-office staff began calling Artest's illness "The Shawn Marion Flu." Even had Weis been unavailable when the Knicks drafted fifteenth, Tapscott was going to pass on Artest to take James Posey, who wound up in Denver. The morning after the draft, though, Tapscott felt betrayed when he saw a quote in the newspaper from Van Gundy alluding to how much he loved Artest's game.

When Layden was hired, Checketts begged a devastated Tapscott to come to the news conference. "We have to show we're united in this," Checketts told him.

Tapscott, who had three years left on his contract, wanted nothing to do with it. But he sought to make a deal with Checketts. If he went to the press conference, Checketts had to agree to let him work one more season with the Knicks as a college scout with scant office duties, then get paid for the final year left on his contract. Checketts opposed the idea. He felt he needed the popular Tapscott to be a visible presence at Penn Plaza, working alongside Layden as the No. 2 guy in the transition.

"I need you to build bridges for Scott," Checketts told him.

Tapscott felt that if Layden was getting paid more than $1 million a year, he could build his own bridges. Otherwise, Checketts had picked the wrong guy. Checketts finally gave in to Tapscott's demands.

The Tapscott issue had overshadowed Layden at the news conference, and Checketts was caught off guard. The first five questions were hurled at Checketts like a grenade: "What does it say about the Knicks organization to pass on a highly-qualified African-American for a visible front-office post in New York City?" reporters asked.

Checketts was sickened to be painted with a racial brush. Less than two months later, he hired Steven Mills, an African-American, as executive vice president of franchise operations.

Meanwhile, Tapscott faded away. He stopped getting invited to meetings at Penn Plaza. His phone calls were never returned. He then learned he was not put on the Knicks' credential list for the All-Star Game in Oakland. Tapscott had never missed an All-Star Game while working for the Knicks. It was a time to gather information from other club officials. Tapscott decided to pay his own way and brought along his wife and daughter. Checketts seemed startled to see him in the hotel lobby of a San Francisco hotel. During the game, Tapscott sat in the Bucks' seats next to Grunfeld and Grunfeld's family, three rows in front of Checketts' contingent.

Two days later, Tapscott was summoned to Layden's office. "Tap, we're going to go in a different direction," Layden said. "I think the communication has broken down."

Tapscott knew there was no point arguing. This directive wasn't coming from Layden. Tapscott had learned from an ally in the office that Checketts was fuming about him sitting with Grunfeld. But, as a final insult, Layden told Tapscott he wouldn't get his $60,000 playoff bonus.

"I just have one thing to say to you, Scott," Tapscott said. "I just want to wish you luck because I know there's a lot of shitty things they make you do around here."

■ ■ ■

Rice did not suit up for the victory against Milwaukee because of the knee injury he had aggravated again in Hartford. The Knicks moved to 4-0 as Camby, with Grunfeld watching proudly, notched his third straight double-double (18 points, 10 rebounds).

October 19

The movie *Black and White* had just hit the video rental stores. The basketball movie featured a star-studded cast and one NBA All-Star, Houston.

"If you're going to rent it," Houston told me, "don't watch it with your kids."

"Really," I said.

"Yeah, really," Houston said.

Ben Stiller, Brooke Shields, Mike Tyson, Robert Downey Jr. and Claudia Schiffer were all featured in the flick. Houston, in his acting debut, did the movie during the 1999 lockout. Stiller remained friends with Houston and was a frequent guest on Celebrity Row. He occasionally stopped into the locker room to visit Houston.

In the movie, Houston plays a star college point guard named Dean who accepts a $50,000 bribe from the Stiller character to shave points. That was the tame part of the film. The opening scene shows two white teenaged girls having sex with a black gangsta rapper in the woods.

When Iverson caught heat for his gangsta rap CD, Houston, a devout Christian who attends Ward's bible study sessions on the road and is a diligent participant in the pre-game chapel, started feeling guilty himself.

"I probably wouldn't do it if I had to do it over again," Houston said. "I wouldn't have played that kind of a role. I wouldn't want my daughter to see that movie, even though it's just a role. I can't say there's a big difference between the movie [and Iverson's CD]. But the bottom line is, if I did music, what I say in the music wouldn't be what I did in that movie. Allan Houston wouldn't have taken the bribe."

October 20

Their exhibition game against Utah was still nine hours away and already Van Gundy was in a lousy mood. His unbeaten club had arrived at the Pepsi Arena in downtown Albany, New York, at 9:30 a.m. for the morning shootaround. As the players walked onto the court, the baskets were not up. Instead of sticking around to ask for help, Van Gundy and his players bolted the arena.

"All he had to do was contact someone and we could've gotten the problem fixed right away," said an arena official, who claimed the team arrived a half-hour earlier than scheduled.

As Van Gundy held court with the writers before the Jazz game, ex-Knick John Starks strolled by. Starks, a huge Garden favorite, and Van Gundy had a love-hate relationship during his tumultuous, but mostly productive, stint with the Knicks. No one got on Van Gundy's nerves more than the erratic Starks, but Van Gundy also loved his defensive grit and competitive spirit. And when his perimeter bombs were scorching through the hoop, he was among the most explosive shooting guards in the league.

The other night in East Lansing, Michigan, Starks, who signed with Utah as a free agent over the summer, was ejected for arguing with an official. He also had missed the team bus that day and arrived late to the Albany arena. Van Gundy couldn't help himself.

"Hey John," Van Gundy called out. "The writers all want to know how many practices you're going to miss this season."

Starks ignored him. One of Ewing's closest friends, Starks later told reporters in the locker room how sorry the Knicks would be to have traded Patrick. "Most people disagree, but I feel keeping him here would've given them a better chance, probably a favorite to come out of the East without Mourning," Starks said.

The morning shootaround snafu was a bad omen, as the Knicks lost, 96-90, and dropped to 4-1. Rice did not play for the second straight game after missing the last few days of practice with a bum knee.

The Big Backcourt experiment was on life support. Injuries to each of the three Gotham Guns had torpedoed Van Gundy's plans. Just nine days remained until the season opener. Sprewell shot one-of-nine against Utah and Van Gundy decided his dabbling at point guard was hurting his overall game.

In addition, the two point guards, Ward and Childs were having strong camps. Childs, in particular, had so outplayed Erick Strickland that Van Gundy no longer viewed Strickland as a point guard. Strickland, sloppy with the ball, would now have to scrape for minutes at shooting guard.

"I think it's something I have to evaluate," Van Gundy said about Sprewell's rhythm being disrupted at point guard. "Certainly, you don't want to take someone away from what they're good at."

October 24-25

The time had come for the Knicks' first-year assistant coach Kevin O'Neill to clear the air with Houston. The 43-year-old O'Neill had heard through the grapevine that Houston held a grudge against him since 1993, when O'Neill became Wade Houston's successor as coach at Tennessee. When O'Neill took over after Wade Houston's dismissal, he made remarks about the past coaching staff that Wade took as a slap in the face. Houston had played for his father at Tennessee but had been drafted into the league by the time he was fired and O'Neill was hired.

O'Neill, the third assistant under Van Gundy behind Don Chaney and Tom Thibodeau, talked with Houston to make sure bygones were bygones. Houston told O'Neill he held no grudge.

With that out of the way, O'Neill could continue having the most fun as a coach he'd had in more than 10 years. O'Neill had coached Marquette, Tennessee and, most recently, Northwestern. He had grown sick of recruiting and schmoozing with alumni at countless fundraisers. When he was at Marquette in the early 1990s, O'Neill gained notoriety as the coach depicted in the Academy-award winning documentary, *Hoop Dreams,* a tale of two basketball recruits from Chicago's rough Cabrini Green projects whom O'Neill attempted to recruit.

Entering countless strangers' living rooms like a life insurance salesman had eroded O'Neill's joy of college coaching. He found the routine demeaning. Every recruit, even if he was marginally talented enough for Division I basketball, asked the same question: He wanted to know his chances of getting to the NBA. The parents, too, grilled O'Neill on how he would help their son get there. O'Neill knew that 99 percent of these inner-city recruits with barely acceptable grades had a better chance of becoming Rhodes Scholars than of making the NBA. He tried to speak to them honestly without crushing their dream. His stock response was, "If you're good enough, they'll find you. That will be up to you."

O'Neill was angry that using basketball as a vehicle to get a free college education that cost other families upwards of $100,000 wasn't good enough for many parents. The parents wanted to use basketball as the avenue to turn their sons into millionaires.

O'Neill also despised sucking up to the alumni. At Tennessee, he spent all of May riding around in an orange Winnebago attending alumni golf outings across the state. O'Neill is a schmoozer by nature, but even this became too much for him.

Although he had limited authority as a third assistant for Van Gundy, the job was all about basketball, a refreshing change. The players' off-the-court issues unrelated to basketball were handled by their agents, not the coaches. There was no next level to worry about. O'Neill was enjoying himself. He wished he had quit the college game sooner.

■ ■ ■

With three days off before the next exhibition game against the Nets, Van Gundy met with Rice, Sprewell and Houston in his office before practice to tell them about the personal sacrifices in store for this season. Unable to fully experiment with the Big Backcourt alignment that put them on the court together, Van Gundy knew he'd have to start the season with a conventional point-guard lineup. That meant Rice, for the first time in his career, would come off the bench as the Sixth Man.

Van Gundy told Rice, "Listen, you could choose to be an asshole this season if you want to be and there's nothing I can do about it." Van Gundy told Rice that if he made sacrifices, he could win a second championship ring.

Rice had a four-year guaranteed contract worth $36 million, most likely his last contract at age 33. Van Gundy realized Rice would not be motivated by the league's biggest incentive: playing for a new deal. If NBA contracts were not guaranteed, as NFL contracts are, Van Gundy's job would be easier. He understood he had to be careful with Rice, who grew to hate Phil Jackson because of playing time issues. Van Gundy knew keeping Rice happy could be a key to the season and maybe his biggest test as the Knicks' coach.

Van Gundy reminded Sprewell of the sacrifice he made coming off the bench during his first season in New York in 1999, when the Knicks made the finals. Van Gundy mentioned to Houston that he also had sacrificed, when Starks was with the team. Some nights, Starks finished games at shooting guard. Van Gundy told his star-studded trio that he was not comfortable with the big backcourt to start or finish games and that there would be times when only two of the three would be on the court at the end.

"There are going to be tough times," Van Gundy said to the writers after the meeting with his Gotham Guns. "If we finish with just two of the three and we lose, the other guy is going to think he should've been in there. One thing you can't hide in this league is if you're a team guy or not. I think we have a chance for a special season if we have team guys."

Against the Nets at The Meadowlands, Van Gundy didn't have to worry about getting the three on the court together. Rice missed his third straight game with a bruised knee in the Knicks' 90-81 win.

After the game, Van Gundy made an eyebrow-raising announcement. The next night, they would play the Wizards and their big center, Jahidi White, at Nassau Coliseum. Van Gundy said he wanted a bigger body on White and would start 330-pound Felton Spencer, he of the 19 percent body fat. It was clear Van Gundy was playing motivational mind games. If Camby felt he "was not a center," as he claimed after getting pushed around by White in Hartford, then the coach would start a player who thought of himself as one. After his bout with White, Camby had also complained of a bad back. Van Gundy and the coaching staff felt Camby's remark meant he was not ready to mix it up with the big boys.

October 26

Sprewell's trip to Long Island turned into a nightmare. He didn't know how he got lost, but as he drove from Westchester, he took a wrong exit that put him somewhere in unfamiliar Queens. He got assistant trainer Said Hamdan, a Long Island resident, on the cell phone, and Hamdan directed Sprewell to safety.

Other than Manhattan and Westchester, Sprewell knew little about the New York area. Fighting through rush-hour traffic and getting lost put him in a frantic state. Sprewell thought he would not make it to the arena in time for the game, and that there would be hell to pay from Van Gundy.

Sprewell felt fortunate to arrive at Nassau Coliseum 20 minutes before tipoff. But by that time, the pre-game meeting had been held and Sprewell had lost his starting job for the evening to Strickland.

Sprewell's tardiness for home games at the Garden had become an issue with Van Gundy. Players are supposed to show up 90 minutes before the opening tipoff. That meant they were supposed to be in the locker room at six o'clock for the usual 7:30 start at the Garden. Otherwise, they'd be fined.

Ninety percent of the time, Sprewell was on the West Side Highway at six o'clock. He usually showed up 15 minutes late. Eyebrows would raise in the Knicks' locker room only if he sauntered in a half hour late. Trainer Mike Saunders, the official attendance taker, usually looked the other way unless the player was more than 20 minutes late. Saunders never told Sprewell whether he'd be fined. The few hundred bucks were automatically deducted from his paycheck.

Sprewell thought the fines were petty. "If they had to get it from me, they'd have to sue me," he said.

Before Sprewell's arrival, the locker room was filled with lively banter. Players ranked on each other from across the room. The writers had noticed that with Ewing gone, the byplay in the room had increased. Rice and Strickland, both outgoing and loud, had added to the jocularity. Ewing's locker room demeanor had consisted of putting on headphones, listening to reggae or hip-hop music, bouncing a basketball and tuning out the world. His policy was written in stone: He never granted interviews to reporters before games.

On this night, the players bragged about their alma maters. "Where'd you go?" Michigan scholar Glen Rice barked across the room at Kurt Thomas. "Wagon Wheel State? I won a [NCAA] title."

Thomas had gone to Texas Christian University and was very proud of it. Thomas led the NCAA in scoring and rebounding his senior year in 1995 and liked to remind his teammates of the fact. Johnson, the ex-UNLV hotshot, and Thomas, buddies from Dallas, often sparred about the issue.

"About every other day, I have to hear how he got his 30 and 20 at TCU," Johnson said. "I mean, they played Rice like eight times a year. Rice and SMU. You gotta get 30 off those guys."

51

Strickland started at small forward and Sprewell sat out the first ten minutes of the first quarter to the dismay of the Long Island fans who had plucked down $20 or $30 a ticket partly to see Sprewell. They had no idea why Sprewell had suddenly became a reserve.

■ ■ ■

At halftime, Layden met with the writers about Minnesota's Joe Smith, whose contract had been terminated by the league because of an under-the-table agreement with Wolves' management. Smith, a power forward, hadn't lived up to his status as the first pick in the draft in 1995, but he could help the Knicks at their weakest position. Sprewell's presence was another selling point. They were close friends and roommates at Golden State.

But the Knicks were well over the salary cap and could only offer Smith a $2.25 million cap exception. Teams which were over the cap were granted a $2.25 million cap exception to try to lure free agents. Layden admitted the Knicks had heavy interest in Smith. "He's certainly a great player," he said. "We will certainly see if we can get him here. With any free agent, we have to show him who we are."

The writers thought they had their story for the night. But when the Knicks lost, 87-86, on a three-pointer by Washington's Chris Whitney with 2.4 seconds remaining, things turned interesting during Van Gundy's post-game meeting with the media.

"We're a bullshit team right now, the way we conduct ourselves," Van Gundy said, fuming. "Poor execution in the fourth quarter, shots we take down the stretch, temper tantrums on the floor, not knowing coverages, blown sets, not being ready to play on back-to-back nights. It's a fucking loose atmosphere the last two weeks. They were more worried about the fucking World Series than about our own team. I'm not talking just about the players. I've got to fucking coach better."

The glowering Van Gundy called the Knicks a "bullshit team" four times and said Ward was the only player who competed. When a radio guy asked Van Gundy for any positives, Van Gundy snapped, "I just said Charlie Ward played hard!" He cut off the interview and bolted in a huff, angry at the world. When he left the coach's room and headed for the bus, he slammed the door behind him, loud enough for the players in the adjacent locker room to hear.

Sprewell's lateness was only a contributor to Van Gundy's ire. He had heard a couple of players on the bench talking about the Mets-Yankees Subway Series scores that flashed on the scoreboard during the game. After four straight wins, sloppiness had infested the Knicks' play in two straight defeats.

Van Gundy's reaction did not sit well with some of the players, but Sprewell was used to it. If this had been his first week as a Knick, he would have been peeved. But he knew Van Gundy was simply trying to motivate them with the season-opener just four days away.

Van Gundy's negativity got to Houston, who stuck up for his teammates.

"I wouldn't call us a B.S. team," he said. "We try to treat our jobs seriously."

October 27

Before the Knicks flew to San Antonio for their final exhibition game against the mighty Spurs at the Alamodome, the Knicks waived Stepania and Lazaro Borrell, two players acquired in the Ewing deal. Van Gundy hadn't played them at all in any of the exhibition games.

■ ■ ■

Hanging from a blue curtain in the Alamodome was a huge black-and-gray 1999 NBA championship banner. The banner caught Houston and Sprewell's eyes every time they came here and reminded them of the Knicks' loss to the Spurs in the 1999 finals. The sight made them feel uneasy.

Before the game, Van Gundy agreed to participate in an interview with a German television crew doing a documentary on the NBA. The first question threw Van Gundy for a loop.

"We read you are after Mutombo. Is that true?" the reporter asked. It was a question Van Gundy could not answer on the record, and a question an NBA beat writer would not ask unless it was off the record. Any positive response by Van Gundy, especially on videotape, would be immediate grounds for being fined by the league for tampering. Mutombo was under contract to the Hawks. Officials from other teams are forbidden from commenting on their interest in obtaining another player.

Van Gundy retained his poise and answered, pointing to a couple of beat writers giggling at the awkward moment. "I don't know, why don't you ask them," he said. "They're the ones making up the rumors."

The next question was, "Why do you drink Diet Coke?" Van Gundy's swilling of Diet Coke, which he props on the press table next to the bench, is one of his trademark habits. He goes through about four cans a game. Van Gundy is adamant about not doing commercials or print ads. The Coca-Cola marketing department is well aware of this but sent Van Gundy cases of Diet Coke periodically. Having the Knicks coach guzzle its product during games is better exposure than an ad anyhow.

"I guess because I like it," Van Gundy responded.

The interview was painful to watch. "Much is made of your brother being on the arch-rival Heat," the reporter asked. "Do you talk to him a lot?"

"Yeah, he's my brother," Van Gundy said. He would not cave in. If the German reporter was looking for any thoughtful answers, none were forthcoming.

When the interviewed ended, Van Gundy looked over to PR chief Lori Hamamoto and said, "You owe me big-time for that one."

■ ■ ■

When he met with a couple of the beat writers, Van Gundy addressed Sprewell's tardiness. Van Gundy had said before that if Sprewell showing up 15 to 20 minutes late on game night was his worst transgression, he'd gladly take it. But his tardiness for the game on Long Island had been excessive.

"Professionalism is important," Van Gundy said. "Your best players set a tone. Good or bad. Latrell helps set a great tone, but better time management on days of home games would be a help."

Sprewell's stomach had turned even before he got onto the court and saw the Spurs' championship banner. The sight of P. J. Carlesimo made him queasy.

Sprewell found out before pre-game warmups that Carlesimo was announcing the game for the Spurs' local cable television network. Larry Johnson had given him the heads-up after spotting Carlesimo at the broadcast table chatting with two writers. Carlesimo, out of coaching since Golden State fired him during the 1999-2000 season, had signed to broadcast 55 Spurs games this season in an attempt to fill the basket-ball void in his life.

Sprewell and Carlesimo had been under the same roof just three times since "The Choke," once at the arbitration hearing and also at the two Golden State-Knicks games during the 1999-2000 season. They had not spoken a word to each other since Sprewell yelled, "I'll kill you" as he throttled Carlesimo's neck. In the first meeting in Golden State during the 1999-2000 season, Carlesimo walked toward midcourt, intent on shaking Sprewell's hand. But Sprewell remained under the basket, ignoring him.

A gruff Jersey guy who talks fast and freely with a *Soprano's* accent, Carlesimo told reporters before the Spurs' game, "In a different set-ting, I'd like to talk to him. Somewhere else where we could sit one-on-one in private and not have the cameras. That's the only situation we've been in together so far."

A surreal scene developed during pre-game warm-ups. Carlesimo stood on the sidelines on the Knicks' side of the court, gearing up for a spot for the pre-game show. While Carlesimo waited for the red light of the camera, Sprewell waited his turn on the layup line. The two men linked forever in sports history were within two feet of each other, their backs nearly touching. Neither turned around. They never made eye contact the whole night. Afterward, Sprewell said, "I don't think it's ever going to be closed. I don't think anything would be helped by talking."

Sprewell truly resented Carlesimo. He considered him a hard-headed dictator who never paid any mind to a player's feelings or advice. He would pick up the phone if Carlesimo called him, as long as nobody would find out. But he didn't think Carlesimo had any desire to rec-oncile their differences other than for his own public relations pur-poses. In Sprewell's mind, Carlesimo wanted to patch old wounds only to enhance his chances of getting another coaching job. Sprewell wanted no part of that.

■ ■ ■

In a 90-79 loss to the Spurs, the Knicks were no match inside for the Texas Towers, David Robinson and Tim Duncan, particularly because Camby had back pain and did not play, making him a question mark for the season opener in four days. The six-foot, six-inch Johnson was forced to play center. Rice played power forward for the first time in his career. That allowed Van Gundy to play the three Gotham Guns at the same time. Finally.

October 30

The just-released *Sports Illustrated* basketball issue contained a long feature on Van Gundy by the gifted writer Scott Price. "He was a nice guy, but you never know how those things will come out," said Van Gundy, clearly pleased by the way the article turned out.

All of the classic Van Gundy tales were in it, replete with his decision to drop out of Yale after getting cut from the basketball team. He had left the Ivy League to attend Menlo Junior College in Menlo Park, California so he could resume being an overachieving five-foot-nine point guard.

The legendary popcorn story involving Yalie Jodi Foster, the actress, was mentioned. Van Gundy and 12 dorm buddies had thrown in $100 each. Whoever landed a date with Foster would win the entire $1,200. One day, Van Gundy was munching popcorn outside a candy store when sirens roared by. Van Gundy stopped to watch when he heard a flirtatious voice: "Boy, that popcorn smells good."

Van Gundy turned around and saw Foster standing by herself. All he had to do was offer her some popcorn, hang out a few minutes and the $1,200 surely was his. But Van Gundy couldn't get a word out, except to say, "Uh-uh." Then he turned and ran away. The moral? He vowed never to get overwhelmed by a moment again.

After the final practice before the season opener, Van Gundy spent several minutes laughing with the writers about his Yale days. To this day, he holds a grudge against the Yale coach that cut him after watching Van Gundy play a pickup game. Van Gundy said that back when he was a Knicks assistant, in the early 1990s, the Yale coach came up to him at the Garden by the bench, extended his hand and asked, "Remember me?" Van Gundy said he made a quizzical face for several seconds. "I made believe I didn't know who he was," Van Gundy said. "The son of a bitch cut me."

It was a relief for Van Gundy to talk about something besides the onrushing season. The opener was a day away, and the slew of questions that faced this undersized team when training camp opened hadn't disappeared. How will Sprewell, Houston and Rice share two positions? Will starting center Camby stay healthy for the first time in his career? Will Johnson's back hold up now that he slimmed down by 22 pounds? And even if Johnson's back does hold up, is his game still good enough to be the team's first low-post option? Will they rebound enough? Will Luc Longley ever recover from his Olympic injury and learn the playbook? Can the Big Backcourt flourish if given practice time?

No trades were on the horizon. The Mutombo talks were at a standstill with Camby and spare parts being offered as booty. Joe Smith wasn't ready to take less money to play with his buddy Sprewell. Initially, Sprewell sounded optimistic about the chances of Smith choosing the Knicks because of their need for size. He had called Smith on the cell phone the day after he got his contract voided.

"I was being the old GM," Sprewell said.

But Smith's first priority was money, and Dallas and Detroit could pay him more handsomely in the future than the capped-out Knicks. Smith was leaning toward the Pistons. "A lot of it depends on money issues," Sprewell said. "Joe's played for a number of years for a lower amount than he deserves."

"The big question going into training camp was whether this is our team," Layden said. "As it looks now, this is who we are. And we like who we are going into the season."

For weeks, Van Gundy had tried to lower expectations for the Knicks. During a conference call with the national basketball writers the week before, Van Gundy had said, "We know when you're talking about dealing with the loss of a Hall of Fame, All-Star, Top-50 player, it's not easy. You watch teams who lose their franchise players and it usually results in the lottery. We're going to try to avoid that."

Avoid the lottery? Not exactly a statement usually associated with a club coming off an Eastern Conference Finals appearance. But nobody had ever heard Van Gundy embrace the Ewing trade. In fact, more than once, he had called it "a risk."

"This year we have more challenges and more questions than in years past because we've had more change than in the past," Van Gundy said.

He was more blunt in the *Sports Illustrated* article, saying, "Oh, there's a huge doubt. We've got a glut of perimeter players, all our inside players have durability issues and, other than Larry Johnson, none of the inside players have averaged more than 11 points a game. We took our best rebounder and traded him. Hell, there are a lot of worries. It's my job to make it work."

Before their last dress rehearsal, Van Gundy again reminded the team about not using the Patrick trade as a crutch. "You can't run forward very fast if you're looking behind you," Van Gundy told the players. "We made a decision. We just keep moving forward."

After the past two practices, Sprewell had spent two hours lifting weights. He was ready.

"Patrick isn't here to blame," Sprewell said on the eve of the opener. "If things are not going well, people will look at the guys who are supposed to be leading us. That's me, Allan, Glen and Larry."

The new era was about to begin for real. On April 13, 1985, Pat Cummings was the center and the Knicks lost in Milwaukee, 88-84, to finish the 1984-85 season with a record of 24-58. Their average attendance was a paltry 11,154. That was the last regular-season game the Knicks played before Ewing became the pillar for the franchise. The last one until tomorrow.

CHAPTER 4

Halloween Night
Horror Show

October 31

The six Knicks fans from Manhattan sitting a third of the way up in Madison Square Garden couldn't be missed on this Halloween Night. The men, all in their late twenties, carried Ewing masks held up to their faces with wooden sticks.

The Knicks wore costumes, too, for their hotly-anticipated season opener against Philadelphia. They were disguised as a minor league team. The boos from the Garden crowd began in the second quarter. The first "PAT-rick EW-ing" singsong chant came cascading down with 29 seconds left in the third quarter. The rhythmic chanting was loud and lasted about 20 seconds. The Knicks were down by 25 points, 77-52. By then, the surly throng had grown tired of booing.

All night, Toni Kukoc drove around Camby at the perimeter like he wasn't there. Kukoc scored 23 points. Ratliff overpowered Camby in the post. The Knicks threw the ball all over the place, committing 22 turnovers. The onset of the Camby era looked a lot like the Cummings era. The Knicks seemed to quit in the third quarter, when they were outscored 29-10. They fell behind by as many as 32 points.

Fans started leaving one minute into the fourth quarter. There was no end to the misery. Sprewell, who shot one-for-nine, dribbled harmlessly 25 feet from the basket on the right wing and still got cited for palming. It was the worst season-opening defeat in franchise history.

The only person having a good time during the 101-72 destruction was a loud woman sitting in the first row behind the press table. She wore a gigantic necklace with a diamond-studded gold "3" that bounced around each time she jumped out of her seat to scream joyously. It was Allen Iverson's mother.

The only cheer from the rest of the gathering came when former St. John's University star Lavor Postell entered the game in the fourth quarter during garbage time. Before the game, Postell had been awarded Ewing's old locker.

"Right here?" Postell said when told by writers that his new cubicle was where Ewing had planted his feet in huge ice buckets. "Well, hopefully I'll be around 15 years, too."

The players couldn't believe how badly they were beaten. "We had no defensive intensity," Johnson said. "It was the worst possible scenario. No defense, period: exterior, interior, in the paint, at the perimeter."

As if the players needed another shock, Van Gundy wrote in a black marker on the white eraser board the time for the next day's practice: six p.m. A night practice. Van Gundy explained that he needed a full day to examine the film.

"We played a horrible game, we gave a horrible effort," Van Gundy said in a whisper.

Layden, standing in the hallway outside the locker room, looked devastated. Sedric Toney, the Knicks' player personnel director, looked like his dog had died. His head down, Layden was too dejected to say hello to the writers as they walked past him on their way to the locker room.

Even if Layden had traded for Mutombo, it wouldn't have made a difference on this night. Mutombo had come down with malaria. The Hawks were coming to town next and Mutombo was sidelined.

November 1

On WFAN radio's pre-game show with Spencer Ross before the season opener, Sprewell had continued his Webber campaign, saying, "Web wouldn't lie to me. If he didn't want to be here, he'd tell me. He came out and said this is where he wants to be." The quotes were picked up by the newspapers. Sprewell, during the second-to-last exhibition game, had said similar things on camera to MSG Network. The NBA office in Manhattan had taken notice of Sprewell's unabashed campaign for a player under contract to another team.

■ ■ ■

A few players, including Sprewell, were irritated by the late practice. Normally, they practiced at noon after a night game. Their egos had been bruised enough by the opening-night loss. They certainly didn't need this type of lifestyle disruption. With a game against the Hawks the next night, Sprewell said, "It's going to feel like we've played three games in a row now."

The Knicks watched film for 40 minutes, then took the court for a two-hour practice. Layden, the lone Knicks executive living in Manhattan—on the Upper West Side with his wife and four daughters—drove north to Purchase College to watch the practice. That wasn't a good sign.

"It gave me plenty of time to really evaluate where we are and where we're hoping to go," Van Gundy said about spending the day analyzing film. "If this game was in February as the fourth in five nights, there would be a bit of an explanation. But I've never seen an opening night like that. Everybody gives effort on opening night. It's unacceptable anytime. It's inexplicable in the first game."

November 2

Before the Hawks' game at the Garden, Layden and Atlanta's Pete Babcock spoke in the hallway outside the Hawks' locker room for 20 minutes. Some of the writers watched from a distance. Layden and Babcock were among the closest GMs in the league, and they were talking about their families. Not once did Mutombo's name come up.

Inside the Hawks' locker room, Mutombo saw a bunch of writers approaching him and joked, "You guys want to sell papers, don't you? You're trying to trick-or-treat me into saying something." Mutombo wagged his finger at the writers, his on-the-court trademark after blocking a shot.

Mutombo was just about over the malaria he had contracted from visiting Africa during the summer, and as the seven-foot-two African center spoke to the New York writers, he sounded like he was also over playing for the moribund Hawks. He said he didn't intend to sign a contract extension with Atlanta. Someone asked Mutombo if he felt he could help bring the Knicks a championship.

"I dream about it," he said. "I think that will weigh a lot on my decision next year."

With Mutombo, the Hawks are a lottery team. Without Mutombo on this night, the Hawks were the perfect get-well medicine the Knicks needed to recover from their opening-night disaster against Philly. The Knicks posted a 94-69 victory over the Hawks. During the blowout, as Mutombo sat in a gray suit on the bench, a fan behind the Hawks' bench yelled to him, "You could wear your same number in New York."

The Knicks realized whom they had just beaten and seemed more relieved than joyous after the game. The most encouraging part of the night was Rice coming off the bench to score 21 points and hit all three of his three-pointers. Rice, never one to embrace modesty, said, "I haven't shown you guys nothing yet. I'm really anxious to see what it's going to be like that one night everyone's hitting. There will be a lot of fireworks out there."

November 3

The league office called the Players' Association first to inform them of its investigation into Sprewell. The NBA's attorneys had grown concerned reading Sprewell's quotes in the newspaper about trying to facilitate a Webber deal. Although it had never been done before, a player could be fined for tampering. Most players and even management didn't realize players fell under the tampering rule just as coaches and general managers in the Collective Bargaining Agreement do. In the convoluted language of the CBA, a player who "indirectly or directly entices, induces, persuades or attempts to entice, induce or persuade any player under contract to another member of the association to enter into negotiation relating to his services shall be charged with such tampering."

The league wanted to discuss the matter with Sprewell. He faced a $35,000 fine and possible suspension. If a general manager had said similar things to the press, he surely would have been slapped with the maximum sanctions. This was different. A player didn't know any better. The NBA did not plan to punish Sprewell unless he acted belligerent during their talk, which was always a possibility considering the league's history with Sprewell.

The league wanted to tell Sprewell to cut off the Webber campaign in the press and let him know that his friendly conversations with Webber should not promote the merits of playing in New York. Although Sacramento did not file an official complaint with the league office, Kings GM Geoff Petrie was furious at Sprewell. Petrie let the NBA know that he felt Sprewell was violating the tampering bylaws. To the press, Petrie simply said he wasn't trading Webber "at any juncture."

Bob Gist, Sprewell's outspoken agent, was livid, too. He spoke to Players' Association officials, angry the league was picking on Sprewell again. Sprewell did not trust Commissioner David Stern any more now than he did in 1997. Sprewell's lawsuit appeal against the NBA to recoup $6 million in lost salary from his season-ending suspension in Golden State was still in the San Francisco court of appeals.

Sprewell told Gist that if the NBA thought this was an important enough matter to discuss on the phone, he'd rather do it in person. He wanted Gist and a Players Association representative by his side. Sprewell was taking no chances. His last phone interview with the league's security chief, Horace Balmer, hadn't gone well, following his choke of Carlesimo.

"I want my agent there," Sprewell said to a Players' Association official. "The last interview on the phone cost me $6 million."

A meeting was set up for three days later at nine a.m. Sprewell promised he wouldn't be late. "If they want to talk to me, let them talk," Sprewell said in the visitors' locker room at the MCI Center in Washington.

■ ■ ■

The Knicks' second of two games in two nights was against Michael Jordan's Wizards. The Knicks were dismal in second-night games last season, winning seven out of 20. One of Van Gundy's pre-season goals was to make them stronger in back-to-back games.

Sprewell wasn't in the mood to discuss the tampering charges before the game. Having watched the Lakers get their championship rings on TV, he was more in the mood to taunt Rice.

"I saw the ceremony the other night," Sprewell yelled across the locker room to Rice. "Where's your ring?"

The other players giggled. "I'd like to have it," Rice said. Travis Knight, part of the Ewing deal, was also owed a ring by the Lakers. "No hard feelings, but when I get it, I'm going to wear it," Rice said.

"Just let me see it," Sprewell said.

■ ■ ■

Sitting courtside for the game was superagent David Falk, whose offices were within a mile of the arena. For the first time, he acknowledged he would push Atlanta to trade Mutombo if he didn't hear what he wanted to hear in a meeting planned with Babcock when the Hawks were in Washington next month.

"I think if the decision is made that he won't be in Atlanta next year, we'll explore trades with them mutually," Falk said. "I have a great relationship with Dave Checketts. Obviously, New York would like to have a premier center. Until I visit with the Hawks, I'm not going to discuss other teams with them."

■ ■ ■

The Felton Spencer pre-season experiment was just that. Van Gundy was not about to start Spencer against the Wizards' White now with Camby coming off such a crisp game against Atlanta. In fact, Van Gundy called the first play for Camby, who slithered past White down the lane for a layup.

Camby likes to point out that few plays are ever called for him, which requires him to get his points via putbacks on offensive rebounds. Having the first play called for him was an astute motivational maneuver by Van Gundy, and Camby appreciated the gesture.

"That was definitely good," Camby said later. "I was definitely going to be aggressive all night even if the play wasn't called for me. But it got me going. Great call."

Camby finished with 20 points and five blocks and the Knicks moved to 2-1 with an 80-76 win. Camby played 40 minutes, his most as a Knick in a regular-season game.

"I'm definitely tired of criticism, saying I can't do this, can't do that," Camby said. "The guy in the middle is always the focal point. I see how Patrick experienced it. But you have to look at my situation. It's not like I'm getting a lot of plays out there to make things happen."

November 5

Van Gundy called the league hypocritical for taking issue with Sprewell for his comments on Webber.

"The NBA has to decide what it wants," Van Gundy said. "If we want players to be accessible and open and honest when they are asked a question and they give an honest answer, we have to live with that. A coach and management is much different from a player who is friendly with another player, giving an honest assessment that he would like to play with the guy. But you can't have it both ways. You can't ask for open and honest players and then condemn them when they're being what you want them to be. You say we have to have media accessibility for 30 minutes after practice. What's he supposed to do, sit up there like a mute?"

Before Sprewell spoke to the writers, Hamamoto of public relations warned the media ensemble, "He won't be taking any questions about his meeting tomorrow."

Sprewell spoke briefly. "I don't feel like I've done anything," he said. "There's nothing to say."

November 6

Sprewell showed up at the league office on Fifth Avenue in Manhattan wearing jeans and a baby-blue denim jacket. He arrived five minutes early at 8:55 a.m. NBA attorney Joel Litvin and senior vice-president of security Balmer represented the league. Gist and Robert Gaston of the union accompanied Sprewell. They met in a conference room at a long, oak table.

"We're having problems with the many quotes of yours in the paper and have verified that you said them," Litvin told Sprewell. "We want you to know that conduct is in violation of the code section on tampering. We want to put you on notice. We would appreciate if you would refrain."

Litvin told Sprewell he could say generic things, such as that he and Webber are friends and enjoy playing with each other, but that was about all. Litvin said he understood that most players didn't know the tampering rule applied to them, so he found no reason to fine or suspend him, unless he had to talk to him again about the issue.

Sprewell said he didn't realize his comments represented tampering. The meeting lasted 15 minutes. All was going fine until Litvin said, "Sorry you guys had to come all the way into the city to meet today. We could've discussed this over the phone."

"I remember the last time we talked in a phone interview," Sprewell shot back, glaring at Balmer.

"Hey, c'mon, let's not get into that," Litvin said, sensing Sprewell's sudden ire.

Sprewell made it back in time for practice. "It was something I could have done over the phone, but I wanted to have it in person because of the things I've been through with them in the past." Sprewell said. "Now I have to watch what we talk about."

With this tampering episode out of the way, Sprewell could concentrate on getting his shot back. His shooting percentage was 29 percent through the first three games. He took an extra 20 minutes working on his jump shot before he joined the team for the charter flight to Milwaukee, his hometown, where the Knicks would play the Bucks.

■ ■ ■

As Van Gundy had feared after the Ewing trade, the Knicks had yet to establish a low-post presence. That led directly to an increase of double-teams on Sprewell and Houston. Last season, the Knicks' best play was the high pick-and-roll, with Ewing setting for Sprewell. Now teams were trapping Sprewell with the double-team and daring the Knicks to throw the ball inside to the rolling big man, even when the big man was being guarded by a smaller player on the switch.

As much potential as Camby had shown as a high-flying offensive rebounder, he still did not have polished low-post moves to command respect when teams drew up their game plans against the Knicks. Johnson and Thomas had yet to impress anyone on the low blocks, either. In the Bucks, the Knicks faced a team similar to them. The Bucks had accomplished perimeter players in Glenn Robinson, Sam Cassell and Ray Allen, but flimsy low-post presence. This game would be a good time for the Knicks to start causing a ruckus inside.

November 7
Rice called the Lakers to inquire about his championship ring. A Lakers official told him it was in the mail.

"Most of those guys up there are enjoying looking at their rings and all I'm looking at is my wedding ring and Travis [Knight] isn't married," Rice lamented after the shootaround in Milwaukee's Bradley Center. He was certain the Lakers had purposely delayed sending the ring. "I'm going to act like a kid in a candy store when I get it," he said.

As a peacemaking gesture, the Lakers' official asked Rice if he'd be willing to have a ring presentation involving him and Knight before the Knicks-Lakers game at the Staples Center in April. Rice said he'd think about it.

■ ■ ■

It was Election Day and the Knicks were in the swing state of Wisconsin. Not that many of the players were heavy-duty voters. Although most of them had been brought up in liberal households, sons of poor-to-working class parents, their riches made them want to vote Republican. It was cognitive dissonance in its purest form. Nobody filled out absentee ballots.

Van Gundy, a staunch Republican, pulled for George W. Bush, although he lived blocks from Bill Clinton's new mansion in Chappaqua, New York. Van Gundy did not fill out an absentee ballot, either.

"It doesn't matter," Van Gundy said, knowing Al Gore couldn't lose in New York. "I know the Electoral College and see the polls. In New York, it's over."

■ ■ ■

Sprewell relished the trips to his hometown and considered it the biggest benefit of playing in the Eastern Conference. At Golden State, the Warriors made one trip a year to Milwaukee. With about 50 relatives and friends at games in Milwaukee, Sprewell spent most of his pre-game stuffing tickets into the right envelopes for the will-call window.

The amount of time players spend on gathering complimentary tickets, making sure the right names are on the envelopes, is astonishing. The players don't enjoy accommodating all the friends who call for tickets. They have to pay for any tickets beyond the two comps they get for each game. So, throughout the season, teammates routinely trade their two comps with each other. For instance, Camby gave his two comps for the Milwaukee game to Sprewell, who would reciprocate when the Knicks were in Boston. That's where Camby, a UMass grad and Hartford native, would need extras. Most of the Knicks can afford to buy out the whole arena if they wanted, but exchanging favors is a way of team bonding. The exception was Ewing, who was known as a ticket hog. He always grubbed tickets from players and rarely reciprocated the favor. And although players were supposed to be allowed just two, he always finagled a few extra tickets out of management.

As he stuffed envelopes, Sprewell learned from the writers that his $30 million lawsuit against the NBA had been thrown out of federal appeals court in San Francisco. He shrugged.

"That means it's pretty much over," he said. "If that is the case, I've got a game to play tonight so there is no sense in getting all distraught about it."

Sprewell didn't need the $30 million. He just needed more tickets.

■ ■ ■

That night, Ewing and the Sonics were in Miami facing Riley and the Heat. Ewing held court with a small group of New York writers who had come to see his first game against an Eastern foe. In four days, he would be in New Jersey to play the Nets, and in a week, the Knicks would be in Seattle.

In September, Ewing had become the godfather of Mourning's infant daughter, Myka Sydney. During the Olympics in Sydney, Mourning had flown home to be with his wife, hence their daughter's middle name. There was initially speculation that Mourning's illness was caused by flying back and forth to Sydney four times in two weeks, but that was wishful thinking.

Speaking about his Georgetown buddy, Ewing repeated a message he had conveyed to Mourning: "He knows I'll always be there for him and if my kidney matches, I'd be happy to donate one if it comes down to that," Ewing said.

Though the Knicks routed Milwaukee, 103-89, for their third straight victory, *The Post*'s back page headline blared, "Patrick's Gift to 'Zo.'"

Houston scored 24 points and Camby had 12 points and 13 rebounds, but the news afterward was grim. Sprewell left the game late in the fourth quarter with back pain, having twisted it as he leapt for a rebound after the game was out of reach. Sprewell's status was in doubt for the next night's home game against the Cavaliers.

Most coaches would not have had Sprewell on the floor with the Knicks comfortably ahead and a few minutes remaining. Van Gundy's policy of playing starters deeper into the fourth quarter of blowouts than any other coach had backfired. Believing the risk of losing a big lead with the eleventh and twelfth men on the floor is greater than the risk of a starter getting hurt. Van Gundy refuses to waver from his practice.

"I'll never be accused of blowing a game because I took out my starters too early," he said.

But, in this case, maybe he had blown a game: the next one.

CHAPTER 5

The Jersey Guy Comes Home

November 8-9

The History Channel, in conjunction with the Knicks, launched a promotion for the fans to vote on the three greatest moments in Knicks history. Ten events were listed on the ballot, including the Knicks winning the draft lottery in 1985 and drafting Ewing.

Post columnist Kevin Kernan, who was harder on Ewing than any journalist in New York, had some fun with the promotion and decided to compile his Top 10 Worst Moments in Knicks history. The Knicks' drafting Ewing had the lone distinction of making both lists, with Kernan rating it as the ninth-worst moment in Knicks history.

The Knicks' game that night against the Cavaliers also could have been ranked among the worst moments in Knicks history. The Cavs, expected to be an also-ran, beat the Knicks, 99-97, to end New York's three-game winning streak. Back spasms ended Sprewell's streak of 146 consecutive games played. The Knicks fell to 1-2 at the Garden.

"Players used to come in here and wonder, 'How are we going to score on this team?'" Childs said. "Now it's how many are they going to score?"

Van Gundy's fears about his team's mind-set changing in the post-Ewing era were coming too close to fruition. He believed the Knicks now thought of themselves as an offensive team.

"We've already lost two games at home because we didn't guard anyone," he said, fuming over the loss.

■ ■ ■

Following the loss, the Knicks announced that they had supplanted the Bulls for the longest active home sellout streak in the NBA: 350 games. The Bulls' streak had ended at 610 two days earlier when they fell 311 fans short of a sellout.

These sellout streaks are partly contrived. The Bulls purposely ended their streak as a way to tell the public that tickets were available. The Knicks, too, could end their streak any time they wanted. They kept in reserve several dozen tickets for players, celebrities and VIPs that go unused, even though they try to sell them at the box office one hour before game time. But the Garden prefers to sustain the image that a Knicks game is the hottest sports ticket in town.

The team's announcement did not mention that the Knicks led the league in something else: highest average ticket price, $51.

■ ■ ■

An arbitrator upheld the NBA's decision to terminate Joe Smith's secret contract. Layden again phoned Smith's agent, Dan Fegan, to reiterate the Knicks' interest and invited Smith to New York for a visit. But Layden viewed the Knicks as long shots for the player, behind Dallas, Detroit and Miami. Their salary cap situation was one of the worst in the league.

■ ■ ■

The Knicks' visit to Seattle was five days away, but first Ewing would play in the state of his residence, New Jersey, against the Nets at The Meadowlands.

In his later years, Ewing always started the season slowly, but his slow beginning was worse than usual. Ewing figured to need an adjustment period to mesh with his new teammates, but his lack of speed in getting back on defense and joining the attack had become alarming to the Sonics.

"Right now, it's obvious we're learning to play with one another," Gary Payton said.

Although Ewing's points and rebounds were down, he was getting high grades for opening up the window to his personality. He signed autographs and granted virtually all interview requests, basic things that he had turned into adventures in New York. The difference was that in Seattle, he often was not the focus of the post-game interviews as he had been after every Knicks game. Payton and Vin Baker were the team spokesmen. More than half the time, the reporters didn't bother talking to Ewing after a game.

Ewing seemed to be having more fun than his teammates in an off-beat commercial the Sonics filmed during the pre-season. The filming took place at a dimly lit, dusty Catholic elementary school gym. The spoof had the Sonics' starters playing an exhibition game against a team of Catholic school girls and boys aged eight to 10.

Ewing and his teammates were told to go full bore. The commercial showed Ewing swatting the shots of a four-foot-tall ponytailed girl and lining up against an eight-year-old boy for a jump ball and winning the tap. In another scene, Ewing and Payton exchanged ecstatic high-fives after Payton drove the lane for a layup past the little kids. Ewing had never been this funny in New York.

Ewing had also become interested in hosting a reggae show for a Seattle rhythm and blues station. Ewing, a Jamaican, was a big fan of reggae and Wyclef Jean. He mentioned his music interests in a pre-season interview with Seattle's most prolific radio personality, Tony Benton, who had four different shows on four different stations. Benton convinced the program director at the station to have Ewing host a show on Sunday nights. Ewing's radio D.J. career was put on hold when the Sonics' season began to unravel. He kept postponing his debut as the Sonics kept losing games, then through coach Paul Westphal's eventual firing and the sale of the team. Ewing didn't want a music show to be perceived as another distraction to the club, especially by the outspoken Payton. He was trying to fit in quietly.

During an assembly early in the season, Ewing dazzled more than 400 elementary school kids in Seattle with his playful personality. The appearance was kept secret from the media. After watching Ewing's smile light up the hall, Walker, the Sonics GM, walked out of the school thinking, "Why did he get a reputation in New York as being aloof?"

■ ■ ■

During the morning shootaround at FleetCenter, Rice and Knight were joking about the "Bling Bling" inscription on the championship rings they had received in the mail the day before. "Bling, Bling," a reference in a popular hip-hop song meaning diamonds or money, had been requested by Shaq. Rice should have appreciated the inscription. After all, his nickname, "G-Money," is part of a tattoo on his left arm.

"I guess if it was up to me, it probably wouldn't be on it," Rice said. "Whether it has 'bling, bling' or 'thing, thing,' it's a championship ring."

■ ■ ■

With Sprewell's back still ailing, Houston went wild against the Celtics, scoring 37 points as the Knicks held on to win in overtime, 103-101. Ward stole the ball in the final seconds to preserve the win. Chris Carr, the Celtics' little-used reserve seeing his first action, had sent the game into overtime by hitting a three-pointer from deep in the left corner.

Van Gundy would have kicked himself if the Knicks lost. He blamed himself for not having a smaller lineup on the floor for the last play, having Johnson assigned to Carr.

The Celtics' point guard was Rick Brunson, who had been the Knicks' third-string point man for the past three years. There was no room for Brunson on the guard-glutted Knicks, so Brunson wound up in Miami, got cut, then latched on in Boston. During the game, Brunson became the victim of a Camby rejection.

"If he made that shot, I would've had to hear about it the whole year," Camby said.

Brunson was tight with Sprewell and Camby, and they both missed his presence. Van Gundy loved how Brunson made the most of his limited skills with a competitive fire sometimes lacking in more-gifted players.

For the first time this season, Postell got non-garbage-time action as Childs missed the game with a bruised knee. Van Gundy rode the rookie ferociously. In the second quarter, Adrian Griffin swooped past Postell for an easy layup. When Postell ran downcourt in front of the Knicks' bench, Van Gundy screamed, "If you want to fucking play, you'd better guard somebody."

In the third quarter, Postell chased down a loose ball deep along the right sideline, keeping it from going out of bounds. Instead of passing, he hoisted a wild, off-balanced shot. During the next timeout, Van Gundy intercepted Postell on his way to the bench.

"Did you know you had 14 seconds left on the shot clock?" Van Gundy screamed.

A younger rookie might not have accepted Van Gundy's heckles. Unlike many rookies, Postell had spent the full four years at St. John's and knew Van Gundy was hard on first-year players.

"If he doesn't get on me, there would be a problem," Postell said. "He's coaching. He's teaching."

■ ■ ■

While the Knicks were in Boston, Ewing was in New Jersey preparing for the Nets. Ewing did not stay at the team hotel in Manhattan's Columbus Circle. He went home to Montclair, New Jersey, to see his wife, Rita, his nine-year-old daughter, Randi, and his five-year-old son, Corey. Ewing had circled the Nets game on his calendar before either of the two Knicks meetings because it would be his first time back home since rushing out to Seattle a week after the trade.

November 11

There were more fans wearing blue Knicks jerseys with the number 33 than wearing Nets' apparel. The crowd at The Meadowlands was 5,000 short of a sellout, but the game felt like a big event.

As a tribute to Ewing's return to the New York area, Gary Sussman, the Nets' publicist and public address announcer, planned to introduce Ewing with the same inflection and tone that the Knicks' P.A. man, Mike Walczewski, had used for years, with a heavy accent on "Pa-."

"I want to make him feel at home," Sussman said before the game.

The heavy cheers from the Meadowlands crowd drowned out Sussman's "Paa-trick Ewing" intro. After receiving a warm greeting from the fans, Ewing and his Sonics were run over by a freight train disguised as the Nets in a 126-91 blowout that dropped them to 2-5. Ewing was outplayed by the Nets' second-year center, Evan Eschmeyer, who blocked one of his shots, and was held to 13 points. The Nets' Stephon Marbury, miffed at the adulation afforded Ewing, scored 41 points.

"I don't take it personally, but I hate when somebody else comes to our home court and they're cheering for him," Marbury said. "That bothers me."

■ ■ ■

That night, the Knicks faced Charlotte in a Saturday-night game at the Garden that illustrated how the NBA's reliance on back-to-back regular-season games hurts the product. Both teams were playing for the second straight night. The Knicks held the lackluster Hornets to 19 points in the second half and posted an 81-67 victory without Sprewell or Childs. The 19 points tied an NBA post-shot-clock era record for lowest points allowed in a half, but it was ugly to watch. Of course, Van Gundy loved it.

"I thought for the fourth game in five nights, coming off an overtime game in Boston, that was the most ready I've seen the guys in a long time," Van Gundy crowed.

The post-Patrick Knicks had begun the season 5-2, the flip-flop of the Sonics' record. Ewing, in particular, was out of step with his new team. It had taken him all of training camp to stop wearing his old Knicks' shoes, the Nike basketball sneakers with blue and orange trim that matched the Knicks' uniform. Meanwhile, Camby was thriving, averaging a double-double (11.9 points, 11.3 rebounds). There was no finer time for the Knicks to fly to Seattle to go face-to-face with Ewing in three days. The separation had been going smoothly so far.

November 12

Van Gundy issued another warning to his club before practice.

"We're coming off a good week and we want to build on it," he told the players. "We don't want to get our minds focused on one player. It's obviously big playing against Patrick for the first time, but we have to prepare for their whole team. We can't be distracted by Pat. We have to make sure we stay focused on the game and prepare to win."

Camby was ready. Although he was having a better season than Ewing, he knew his efforts would be for naught if Ewing outplayed him in Seattle.

"I'm going to be pumped up," Camby said. "We've been hearing about Patrick all summer long. We're going to be ready to go."

Camby had gone through a tough summer and still showed traces of paranoia about Ewing.

"If I have a good game against him, people will say, 'Oh, he's too old,'" Camby remarked. "I played against him all the time in practice. I know what he's going to do. I'll make him work for his shots and make him chase me around on the offense end."

CHAPTER 6

We Meet Again

November 13

The Knicks practiced in the morning and prepared for the six-hour flight to Ewing country. After his press briefing, Van Gundy met privately with one of the few journalists in New York he trusted, columnist Ian O'Connor of Westchester's *Journal News*. Earning Van Gundy's trust is difficult because he takes printed criticism personally. He doesn't mind negativity—after all, who is more negative than him?—as long as it is pointed in the right direction and not at him.

O'Connor kept Van Gundy's "Joe-Bag-of-Donuts" character alive, even if there was no more Honda Civic, the symbol that embodied the coach's down-to-earth personality. The old, trusty Honda Civic was totaled, blown to bits last spring when the team charter's thrust got too close to the waiting cars on the tarmac at Westchester Airport. Now, Van Gundy often could be seen ducking into a black Lincoln Town Car with his very own driver, provided by the Knicks to take him to games. Otherwise, he drives a trendy white sport utility vehicle he purchased after he got his $14 million contract. Not exactly a Honda Civic.

Van Gundy, whose office wall is adorned with three framed back pages of *The Post*, each alluding to his potential dismissal, showed

O'Connor a newspaper clip from several years ago when he was the interim coach and Ewing lobbied for him to remain in power.

"Forget all this stuff about a name coach," Ewing said in the article Van Gundy showed O'Connor. "Jeff works as hard as anybody. Look, I just think [management] should go ahead and let the man stay. We need young blood and that's what Jeff brings. Forget all those recycled guys. We don't need that."

Before boarding the plane to Seattle, Van Gundy said to O'Connor, "Patrick thought we needed young blood. And that's why he ended up having to leave."

■ ■ ■

Sprewell was ready to return from his back injury. He did not want to miss the reunion. On the plane ride, he sat next to Camby and tried to pump him up, saying, "You know Patrick's going to be really motivated. He's going to want to get 40 on you. You know that."

Ewing wasn't saying much to the New York press that had traveled with him for the past week. But his Seattle teammates knew the deal.

"We couldn't face the Big Fella if we lost this game," Vin Baker said.

The Knicks checked into the Four Seasons Hotel in Seattle at six p.m. Childs, Houston and Ward received phone calls from a visitor downstairs in the hotel restaurant. It was Ewing on his cell phone. He was dining with John Thompson, who was working the game as a color commentator for TNT. Ewing couldn't help talking trash to his old teammates. "We're going to whip your butts," Ewing told Houston on the phone.

"It's going to be very strange," Ewing had told the New York reporters a few days earlier. "I just have to go out there and forget all the sentimental things and play basketball."

Ewing just wanted to make sure he went to the right bench. He remembered Charles Oakley's first game against the Knicks after being traded for Camby before the 1999 season. At the first timeout, Oakley walked toward the Knicks' bench. Ewing wanted to avoid that if he could.

"I'm so accustomed to being announced as a New York Knick, sometimes I still hear it in my head during intros," Ewing confided.

November 14

The Knicks' bus rolled into Key Arena at 10:30 a.m. The Sonics were on the court having their morning shootaround. Every Knick headed for the visiting locker room except Childs. Wearing a black wrap around his head, Childs veered past a security guard and walked to the edge of the court. Ewing caught Childs' eye and came over, smiling and laughing. They shook hands and spoke for a few minutes.

"Long time no see," Childs said. "It's going to be fun tonight." Childs was the lone Knick who had bothered to call Ewing over the summer.

The Sonics' David Wingate received a more-enthusiastic greeting from his former teammates than Ewing did. Wingate had played an ambiguous role for the Knicks the past two seasons, playing in only 27 games because of bad knees. He was mostly a practice player. He was also the team's unofficial social director, knowing where to find the attractive and available ladies in every NBA city.

Though he attended Georgetown with Ewing, Wingate was much closer to Johnson. Because of his bum knee, Wingate was unable to play at a high level anymore, but he managed to become a valuable part of a team without having to play. He gave his all in practices. He was an enthusiastic cheerleader on the bench. And his engaging personality made the club looser. He ran three-point shooting contests for money with Thomas and Camby at the end of practices.

But the perception that Wingate returned to Seattle to serve as Ewing's babysitter was untrue. Actually, he was back in Seattle on Payton's recommendation. Wingate and Payton were close friends.

As he walked to the court for the shootaround, Sprewell spotted Wingate across the long hallway. Wingate was standing outside the Sonics' locker room, speaking to writers about Ewing.

"Hey, Win!" Sprewell bellowed. They screamed back and forth, two guys happy to see each other. Larry Johnson soon came over to visit Wingate in the locker room. Ewing had already left, sneaking out a back door to avoid the media. He never spoke at morning shootarounds. Apparently, that meant he never spoke to his former teammates, either.

■ ■ ■

That night, a Ewing lovefest occurred spontaneously at midcourt during pre-game warmups. First, Ward sauntered over to break the ice and hug Ewing. Following Ward's cue, Camby and Sprewell gave Ewing big bear hugs. Ewing smiled broadly. A line formed to get at him. Thomas, Houston and Strickland, who never played with him, queued up at midcourt to embrace Ewing. All the guys who inexplicably forgot to phone Patrick in the weeks after the blockbuster trade were paying their respects seven weeks later.

There were more hugs as the players lined up for the opening tip. Ewing embraced each member of the Knicks' starting lineup. Ewing then pointed to Van Gundy at the bench.

But in the opening few minutes, sentimentality gave way to cold reality. Ewing looked out of place in the Seattle offense and slower than in his final days as a Knick. Ewing missed his first four shots while Camby went on a dunking rampage. The contrast in athleticism between Ewing and Camby became striking. With Ewing trailing by several yards, Camby skied for a fast break dunk off of a Ward pass midway through the first quarter. Later, Camby flew high and rammed home an alley-oop pass by Ward. As he came down, Camby howled to the fans behind the basket. Camby spent the first half running circles around the creaky Ewing. The Knicks challenged Ewing by penetrating the lane, and Ewing instilled no fear in them. Ewing didn't score for the first 22:46 of the game.

While the teams took warmups prior to the start of the second half, Van Gundy sat on the bench concentrating on his play board. Ewing sidled up next to Van Gundy and took a seat.

"What's up, Pat?" Van Gundy said, startled. Ewing lunged at his chart. Van Gundy playfully fought him off. They shared a few more words and laughter before Ewing walked back onto the court. Van Gundy sat alone on the bench, staring at the floor and smiling wistfully for several seconds.

Ewing had a stronger second half and finished with 10 points, nine rebounds and two blocks, not bad unless you compared him to his spry counterpart. Camby racked up 20 points and 17 boards.

The Knicks won the center battle in a landslide but lost almost everything else. Camby was the only one who played with zeal. Everyone else seemed to have their intensity level set on low gear, perhaps feeling awkward in Ewing's presence. Sprewell, Houston and Rice played terribly. Camby was the only one ready to combat the force which Ewing's souped-up Seattle teammates brought. Even when he wasn't playing, Camby rose from the bench and clapped and waved his arms after every Knicks basket. He wanted this game badly.

Payton was magnificent with 26 points and 13 assists. The Knicks failed to cover the three-point line on defense and Seattle rang up 11 treys. Ultimately, the Sonics allowed Ewing to save face as they pounded the Knicks, 96-75.

"Marcus played very hard and well," Van Gundy said. "As a group, we didn't. He was one of the guys who played hard and the only one who played well."

After the game, Ewing said above the locker room din, "I just want to thank you guys for this."

In case anyone was getting too sentimental, the Sonics' Brent Barry cracked, "We really wanted to win this one for David Wingate."

Ewing met the press in an auxiliary room. Hamamoto, Ewing's most trusted friend left in the Knicks' organization, strolled out of the Knicks' locker room to watch the proceedings. Ewing felt like an elephant had been removed from his back. Clearly touched by how hard his teammates had fought, Ewing said, "They wanted to win this game for me. They said that when I first came and they said it before the game. I'm very relieved it's over. Now the New York media can all go home."

Ewing was tired of the hype. He was thrilled to get the game over with. He just wished he hadn't rushed his shots in the first half.

Several writers from New York had followed Ewing for the week leading up to the showdown. They would leave him alone now, but not for very long. Eventually, they would be back. The rematch at the Garden was three months away.

CHAPTER 7

Gotham Guns Growling

November 15-18

It was one thing to lose to the hyped-up Sonics and quite another to go down without a fight against the woeful, inexperienced Los Angeles Clippers, who crushed them at crunch time the next evening at Staples Center. Lamar Odom, a former New York schoolboy legend, finished off the Knicks by hitting big shots over Johnson late in the fourth quarter of the Clippers' 78-74 victory. The Knicks, playing their second game in two nights, had never scored fewer points against the Clippers.

The giddy crowd at Staples, home to both the Clippers and the Lakers, even booed Rice. A Clippers' crowd booing a Laker for leaving La-La-land? It was a first.

"I don't even think they know why they're booing," Rice said.

The Knicks' locker room was morose. Sprewell was off to the worst start of his nine-year career and openly wondered whether the Gotham Guns troika was going to work. Playing his second game since the back injury, Sprewell was shooting a horrendous 31.2 percent for the year, including his seat-of-the-pants bucket against the Clippers. In a wacky hoop that made all the highlight shows, Sprewell hit a shot while on his rump by the foul line. That the Globetrotters-type basket did not propel the club to victory was a bad omen. Houston and Rice, too, were struggling with their shots. And Van Gundy remained reluctant to have the threesome on the court together.

"It's just one of those things where we have three guys playing the same position," Sprewell said. "We have to rotate and it's hard for guys to find their rhythm. A lot of times if Allan is going good, Jeff doesn't want to take him out, but he has to give either myself or Glen minutes. So it's kind of hard to get into a rhythm."

Sprewell seemed to be aiming this salvo cross-country, all the way to Checketts' office at 2 Penn Plaza.

"That was the big question, was it going to work?" Sprewell said. "I'm not saying it can't, but it's difficult."

A few lockers over, Rice complained about the adjustment he had to make when coming off the bench. He explained the difficulty of getting loose right away and being productive. It was harder than he had envisioned. The Knicks were 5-4 heading to the Arizona desert, but the heat was already on.

■ ■ ■

After an off day in Phoenix, the Knicks bused to America West Arena for their morning shootaround. During the bus ride, Van Gundy read the newspaper clips faxed from New York and sensed the uneasiness Sprewell, Rice and Houston were feeling. Van Gundy knew he would have to address the problem. Before the shootaround, Van Gundy read aloud the quotes attributed to Sprewell, Rice and Houston and told the team the quotes sounded like excuses.

"We can use our roster makeup as our excuse or we can win," Van Gundy said. "Every sentence starts with, 'It's hard, it's hard to block, it's hard to rebound.' We're an excuse team right now."

When he spoke to the writers, Van Gundy exonerated Rice to a point, believing he indeed had an adjustment to make, coming off the bench for the first time in his career. But he would not let Sprewell off the hook.

For Sprewell, getting second-guessed by Van Gundy about his quotes hit a raw nerve. His back was so sore, he probably shouldn't have been playing. But sitting and watching was even more painful. Being labeled an excuse-maker made him angry and was hardly motivational when putting on his pants and shirt was painful.

"When I say things are tough, I'm just saying you have to deal with it," Sprewell said. "I never make excuses. I know I'm not playing up to my potential. I'm playing with pain. That's not an excuse. That's how it is. But you know how Jeff is. We still love him."

An angry group of Knicks took the court against the Suns, who had not lost at home. Salvaging the three-game Western trip, the Knicks decreased their excuse making and increased their production in a 90-85 victory. Their gritty defense forced the Suns into 29 turnovers, 14 by superstar point guard Jason Kidd.

The only damper came when Camby collided with Rodney Rogers on a drive through the lane midway through the fourth quarter. Camby sank the basket and drew the foul, but landed on the side of his foot. He left the game with a twisted ankle. X-rays were negative, but Camby was unsure of his status for the home game against Golden State in two days.

"It would've been a miserable flight home if we would've went 0-3," Camby said.

The dissension in the locker room had been replaced by players too beaten up to say much at all. Camby hobbled like a cripple and Sprewell clutched his back with a pained expression as he walked into the locker room after the victory. Ward's left knee had throbbed for days. He sat out the morning shootaround but managed to play. Afterwards, he walked around the locker room like a gimpy quarter-back. Half the team had already boarded the bus that would take them to the red-eye flight back to Westchester Airport.

"It's the walking wounded in here," the former college football Heisman Trophy winner shouted across the room to nobody in particular. "It's like after a football game."

November 19

Camby's goal was to play all 82 games this season and, once and for all, erase the reputation he had earned for being a brittle player. The sprained left ankle he suffered in Phoenix ended that dream. Camby sat out the Warriors' game.

The Knicks more than made up for his absence on the glass. Johnson had one of those yesteryear moments, grabbing 16 rebounds. Kurt Thomas stepped up with 17 points and even Spencer contributed seven rebounds and one block in a rare appearance. Sprewell played his best game of the season with 22 points, five rebounds and five assists against his former club. Sprewell's emotions when facing the Warriors were not nearly as fierce without Carlesimo on the sidelines anymore. But he still enjoyed having a good game against the club that tried to terminate his contract. Surely, Sprewell did not want to lose to them. But the game was never in question.

November 21

The Knicks couldn't help but feel disappointed when Grant Hill signed with Orlando over the summer, especially after the staff flew all the way to Detroit to meet with him. But they didn't have to stare their disappointment in the face when they played the Magic in Orlando. Hill sat out his eighth straight game with an ankle injury.

Instead of having Hill as the featured star at the newly named T. D. Waterhouse Arena in Orlando, the Magic boasted Tracy McGrady, a former Raptor who had also signed a whopping contract over the summer. McGrady, like Hill, was a slasher whom the Knicks routinely had trouble guarding at the perimeter.

■ ■ ■

The Knicks were in a playful mood before they took the court for their morning shootaround.

"You faggot motherfucker," Johnson yelled at Childs.

Johnson looked at the devout Ward. The Knicks tried to watch their language around Ward. Apologetically, Johnson said, "I'm sorry, C. My fault." Turning back to Childs, Johnson said "Chris, you stupid homosexual."

Ward was the Knicks' Holy Man, the unofficial preacher of their pre-game chapel and hotel Bible sessions. Indeed, you had to watch what you uttered in front of Ward. During the West Coast trip, inside the Staples Center dressing room, I made the mistake of saying loudly, "Jesus Christ," after watching Darius Miles dunk on the locker room television which was playing a video of the Clippers' prior game. Ward and Houston, sitting together in the corner of the room, looked up at me, startled.

"What did you say?" Ward asked, seemingly offended. He explained it wasn't proper to use God's name in vain. That was the last time I used that expression in the Knicks' locker room.

■ ■ ■

The Magic shot 57 percent from the floor in the first half and built a 16-point halftime lead. The Knicks were without Camby for the second straight game because of his ankle injury. McGrady was sensational, driving past Houston repeatedly or pulling up for jump shots with space to spare. Trailing badly, the Knicks easily could have looked ahead to tomorrow night's game in Atlanta, but Sprewell wouldn't let them.

"We can still win this game," Sprewell barked at his teammates four times in the locker room at halftime.

The fantasy finishes were supposed to happen 10 miles down the road at the Magic Kingdom. But at the building formerly known as The O-Rena before Corporate America reared its ugly head, the Knicks staged a miracle at T. D. Waterhouse. They closed to within three points in the final minute. Then Sprewell sank a three-pointer that would have tied the score, only it didn't count. Van Gundy had signaled for a time-out moments before. The coach felt terrible about it.

With 18.3 seconds left, Orlando clung to a one-point lead. McGrady inbounded from midcourt to point guard Darrell Armstrong, one of the league's top foul shooters. Instead of holding onto the ball and trying to get fouled, he panicked when he got double-teamed by Knight and Childs. Armstrong jumped and flung a pass back to McGrady, who had just stepped back onto the court and wasn't expecting the ball. Strickland poked the ball away. Childs tracked down the loose ball and soared in for a layup with 12.3 seconds remaining. The Knicks had their first lead of the game, 85-84.

But they almost gave the game away. On Orlando's final possession, McGrady tossed up an airball, and Pat Garrity caught it underneath the basket. He went up for an uncontested layup that would have given the Magic the win at the buzzer. The ball rolled off the rim and out. The buzzer sounded and Van Gundy high-fived Camby and raced toward the tunnel, laughing all the way. He nearly mowed over two security guards. It was quite a departure from Van Gundy's normal demeanor. He normally trudges off the court, win or lose, with a blank, sad-dog expression. Van Gundy rarely displays joy after a win, partly because he does not want to rub it in to the other team and partly because he expects to win.

The players mobbed each other at midcourt to celebrate one of the wildest finishes in recent memory. Outside the locker room where the whoops of his 8-4 club could be heard, Van Gundy said, "I didn't mean to look like the cat that ate the canary. I was just happy to get the win."

For Strickland, this was a special night. Saddled with sporadic playing time, he had finally made a large impact on a victory, and not just with his last-second steal. For parts of the second half, Van Gundy assigned Strickland to McGrady, who had overmatched Houston. Strickland did a much better job of staying in front of the super-swift swingman.

Despite playing a limited role, Strickland never sulked openly and remained one of the most engaging guys in the locker room. But he was perplexed at how quickly Van Gundy had decided he was not a true point guard for the system, particularly because the coach had lobbied to trade for him. The trade now appeared to be terrible timing. Strickland had been a starter for resurgent Dallas last season and was now in a contract year.

Strickland had a rough training camp, committing too many turnovers and losing Van Gundy's trust at the point. He was slow to adjust to the structured sets, having enjoyed the free-wheeling fastbreak system employed by Mavericks coach Don Nelson. Now, at six-foot-three, he had to fight Rice, Sprewell and Houston for minutes at the crowded swingman position.

Van Gundy loved Strickland's toughness. A walk-on defensive back at Nebraska, Strickland played with as much defensive grit as anyone on the Knicks. Perhaps Strickland's breakthrough game against McGrady would nudge Van Gundy into using him as a defensive stopper.

"It's what I do," Strickland shouted to reporters above the noise in the locker room. "McGrady's a great player and I have a lot of heart and I go after people. Jeff put me in there for that reason. He told me to put a stop to it."

CHAPTER 8

Thanks for Nothing

November 22

In what had become a ritual, Mutombo met with the New York writers trying to get a fix on the trade talks. Mutombo said he had spoken to Ewing about what it's like to play in New York. Was his response positive?

"C'mon, he played 15 years there," Mutombo said. "He's still living there. He loves New York."

With malaria out of his system, Mutombo was back on the court and swatting shots, showing a trace of what the Knicks coveted. With a crowd of less than 10,000 showing up on Thanksgiving Eve to watch the 1-10 Hawks, it was no wonder Mutombo wanted to try a different environment.

For one night, though, the Hawks outclassed the Knicks. They built a 21-point lead in the third quarter and won, 78-74. Mutombo had three blocks, rejecting a Knight runner, a Thomas drive and a Strickland fast-break layup. All the giddiness gained in Orlando had evaporated. The Knicks fell to 8-5. Camby missed his third straight game. Spencer injured his knee crashing to the floor. Ward didn't play, and whispers inside the locker room indicated he might need arthroscopic knee surgery. Houston didn't guard anyone for the second straight night. And Van

Gundy insulted one friendly radio reporter from Atlanta during the post-game media session.

The radio guy had asked several of the Knicks before the game what they had to be thankful for on Thanksgiving. Toward the end of Van Gundy's gloom-and-doom post-game press conference, the radio man piped up, "Despite the loss, do you have anything to be thankful for?"

Van Gundy shook his head in disgust as he digested the question. He looked over to Hamamoto and said, "I should get paid extra for this."

Van Gundy abruptly ended the session. Later, in the pressroom, the radio guy asked the writers why Van Gundy acted so Grinch-like while all the players he had asked gave thoughtful responses. He was told that after a bad loss to a bad team, Van Gundy would sooner slug his grandmother than answer a question on being thankful about Thanksgiving.

November 23

He had taken a lot longer than expected, but seven-foot-two Luc Longley was finally ready for his first Knicks practice. When training camp opened, the Knicks had hoped Longley's bruised knee, suffered in the Olympics, would heal in time for the season opener. Nearly four weeks into the season, Longley was still on the injured list and not exactly rushing to get back into the fray.

In September, Longley was seen as a key component to the Ewing blockbuster. Now, Van Gundy didn't know what to do with Longley, considering Camby's dynamic play as the starting center.

"Hopefully, he can give us some quality minutes," Van Gundy said. "How many minutes, I don't know. I don't know if he'll play every day or not."

Set on his eight-man rotation, Van Gundy deviated only when the Knicks were beset with injuries or foul trouble. Longley did not figure to slide into the group. Still, Van Gundy hoped his size would come in handy on the rare nights they needed him on defense and maybe he'd get some buckets in the post.

Longley's three championship rings earned while playing for Jordan's Bulls seemed irrelevant to Van Gundy. He hadn't learned Van Gundy's playbook, let alone his trust, which Van Gundy spoons out in tiny dollops. As he was not part of the team's normal routine of shootarounds, practices and pre-game warmups for the first seven weeks, Longley had trouble fitting in.

The big Aussie redhead charmed the writers with his heavy accent and witty lines but hadn't yet won over his teammates. He spent most of his time on the road hanging out with rookie center Jonathan Kerner, who surprisingly made the team out of training camp and was being carried on the injured list. How obscure was Kerner? One of the Knicks' veteran players didn't know his name six weeks after training camp opened.

The two key guys in the locker room, Camby and Sprewell, hadn't made much of an effort to befriend Longley. Camby, still bothered by a cranky ankle, viewed him as a threat to his playing time. Sprewell was Camby's closest friend on the team and was perplexed by why it took Longley so long to rehab a bruised knee.

"I don't know nothing that's going on with that guy," Camby said during the days leading to Longley's practice debut. "I don't know anything about him."

Longley was aware of his awkward position on the team. In fact, with all the rumors swirling around the club about another trade, he hadn't unpacked many of the boxes sitting in the garage at his new place in Westchester.

Longley had belonged to the close-knit, championship Bulls teams that revolved around Jordan like the Earth revolves around the sun. Although Longley became Jordan's whipping boy, they had a great understanding and Jordan knew that, unlike others, the big Aussie could take the ribbing.

"It's been tough finding my way around this team," Longley said. "I feel like a wallflower. Certainly, it would be easier if I was playing. We have a good bunch of guys on this team, but it always helps to be out there with them."

If any of the Knicks got to know him, they would have found that Longley was one of the most interesting players in the league. Few players on the team knew he owned a professional basketball team back home in Perth, Australia. His six-foot-ten father played for the Perth Wildcats many years ago. Longley played for the club when he was 16. When his NBA career ended and the three years left on his contract expired, Longley planned on heading back to Perth to live the rest of his life with his wife and two young daughters. If the Aussie

Olympic team had won a gold medal in Sydney, he might have retired on the spot. That would have been the ultimate achievement of his career.

After the season, Longley had planned a three-week trip with a group of friends from Australia to visit a Third World Nation, where they would hunt and fish for their own food. In Longley's profile in the Knicks' media guide, he said, "If I could change one thing in this world, it would be Australia's proximity to the U.S."

Longley was amused when reporters asked him about the quote. "I don't know where that came from," Longley said during training camp. "I think a young PR assistant made it up a few years ago and it's just stuck. I never said that." Another piece of misinformation printed in every media guide, program and rosters was that Longley weighed 265 pounds.

"That was my weight coming out of college," said Longley, who actually weighed 295 pounds. Van Gundy now had every one of those pounds available to use against the beefier centers in the league. Would he?

"Minutes are earned," Longley said diplomatically. "You don't get them by just showing up."

November 24

The news regarding Ward's knee became more alarming. He underwent an MRI and was declared out of the next day's game against the Toronto Raptors. Ward has had knee problems since high school, when he needed surgery. Van Gundy knew something was terribly wrong. Ward had a higher tolerance for pain than anyone on the club.

Ward had been playing in intense pain for weeks. In the past, Van Gundy, seeing his point guard in pain, would beg Ward to sit out a practice or shootaround. But, in this case, Ward came to the coach for time off.

The Knicks expected the MRI results before the Toronto game. Van Gundy realized he probably wouldn't have his point guard for a long time. Before practice, the Big Backcourt idea had resurfaced in Van Gundy's mind. He figured he might as well give it a shot against Vince Carter's Raptors, always a tough matchup because of their size and athleticism. The alternative was starting Childs at the point.

The Big Backcourt plan was scrapped when Van Gundy got a call from Sprewell the morning of practice. Sprewell sounded as if he was on his deathbed. He had an upper respiratory infection. Van Gundy wasn't ready to use the big alignment without at least one practice.

November 25

The Knicks activated Longley before the matinee game against Toronto at the Garden. Spencer, whose knee was bruised in Atlanta, replaced him on the injured list. Although Spencer had a legitimate injury and expected to be healthy in two weeks, he knew the deal. Months could pass before he returned to the active roster.

The Knicks suffered a bitter 79-75 loss to the Raptors. Down by two, Rice had a chance to win the game in the final seconds. Standing in the left corner behind the three-point arc, Rice released a perfect spinner, a shot he'd hit many times in clutch situations. This would be Rice's moment to win over the fans and stake claim to his belief that he deserved a much bigger role in Van Gundy's offense. But the ball hit the side of the rim and bounded away.

Oakley, the ever-popular Knick immortalized for his Garden floor-burns and rebounds, had been hard on his former team ever since they shipped him north of the border. At every opportunity, Oakley used his trademark array of mixed metaphors to criticize the Knicks. The comments never sounded like sour grapes because his word choices were so zany.

Oakley did not disappoint before and after the game. The Oak Man took a verbal poke at Camby, the player for whom he was swapped.

"They still need a center, so he can't be off to too good a start," Oakley said. "They traded the mobile home in their driveway for a Yugo that can't go many places. If you go to the store and buy eggs, when you get home you still have eggs."

Following the game, Oakley said, "I like some of the guys on the team, but there aren't too many left from the warrior days."

Rice, who went three-for-12 from the field, fretted about the missed shot and his lost season. "Right now, I'm killing myself mentally," he said. "I'm pressing too much. If I don't relax, it will have a snowball effect."

The worst news, though, didn't come until after the game. The PR staff had remained mum on the topic, which was no surprise. But as Ward left the locker room, two writers stopped him. Ward had learned the MRI results. He would need arthroscopic surgery on his right knee to clean out more loose cartilage. He was told he could miss two months. Team doctor Norman Scott would invade Ward's knee again, just like he had in the summer of 1998. Ewing set the Knicks' record for the procedure, having four scopes, three during the summer.

"They said six-to-eight weeks, but whenever it feels good, I'll be back," Ward said. "The Lord has let me play with it for a very long time. I've been blessed for a long time since my knee surgery in high school. Nobody expected me to be playing, especially the doctors who did that first surgery."

No one said it at the time, but perhaps this would be Rice's break. Van Gundy was thinking "big."

November 26

Van Gundy felt his players needed a motivational kick in the shorts, so he went after them hard in his talk to them before practice and to the media later.

"I really have a problem when all I ask is that you come on time, be ready to play, play hard, play to win," he told the players. "I think we have to look ourselves in the eyes and say, 'Are we doing that?' The answer is no."

Van Gundy was at his cranky best. To the media, he brought up the Oakley quote about not having enough guys from the "warrior days" and made it an issue. Instead of defending his players against an unfair taunt by an opponent, he embraced it as fact.

"Oakley said something very telling after the game," Van Gundy said. "He said, 'Where are the warriors?' And it really upsets me when somebody says that. That's basically saying, 'They don't play hard.' It disgusts me that's how we're looked upon, that we have a bunch of these soft guys. I think they just assume we'll be in the playoffs because we've been there before. We're older, we're all taken care of contractually, some guys may be unhappy with their roles. Whatever the reason, we have no edge to us."

Of course, Van Gundy was talking about a crew whose nucleus had made it to the Eastern Conference Finals last spring and the Finals the spring before that. This soft nucleus had whipped Oakley's Raptors in a three-game sweep six months ago. Any player around the league would say, on or off the record, that the Knicks were beasts and one club you wouldn't want to face in the playoffs. The Knicks were a pedestrian 8-6, but everyone from Checketts to Layden to the video coordinator had figured it would take time for the new blood to develop chemistry.

Van Gundy, however, was entranced with "The World According to Oak." If the Knicks' coach wanted to piss off the players, his obsession with the Oakley quotation had done the job.

Sprewell, who played with a respiratory infection and an ailing back against Toronto, rolled his eyes when told Van Gundy thought Oakley's warrior quote was on the mark.

"I don't think it's a true statement," Sprewell said. "We've got warriors. We have guys who compete. Charlie, myself, L. J., Marcus, Allan compete. We just don't have a lot of big, bruising bangers."

Van Gundy confirmed he was going with the Big Backcourt until further notice. But he had one request. He wished the media would retire the "Big Backcourt" phrase.

"I hate that moniker," Van Gundy said. "You don't know how much I hate that, because sometimes we play so small when we are so big."

Sprewell, at point guard, Houston, at shooting guard, and Rice, at small forward, would get their chance to work magic together and resuscitate a stale offense. The Knicks had scored 74, 75, 75 and 74 points in their last four defeats. Childs, who started against Toronto, would return to the bench. He left practice without speaking to reporters.

November 27

The Knicks signed another point guard to fill Ward's roster spot. An old face was returning: Rick Brunson, who had been waived by the Celtics. Brunson's strong relationship with Sprewell, Camby and Van Gundy and his low expectations about playing time made him the perfect choice. Van Gundy liked the former Temple guard's allout hustle.

Brunson played on the same Temple team as Aaron McKie and Eddie Jones. Not a bad threesome for any college program. He had also nicknamed Johnson's trademark three-point sign, the one in which he crosses his arms to spell out the letter "L." Johnson makes the sign only during the playoffs. Brunson coined it "The Big L" after a rapper who had been killed a few years back.

While Brunson was a nice addition to the locker room and the team's leading prankster, he could be abrasive with the media. During his first tour with the Knicks, Brunson had the locker next to Ewing's. When the herd of reporters descended on Ewing after a game, a reporter often had to stand directly in front of Brunson's wooden cubicle. Brunson grew sick of it, and the sound of the third-string point guard bellowing, "Get the fuck out of my locker" was heard more than a few times. Once, a TV anchor made the mistake of saying, "Hi, Ricky." Brunson looked up and said, "Don't call me that again. Only my mother calls me Ricky." Actually, Brunson got on everybody, including his teammates, and was always quick with a putdown. He loved goofing on rookie Postell's wardrobe.

■ ■ ■

Instead of activating Longley's buddy, Kerner, the Knicks were forced into releasing him to make room for Ward on the injured list. Childs held his tongue about the new no-point-guard alignment. Van Gundy had feared telling Childs about his decision before yesterday's practice, figuring his animated point guard was not going to take it well. When Van Gundy finally told him, Childs kept his emotions in check.

"You're the coach," Childs said. "You make the call."

But Childs was fuming. He saw himself as a starter, not just on the Knicks but on several teams. He viewed it as another slight and wished the trade rumors would come true. When he spoke to the media, Childs chose his words carefully.

"Whether I'm happy or not, I keep it to myself," he said. "Even if I don't agree, you'll never hear me voice it to anybody outside this locker room."

It was Childs' way of saying he was ticked off without actually saying it. But he couldn't complain after the Vancouver game. The big backcourt alignment destroyed the hapless Grizzlies. Rice, thrust into the starting lineup, busted out for 23 points, bagging five three-pointers and discovering his lost stroke. Houston added 22 and Sprewell 18. The Gotham Guns were firing deadly bullets against the lowly Grizzlies.

"If it ain't broke, don't fix it," Rice said with a smile about the new alignment.

■ ■ ■

Finally, a Luc Longley sighting. Although he had suited up, Longley had not played against the Raptors three days ago. Against Vancouver, Longley entered in the second quarter and the Garden erupted in a chant of "Luuuc," just as the Chicago fans had so many times during the Bulls' glory days.

After fighting many battles at the Garden as a hated Bull, Longley was touched. After the game he joked, "Were they Luc-ing or booing?" Then he added, "I'm happy to be on the floor as a local and not a marauder." Longley had became the first NBA player to use the word "marauder" in a sentence.

November 28

Falk, Mutombo's agent, met for lunch for two and a half hours at the Four Seasons Hotel in Washington with Hawks general manager Pete Babcock and president Stan Kasten. He told Babcock that Mutombo was concerned with the direction the Hawks were going in. He wasn't keen about signing a long-term deal with a club whose future was bleak. Falk wanted to know Babcock's plans for improving the team. If Babcock didn't think he'd be able to turn the club into playoff contenders within two years, Mutombo preferred to either be traded or go elsewhere when he became a free agent next summer.

Babcock had fielded numerous trade inquiries about Mutombo over the past few months, with the Knicks being the most persistent suitors. Babcock, too, had no plans of making a six-year commitment to a 34-year-old player (and reports suggested he could be older because of spotty birth records in Zaire). There was no talk of a contract extension during the meeting, and Babcock left thinking that trading Mutombo by the February 23 trading deadline was in the club's best interests.

■ ■ ■

If Van Gundy thought he had worries, imagine what Pat Riley was going through. The Heat came into the Garden with five wins in 14 games, by far the worst start since Riley took over in 1995. The team was having a hard time adjusting to life without Mourning. The players were constantly worried about Mourning's physical condition and noticed that even Riley had lightened up a bit. His notoriously vicious, marathon practices had become less taxing.

Brian Grant, once the apple of the Knicks' eyes, had been moved to center in Mourning's absence. That meant Grant would see playing time against Camby. This time, Camby wouldn't be facing a life-sized cut-out poster, but the real deal.

Van Gundy wasn't fooled by the Heat's record. This was the best rivalry in the NBA. Although some of the faces had changed and Ewing and Mourning would not square off, the magnitude of the event remained high. TNT would broadcast the game live.

"Miami is a big-time game for us," Sprewell said.

When the teams last met the previous spring in Game Seven of the second-round series, Miami's Dan Majerle was tugging at Sprewell's shorts along the baseline in the dying seconds. Sprewell had grabbed an errant last-second shot by Clarence Weatherspoon and was falling out of bounds, with help from Majerle. The Knicks were saved when referee Dick Bavetta granted them a timeout, even though Sprewell had never signaled for one. After their third straight heartbreaking play-off ouster by the Knicks, grumbling Heat players referred to the veteran official as Knick Bavetta.

Sprewell remembered the Heat's complaints and couldn't believe that everyone from owner Mickey Arison to Riley had cried about the phantom timeout when Majerle had blatantly fouled him on the play.

"They should have been talking about the execution of their last play instead of the officiating," Sprewell said, clearly ready for the rivalry's renewal at the Garden the next night.

CHAPTER 9

The Heat Is On

November 29

Mourning sat on the bench in a tan suit. Before tipoff, a Garden fan yelled to Mourning,"It's no fun without you. Get well."

The Heat got well at the Knicks' expense. There were a few obligatory "Riley sucks" chants, but the fans otherwise sat on their hands during a drab night. When a few fans razzed Riley in the final seconds, the former Knicks coach turned to his once-adoring audience and shouted, "It's early. It's November. It's the worst month I ever had."

Riley had a big smile as he yelled it. Grant and Mason bludgeoned the Knicks' interior. The final score was 84-81, not nearly signifying the extent of the carnage. Mason, the ex-Knick bulldog, finished with 19 points and 18 rebounds. Johnson was overwhelmed by the guy the Knicks traded to Charlotte to get him. Unable to hold his own again as the starting power forward, Johnson finished with six points, shooting three-of-11. With Ward rehabbing, the "Big Backcourt" struggled. After Childs shot an airball at the buzzer to seal the loss, Tim Hardaway jabbered in Childs' face. Childs just walked away.

The loss was appalling to Sprewell. His teammates had treated the Heat as just another team. Sprewell noticed that some players were joking around in the locker room minutes after the loss. After Van Gundy left the locker room, Sprewell lit into his teammates.

"This is the Garden," Sprewell said. "Nobody comes into the Garden and does it to us like that. Check yourself, man. Let's get some pride. Look within your heart and how much we want it. We weren't fucking ready and that shouldn't be. This was a big game and we didn't treat it that way."

His teammates had never seen Sprewell so angry. Camby, Sprewell's closest friend, considered his buddy so mellow that he believed the man who had choked Carlesimo was an alien who invaded his body for one day. Now Camby saw another side of him.

"Once I'm at the point that I've been disrespected, once that switch has been flipped, I'm really hard to handle," Sprewell had said in a magazine interview weeks earlier. "I get into a whole different mode. It's nothing nice."

When the media entered the locker room after the mandated 10-minute cooling off period, it was clear something big had happened.

"I don't want to be the guy fussing at the team," Sprewell told the writers. "Jeff does it enough, anyway. We have guys from other teams, and I don't know how they went about their business. But when we're serious, when we have a playoff-type atmosphere, when we have guys focused on what their responsibilities are, we win. That wasn't the case. I want a ring. Glen's got one, Travis has one. We have a great opportunity this year. We're not taking these losses personally."

There was edginess in the locker room. Childs was ripping Hardaway for having a big mouth. He sat at his locker, staring at the carpet, then looked up at the group of writers and stopped himself in mid-sentence, noticing my new choice of unconventional eyewear.

"What's with the purple glasses?" he snapped. Then he shook his head, sneered, didn't wait for a response and kept on talking about Hardaway.

December 1

At the end of the morning shootaround at Chicago's United Center, Johnson, the co-captain, gathered the players at midcourt and told them how important tonight's game was. There was a feeling that a loss to the worst team in basketball would send the Knicks reeling.

Johnson hadn't seen the newspaper clip that had been slid under his hotel door. He never read the newspapers. But somebody wanted him to see this one: a column I had written in that day's *Post*.

"TAKE A SEAT, LARRY," read the headline. I wrote, "There is no delicate way to put this: Larry Johnson must be benched for the good of the franchise." The column called for Van Gundy to replace Johnson in the starting lineup at power forward with the taller, healthier, six-foot-nine Thomas. Although he had lost weight, the six-foot-six Johnson wasn't pulling down enough offensive rebounds. He couldn't draw defenders to the outside because he had lost his ability to hit three-pointers. He still had his low-post moves, but he was missing easy inside shots. Back surgery had robbed him of his leaping ability.

Ninety minutes before the game, as the writers spoke to Van Gundy, Johnson walked toward the locker room and shot me a dagger glare. When the writers entered the room, Johnson was stretched out on the floor, doing back exercises with his headphones on. He again glowered at me, a sure sign of trouble: Johnson usually ignores all beat writers.

Johnson went hot and cold with the media. He can be charming or he can be an ogre. Even his best friends called him moody. He trusted one writer in New York, Frank Isola of *The Daily News*. Isola never questioned Van Gundy's extensive use of Johnson.

Johnson soiled his national reputation during the 1999 Finals and nearly lost his sneaker contract when he cursed out an NBA public relations person during a mandated media session at the Garden. Johnson was finishing shooting free throws when public relations assistant Teri Washington went up to him and said, "It's time for interviews, Larry."

"I have work to do," Johnson shot back.

Washington asked him again, but Johnson would not stop shooting free throws. Finally, Washington said, "What happened, L.J.? I loved you when you were at UNLV."

Johnson snapped, "Do you think I give a fuck if you loved me when I was at UNLV?"

He finally caved in and talked to the assembled group of writers, cursing his way through the interview and telling the media that it didn't pay his salary. Johnson got fined $25,000 for the incident.

Johnson realized his moods ran from surly to sublime, much like his three-point shooting touch. Once, when he was on a hotel elevator with a buddy visiting from Vegas, a Knicks PR assistant walked on. Introducing the Knicks employee to his friend, Johnson said, "This is the person who protects me." When the PR assistant said, "I try, Larry." Johnson responded, "No, no, no. You do, because I know I can be an asshole sometimes."

Johnson was the team's sharpest dresser and a lady charmer. He occasionally dressed like an old-time gangster. Al Capone is one of his fashion heroes. Once in a while, he would leave the locker room wearing a stylish, black do-rag. Versace was his favorite designer but Anthony Giovanni, who designs clothes for *The Sopranos,* was a close second.

The paradox of L.J. was beautifully illustrated in a fashion story he agreed to do with *The Post's* Farrah Weinstein. Johnson, who owns a hair salon in Charlotte, had been known to charm the hell out of women reporters.

"I enjoy walking past a woman and smelling sweet," he told her. "The secret to putting on the right amount of cologne is to spritz it once into the air and then walk through it. That way, you don't get it on you, but you smell nice." He also admitted in the story that he no longer wore underwear. Yet, ask him a question about his lost three-point shot and he's liable to tear your head off.

Johnson came out against the Bulls as hot as an electric light bulb left on overnight. He sent lovely spinners through the net and drove to the basket with a fury. From the United Center's press row, the sharp-witted Mike Dougherty of the *Journal-News* cracked, "All Larry sees is a rim wearing purple glasses." The reference, of course, was to my new purple eyewear. Johnson finished with a season-high 24 points and the Knicks prevailed, 91-86.

"Larry gets judged too harshly," Van Gundy said. "He plays good some nights and he plays bad like a lot of our players. I don't think the focus should be on one guy."

In an otherwise giddy locker room, Rice sat slumped at his cubicle, staring into space. His downcast body language stood out like a kid crying at a birthday party. Rice had difficulty hiding his emotions. Why he didn't leave for the bus quickly without the writers seeing him stewing was a mystery. That is, unless he wanted the writers to see him stewing.

Rice had been benched for the final 14:27 in a game not decided until the last minute. He was three-of-seven from the field for nine points. When the writers approached him, Rice didn't have a lot to say. It wasn't so much his words but his look and soft voice that spoke volumes.

"It's hard to get used to and I don't want to get used to it," Rice said of the fourth-quarter benching. "It's a question you have to ask the coach, but, hey, all you could do is support the other guys."

Johnson took his time getting dressed in the off-limits shower area. All of the other players had already left for the bus, but four writers lingered. If he was trying to wait out the media, he wasn't successful. He finally came out and made eye contact with the other three writers, avoiding my glance. "My guys," he said to the other three.

Later, as Johnson trudged to the bus, I caught up with him and tried to clear the air. This was one of the more challenging parts of beat-writing at *The Post*. The bosses encouraged pointed commentary, but you still had to maintain working relationships with the players. Columnists could rip apart a player and not have to deal with him the next day. Beat reporters were with the team every day.

"Larry, if you saw what I wrote today, it wasn't a personal thing," I said.

"You don't worry about it," he said. "You've got a job to do. I've got a job to do."

■ ■ ■

Before the game against the Timberwolves the following night at the Garden, Van Gundy addressed what he saw as a worsening situation. His players were berating the referees too often, and Childs and Thomas were the worst offenders. In Chicago, Thomas was ejected for arguing a foul against Elton Brand.

"Am I waiting for Kurt to mature?" Van Gundy said after the Bulls' game. "I'm not holding my breath. It's not just Kurt's technicals and getting thrown out. That could have cost us big, but we bitch and whine on every call. It's not only hurting the individual players. It's hurting our team. We're not getting the benefit of the doubt."

Notorious for losing his temper during games, Thomas had earned the moniker "Dirty Kurtie" and "Crazy Eyes". On Christmas Night 1999, he secured his reputation as an out-of-control thug when he took a swing at Jalen Rose in a game televised on NBC, drawing an ejection and suspension. Thomas didn't seem to mind the notoriety.

Thomas' savage look after a call goes against him was at odds with his pleasant off-the-court demeanor. He was the most soft-spoken, easy-going guy on the club and didn't have a mean bone in his body. But it takes some time around him to figure that out.

When the Knicks' new public relations manager, Jonathan Supranowitz, started his job over the summer, he was terrified of Thomas because of his look and league-wide reputation as a hot-tempered dirty player. Supranowitz's first interaction with Thomas was to ask him questions for the media guide. During the interview, Thomas was twisting his earring when it got caught. Thomas screamed in pain for a half minute. The Knicks' PR official had no idea what was going on. Supranowitz nearly had a heart attack, thinking Thomas was going crazy on him.

■ ■ ■

Houston was unstoppable and the Knicks battered Minnesota. Houston scored 37 points, much to the delight of his teammates, who whooped and hollered every time he hit a shot, and the fans, who buzzed with anticipation every time he touched the ball..

"That was the best feeling in the world," Houston said. "Every time I touched the ball, they wanted me to shoot. That never happened before."

"What's up, Michael Jordan?" Wolves superstar Kevin Garnett said to Houston as they crossed paths in the Garden tunnel after the game.

Rice again did not play in the fourth quarter but politely declined to discuss the matter.

■ ■ ■

Sprewell hadn't said anything about Webber since the league meeting, but Webber's recently-fired agent, Fallasha Erwin, was quoted in *The New York Times* as saying the Knicks would be his former client's first choice this summer if things didn't work out with Sacramento.

"I know he likes New York and I think that would be a very viable option for him," Erwin said. "The one year he played with Sprewell, they both excelled. Latrell likes to get up and down the court like Chris. He has an endless motor and that's Chris' game. Chris goes to play with players. The one reason he went to Washington was to play with Juwan Howard."

December 4

The Knicks gained their revenge on the Clippers in a game that was decided by the second quarter. Clippers coach Alvin Gentry was ejected before halftime for walking onto the court to confront an official. In the fourth quarter of the 106-78 wreckage, acting coach Dennis Johnson turned to the reporters sitting on press row next to the visitors' bench and asked, "Do any of these phones dial 911?"

Afterward, *Baywatch* star David Hasselhoff visited the Knicks' locker room. Hasselhoff was in New York performing in the Broadway play *Dr. Jekyll and Mr. Hyde.* The tall actor came into the room and strutted around like he owned the place, schmoozing with the players and inviting some of them to see the play. Visitors and media members normally speak softly in an NBA locker room, but Hasselhoff's voice boomed across the room. He made sure everyone knew he was there.

During a season that has so many road trips and night games, players embrace the quiet nights they have to relax at home with their families. They're not looking for a night out on the town. So, when Hasselhoff invited Sprewell to the play, Sprewell knew he wouldn't have the time to go.

"Sounds good," Sprewell said politely, not wanting to insult the famous guest.

December 5-6

Pete Vecsey, the NBA columnist for *The Post,* reported that the Knicks had resumed trade talks with the Wolves regarding point guard Terrell Brandon. With Ward's knee a potential long-term problem, a trade for Brandon made sense. But Minnesota was asking for Houston, who planned to exercise an opt-out clause in his contract to become a free agent next summer. The talks didn't progress much from there, but it was a clear indication that the Knicks were concerned with their situation at point guard. Ward's knee was going to be a chronic problem. Layden kept tabs of the quality point guards available, including former Knick Rod Strickland. After practice, Houston said he had become "immune" to trade rumors.

■ ■ ■

The club flew out to Dallas for a two-game Texas trip that figured to be a major challenge: the upstart Mavericks, emerging as a top-flight playoff contender, followed by the dominant Spurs in back-to-back games.

The night before the Dallas game, as most of the Knicks stayed in their hotel rooms to watch the Lakers play the Sixers, the Associated Press reported that Mavericks coach Don Nelson had been diagnosed with prostate cancer.

Four current Knicks had played for Nelson, but only Ward was left from Nelson's 1995-96 Knicks team. Nelson was fired in March of that season. Strickland and Thomas had played for Nelson in Dallas and Sprewell had played for Nelson in Golden State. Nelson had run his friend Webber out of Golden State, but Sprewell didn't hold a grudge. He liked Nelson's creative offense, even wished Van Gundy applied some of Nelson's tactics.

The Van Gundy-Nelson relationship was a giant mystery. Nelson's firing led to the Van Gundy era. Whether Van Gundy was Nelson's trusty assistant who remained loyal despite the coach turning his back on Ewing or helped undermine Nelson behind the scenes is debatable. Van Gundy certainly respected Nelson's longevity as a coach. In his eyes, anyone who could last that long in the NBA had to be admired.

But Van Gundy and Nelson had completely different basketball philosophies and work ethics. After Riley's tortuous practices and dictatorial leadership, the Knicks did not embrace the laid-back climate Nelson created. Checketts began to think Nelson was more concerned with getting to the golf course early and drinking beer than working his team hard in practice. Beer wasn't even permitted in the Knicks' locker room under Van Gundy.

Van Gundy's ugly 1995 incident involving *Post* reporter Thomas Hill would never have happened if Nelson had stuck around for the whole practice. Hill had written a story that quoted John Starks' grandmother complaining about her grandson's diminished role under Nelson. With practice almost over and Nelson gone, Van Gundy, then a young assistant, shouted at Hill across the Purchase gym, "What are you going to do, call his fucking baby daughter next?"

Starks threatened Hill, getting right in his face. Van Gundy never apologized to Hill. Nor did Checketts, who said he was sorry the incident happened, but felt Hill was wrong to call a player's grandmother. Privately, Checketts admired Van Gundy for sticking up for a player. He hadn't thought Van Gundy had the courage to do so. The incident

103

helped Van Gundy get the job as interim coach when Nelson was fired two months later.

Van Gundy starts work at six a.m., watches tons of film, and has a reputation as the hardest-working coach in the league. He obviously wasn't imitating Nelson. Nor did he steal any strategies from Nelson, a freewheeling offensive coach. Van Gundy stuck to Riley's principles of a structured half-court offense that relied on rebounding, defense and Ewing to win games.

Nelson might have gotten away with the golf, beer and offensive-minded approach had he not decided the Knicks were better off phasing out Ewing, emphasizing Anthony Mason and de-emphasizing Starks. Nelson met with Checketts, GM Ernie Grunfeld and the ITT/Sheraton corporate bigwigs in Manhattan and told them he thought Ewing should be traded and the Knicks should make a big push for Orlando's Shaquille O'Neal, who would become a free-agent that summer.

Nelson's master plan looks brilliant with the passing of time, but back then, his Shaq vision got back to Ewing. To this day, Nelson doesn't know the identity of the snitch who cost him his job, but he knows he was fired because of it despite the Knicks' 34-25 record. Ironically, the current perimeter-oriented Knicks, minus Ewing, were exactly what Nelson had envisioned five years ago.

"Once that meeting got back to Patrick, he and John Starks made it real difficult for me," Nelson told *The New York Times*. "Ernie was very private, so I can't imagine him saying anything. Anyway, once Patrick found out, I was dead in the water."

Another sticking point between Nelson and Ewing was the hotels at which the Knicks stayed. When Riley was coaching, the Knicks went from staying at Marriotts to Four Seasons and Ritz-Carltons. Riley wanted only the best. Once, when the Knicks walked into a restaurant in Charleston, Riley had management change the way the napkins were folded.

"I don't know if Nellie even uses a napkin," one Knicks official said.

Riley used to buy each member of his coaching staff two dozen Ralph Lauren golf shirts that sold for 90 dollars each retail. The ones Riley ordered came with Knicks logos and he bought more than two dozen for himself. When Nelson took over for the 1995-96 season, he told the operations department, "Just get me some T-shirts. And make sure they have a pocket."

When Nelson took charge, he cared only about convenience, not style. The Knicks began staying at Westins, Hyatts and Marriotts again. Ewing wasn't pleased and complained to management. Though it was not specified in his next contract, signed that summer, Ewing would have a lot to say about which hotels the Knicks stayed in during the Van Gundy era. Of course, Van Gundy didn't care if it was the Ritz-Carlton or the Red Roof Inn, as long as he had a VCR to watch game tapes. But he wanted to keep his players happy, especially Ewing.

Nelson believed Ewing stopped giving his best efforts in mid-season to get him fired. One conspiracy theory fingered Checketts as the informant, and Nelson believes it. "Not in a million years," Nelson says about Van Gundy's potential role in the mess. He understood why his top assistant, Don Chaney, was passed over for the interim job. If the philosophy was to make Ewing the centerpiece of the team, Van Gundy had to be in charge.

Van Gundy was wise to team politics when he took over as interim coach. He immediately made Ewing the focal point of the offense. In return, Ewing lobbied hard for Van Gundy to be named permanent head coach.

Van Gundy sings Nelson's praises whenever his name is brought up, but it always seems forced. He benefited greatly from another man's misfortune. Had Nelson read the political landscape accurately and played his cards right with Ewing, Van Gundy may have been a career assistant coach.

But, on this day, Van Gundy's emotions weren't forced. There was genuine sadness when the Knicks arrived for the shootaround at Dallas' Reunion Arena. "Nellie saw something in me and gave me a great opportunity," Strickland said. Two hours before tipoff, Ward knocked on Nelson's office door and presented him with a card, a basket of flowers and a cake. Van Gundy went to Nelson's office before the game and wished him well. Chaney spent 15 minutes with Nelson, his former teammate on the Celtics. They laughed about the wild old days in Boston. For all of Boston's sustained success, the Celtics of Tommy Heinsohn had a reputation as the biggest beer drinkers in the league. And Nelson was the ringleader.

"Cancer's not stunning, but when it hits someone close to you it is," Van Gundy said before the game. "And I'm not trying to portray that me and him are really tight because we only spent a few months together. But I have a great deal of respect for him. He's a really nice man."

Nelson told reporters he was leaning toward undergoing surgery and planned to consult with Yankees manager Joe Torre, another prostate cancer victim.

■ ■ ■

Determined to win for their sick coach, the Mavericks dominated the Knicks with their size. They shot 71 percent from the floor in the first quarter of a 94-85 victory. The victory was Nelson's 938th, tying him for fourth with Red Auerbach on the all-time NBA list.

The Knicks failed to execute the gameplan, which was to help out defending All-Star swingman Michael Finley when he broke past his man on the perimeter. In the fourth quarter, Van Gundy called a time-out to remind them of the gameplan. On the first play after the time-out, nobody moved over to help out as Finley scored another basket on a runner in the lane. Van Gundy called another timeout. He walked a few steps away from the bench., refusing to join his club in the huddle. For the rest of the timeout, he let the players sit by themselves in silence. He stood five yards away with his arms folded.

"We sucked today," Sprewell said afterward.

Rice's season hit a new low. He was scoreless in 26 minutes, missing all six of his shots. It was his first scoreless game since his rookie season, when he left after one minute because of a leg injury.

■ ■ ■

The trip to Dallas was bittersweet for Strickland. He saw his old teammates and spoke before and after the game with Mavericks owner Mark Cuban. Cuban got closer to his players than any other owner. Most Knicks players wouldn't know Cablevision honchos James or Charles Dolan if they knocked into them in a dark alley. Strickland e-mailed Cuban throughout the season. In many of his e-mails, Cuban apologized to Strickland for the draft-day trade.

A fan favorite, Strickland had attended the Mavericks' draft party in late June. He schmoozed with fans and signed autographs until a Dallas official took him aside to let him know he had been traded to the Knicks. Strickland left the party in shock.

Strickland wouldn't be human if he wasn't envious that, as he rode the Knicks' bench, the Mavericks were off to their best start ever.

"I was there while we were building, building, building, and now I'm not there when they've made it," Strickland said.

Strickland expected to escape his contract in the summer to become a free agent. He hoped Cuban would bring him back. Strickland played a season-high 26 minutes against Dallas and was one of the few Knicks who gave an honest effort. But, for all of his trying in Dallas, Strickland sat out the entire Spurs game the following night. After starting 67 games in Dallas the previous season, Strickland was now ninth on the Knicks in minutes played.

■ ■ ■

Spurs commentator P. J. Carlesimo, about to sign a contract to appear on NBC's pre-game and halftime shows, was absent this time as the Knicks recovered from their loss the previous night. "It's a good game for him to miss," Sprewell snarled. Leading the resurrection were Longley and Rice, who scored 19 points with 12 rebounds. Longley, who didn't play against Dallas, was needed against Tim Duncan, and for the first time he showed why Layden wanted him. During the morning walkthrough at their hotel in San Antonio, Van Gundy had asked Longley whether he wanted to guard David Robinson or Duncan. Longley chose Duncan.

Duncan, who has made a habit of torching the Knicks, was going good in the first half. But he went one-for-eight from the floor in the fourth quarter with Longley laying 290 pounds into him.

"It's the reason I'm in the league," Longley said. "The reason I'm on this team is to play defense against big guys. The reason you haven't seen much of me is we haven't played a lot of big centers. Opportunities to play in crucial times like this will help develop trust in me."

December 9
The Knicks returned home and beat the pesky Denver Nuggets. With the game all but over in the final seconds, Sprewell, who scored 29 points, sidled up to Denver coach Dan Issel and told him how impressed he was with their team. Issel, who had been friendly with Sprewell for years, looked at him and didn't say a word.

"You're not talking to me today?" Sprewell asked.

He wasn't, not after Sprewell had buried his club. The Knicks were now 5-1 since Sprewell's heated address in the locker room following the Miami loss and 14-8 overall. But his back still hurt, and he looked forward to the three days off the Knicks had before taking on Toronto at Air Canada Center.

Johnson hit a key three-pointer from the corner to clinch the victory in the final minute. Johnson had missed eight of his first nine shots through the first three quarters and his careless inbounds pass led to an easy dunk for Antonio McDyess. Postell went up to Johnson in the locker room to congratulate him on his clutch trey.

"Thanks," Johnson said. "The first part was kind of ugly, though."

Postell replied: "That's all right. It still counts."

December 10-13

Some of the Knicks spent the lull between games doing charity work. Postell, the rehabbing Ward and Childs knocked down walls at a Harlem tenement and installed sheetrock for the Fannie Mae Foundation to refurbish the depressed area. Houston attended a computer class in the South Bronx. He showed a group of 13-year-old students how to log onto the web, access NBA.com and vote for him in the All-Star balloting.

The rare three-day break gave the Knicks extra time to prepare for a club that had given them fits in the regular season. It also gave them a chance to respond to Oakley's comments earlier in the season. One of Oakley's most-frequent targets was Thomas. Last season, he had called him "a lady" and "a tough-guy wannabe." They nearly fought during a game, pushing each other before the referees intervened. Oakley's reputation as the league's busiest thug was growing. Two weeks ago, the NBA suspended him for taking a swing at the Clippers' Jeff McInnis during a shootaround. There were rumors the fight was over a girl.

Oakley's "warrior" jab wasn't sitting kindly with Thomas, who fancied himself as the Knicks' enforcer. "Oakley's got to define what his definition of warrior is," Thomas said. When asked for his definition, Thomas said, "Me. Plain and simple."

December 14

During the morning shootaround at Air Canada Centre, as his players shot free throws, Van Gundy saw the Raptors waiting in the wings and got his club off the court. He wasn't taking any chances with Oakley around and the players still stinging from his quotes.

After the Raptors worked out, Oakley said his dislike for Thomas was genuine. "It's personal," he said. "He can't say nothing to me. I don't want to interact with him on the court. I don't want him to think he can shake my hand. It's like that."

On the state of the Knicks, Canada's roundball poet laureate said, "You get what you paid for. You go to the store, you buy milk, you bring it back, that's what you wanted."

That night, the Knicks' offense turned sour down the stretch in a 70-68 loss. They didn't score in the final three minutes and Houston was the goat. With 30 seconds remaining and the Knicks up by one, he dribbled to midcourt and accelerated when Carter stripped him of the ball. Houston had a chance to redeem himself, but missed badly on a three-pointer at the buzzer. As he left the court, Van Gundy crumpled the piece of paper on which he had just diagrammed the final play, dropped it to the floor and kicked it.

Johnson left the game in the first half with a sprained left knee. He would need an MRI on his MCL the next day.

The loss hurt badly. The Knicks had a six-point lead with five minutes left and had harassed Carter into a bad game. But they crumbled like novices down the stretch.

"It was right there for us," Sprewell said disbelievingly with a shake of his head.

Knicks general manager Scott Layden insisted that he didn't want to trade Patrick Ewing, but in the end, he had no choice: Ewing wanted to be traded, and Knicks brass felt he no longer would play his heart out for the club if he returned.

Embattled Knicks coach Jeff Van Gundy, one of Ewing's biggest supporters, was left shuffling his lineup all season when he lost his franchise center. Van Gundy tried to motivate his team any way possible to overcome the loss of Ewing, but fell short in the end.

Right: Marcus Camby thought he had problems when the Spurs' Danny Ferry poked him in the eye while battling for a rebound, but his life took a tragic turn when his sister Monica was held hostage and raped.

Bottom: Knicks and Pistons players gather in a prayer huddle after a game on April 18, 2001, at Madison Square Garden. Players bringing their religion into the workplace became an issue after two magazine stories.

111

Top: Many fans thought
Othella Harrington, sur-
rounded by (left to right)
Charlie Ward, Allan Houston
and Latrell Sprewell, should
have received more playing
time after being acquired
from Vancouver, but usually
DNP appeared next to his
name.

Left: Charlie Ward's religious
views became a major issue
when his controversial
remarks about Jews and Jesus
appeared in a Sunday New
York Times Magazine article.
Ward eventually apologized
for his comments.

Patrick Ewing's return to Madison Square Garden on February 27, 2001, as a member of the Seattle Supersonics was the most-anticipated game of the season. Ewing received a spectacular ovation from the crowd, and later went one-on-one with Marcus Camby.

Larry Johnson (left) and Mark Jackson, both teammates of Ewing's in New York, battle with the big man for a rebound in Ewing's first game back at the Garden. Ewing was boxed in all night, outplayed by Camby.

Two players in the Ewing deal: Glen Rice shoots over Ewing in the February 27th game at the Garden. Rice disappointed the Knicks for most of the season because of plantar fasciaitis and was frequently relegated to coming off the bench.

Although his team lost, Ewing's return to the Garden made for an emotional night. Former teammate Mark Jackson, recently reacquired by the Knicks, welcomed Ewing.

Spike Lee, perhaps the most famous and most out-spoken Knicks fan, is a regular on celebrity row at the Garden. Lee criticized the Knicks for trading Ewing and even blamed the media.

Latrell Sprewell drives past Toronto's Vince Carter during the Knicks' playoff series against the Raptors. Sprewell was the most reliable Knick during the regular season and playoffs.

Patrick Ewing returned to the Garden one more time for Game 2 of the Knicks' playoff series against Toronto. By that time, Seattle had been eliminated and questions brewed about Ewing's future.

CHAPTER 10
The Whisperers

December 15

The Knicks do not hold morning shootarounds before the second game of a back-to-back set. On the road, they'll occasionally have a morning walk-through in the hotel ballroom, with the training staff putting tape on the carpet to resemble a basketball court. The walk-through consists of players walking through offensive and defensive sets. No shooting, no balls, no contact.

The Utah Jazz kept getting older, but the Karl Malone/John Stockton band sustained the team's greatness. Van Gundy knew that the Jazz, playing at the same high level that made them back-to-back finalists in 1997 and '98, required some sort of preparation. Van Gundy called for a pre-game walk-through in the Garden's rotunda. Instead of asking his club to arrive early, the walk-through began at six p.m. and lasted until 6:30 p.m., cutting into the time the players and coach were supposed to be accessible to the media.

Though the writers eventually spoke to Van Gundy, they had no time with the players because the locker room was closed to reporters at 6:45, 45 minutes before tipoff. The walk-through during the media access period violated NBA rules, but Van Gundy didn't care. The NBA, often outraged by the way the Knicks treated the media, had fined them several times for violating access rules. But Van Gundy was willing to risk another financial hit if it meant giving his club a better chance at defending the pick-and-roll against Malone and Stockton, something they hadn't done well in recent games against the Jazz.

Van Gundy considered most of the pre-game banter with reporters a waste of time, even though he often was very good at supplying them with interesting material. Although tight-lipped when the topic turned to injured players, he was one of the most quotable, articulate coaches in the league.

The tabloid beat writers and columnists desperately needed stuff for the early-edition stories that had to be filed to their copy desks before tipoff. The beat writers for the suburban papers also needed tidbits for their notebooks. The writers would have tolerated the inconvenience if they been informed about the delay beforehand. That a Knicks' official did not notify the writers Van Gundy would be a half-hour late was mystifying considering that the PR staff was touchy about writers calling the league to complain about the club breaking media access rules. When Van Gundy finally arrived, he was unapologetic and didn't acknowledge his lateness.

But the writers didn't complain to the league and the Knicks proved that the walk-through was a waste of time. The Jazz did whatever they wanted as the Knicks looked tired and ill-prepared. On the first play, Rice drove the lane, got triple-teamed and tossed the ball out of bounds for one of his four turnovers. The Knicks committed 26.

The boos rained down in torrents at halftime and during the second half. During the final minute of the Jazz's 89-58 demolition, a fan behind the Knicks bench yelled at Van Gundy, "You're still using the Patrick Ewing offense. Why not bring him back?"

Sixty-eight points in Toronto, 58 points against Utah in back-to-back games. So much for the big backcourt infusing life into their attack. Van Gundy's lack of imagination in adjusting his offense to suit his new perimeter talent was looming as a prominent issue. Perhaps that's why Van Gundy changed the storyline when he met the media after the game. Van Gundy said the Knicks' problems weren't about X's and O's. They were about a me-first attitude infecting the team.

"We're fighting ourselves right now," Van Gundy said. "There are a lot of internal things that have cropped up this year more than ever before. The game becomes very hard when you're more concerned with yourself than the team. You guys are in the locker room all the time. We have a lot of whisperers. They're bad for your team."

Although Van Gundy did not name names, the "whisperers" in the locker room remark was a sign that Van Gundy thought he was losing control of the team.

Rice, Strickland, Longley and even Childs were unhappy with their roles, but, for the most part, they were honest about their desire for more minutes. Branding them as whisperers made them sound underhanded. The players felt betrayed by Van Gundy's blanket accusations. One thing some players resented about Van Gundy was the double standard. He was allowed to get mad when a player complained to the media about his role, but the same rules did not apply to him. Players such as Rice, Strickland and Childs felt doublecrossed by the "whisperers" remark.

The players had a good idea where the "whisperers" allegation stemmed from. Several of the Knick players watched what they said around Lori Hamamoto, especially when they were discussing Van Gundy. As one veteran said when Hamamoto walked into the locker room before a game one night, "Oh no, there's Jeff's spy."

Players joining the club were warned by their teammates and others close to the team to watch their mouths around Hamamoto because of her friendship with Van Gundy. She acted like a mother hen when it came to the coach and was wary of any reporters whom she felt had it in for him. If she sensed Van Gundy was about to put his foot in his mouth during a controversial line of questioning, she wasn't adverse to stopping the interview. When the Van Gundy-Grunfeld feud ended in Grunfeld's dismissal during the 1999 season, public relations director Chris Weillor, seen as a Grunfeld confidant, was axed. Hamamoto was promoted to lead the PR department. Van Gundy had grown to trust her more than anyone in the organization.

Van Gundy didn't loiter in the locker room before or after games as Hamamoto did. When in the room, he either talked to the team or wrote notations on the board. But before the Utah game, he had approached Rice about Craig Sager of TNT's report during the Knicks-Raptors game. Sager had reported that Rice told him he was unhappy with his role. This wasn't news; the New York papers had been reporting his displeasure regularly. Rice suggested that he wanted more minutes in the fourth quarter and not enough plays were being run for him. He was averaging just nine shots per game. Rice thought Van Gundy could use him more on post-up chances, particularly with the Knicks searching for low-post points.

Using the Sager report as an excuse, Van Gundy confronted Rice. Normally, he didn't like approaching players individually, although sometimes he communicated with notes slipped under hotel doors. When Van Gundy criticized a player, he did it in front of the group. He didn't feel he was wrong to do this because a mistake by one player affected the whole team.

Rice told Van Gundy he never said he was unhappy with his role, and Van Gundy believed him. So when Rice heard about Van Gundy's "whisperers" dig, he wondered why the coach was allowed to air dirty laundry, but no one else.

"This team is perfectly fine as far as attitudes," Rice said. "We all pull for each other. We lost and, when bad things happen, people tend to look at things that aren't there."

But the Knicks had scored 126 points in two games. Was it the attitude? Or the offense?

December 16

The Knicks almost never practice the day after back-to-back games, but Van Gundy had the players come to Purchase for a team meeting. He talked to them for 20 minutes to clarify some of the issues he had addressed with the media after the Jazz game. He wanted to make sure everyone was thinking about the team and not doing their own thing. His concern was attitude.

"We're not doing what it takes to win," Van Gundy said. "We don't come to rebound every night. We're not doing a good job taking care of the ball. I didn't like our attitude toward defense, rebounding, ball-handling or our attitude toward giving in when things get tough. Our problem is our attitude toward the game, what it takes to win."

After the meeting, Rice downplayed his rift with Van Gundy. "Jeff and I are straight," Rice said. "We're on the same page about what happened [with Sager]."

In a private conversation, Sprewell spoke to Rice about the dangers of letting anger build up against a coach. He had been there before once and the result was one of the ugliest moments in professional team sports history. Sprewell told Rice not to have a negative attitude, even if he felt slighted about not playing in the fourth quarter.

Meanwhile, Van Gundy knew the tension around the team was not helped by Johnson's injury. Johnson's MRI was negative, and he was diagnosed with a sprained MCL that might keep him out for two weeks. Johnson was one player Van Gundy could count on to build team morale and unity, but not when he wasn't playing.

December 17

The whispers went away for one afternoon against the Bucks at the Garden. Strickland, one of the supposed disgruntled Knicks, buried a wide-open three-pointer from the left corner with .6 seconds remaining in the fourth quarter to force overtime. The Knicks had blown a 16-point third-quarter lead and trailed by 10 points late in the fourth before staging a stirring rally. Rice was brilliant with 32 points and the Knicks won, 100-97.

"We showed great will when we got down," Van Gundy said.

There seemed to be no middle ground in the Knicks' universe. When they won, they had great character. When they lost, they were dogs. Maybe the New York tabloids were to blame for the shifting perceptions. Or maybe Van Gundy's wildly fluctuating view of his club was the cause.

December 19

Another trip to Atlanta, another chance for the beat writers to question Mutombo. The writers huddled around Pete Babcock in the locker room before the game for an update on the Mutombo trade talks. As the Hawks' GM talked about the chances of trading Mutombo, a surprise visitor burst through the locker room door: Ted Turner, the Hawks owner/billionaire media mogul, accompanied by three VIP companions.

Turner, wearing a white suit, had no idea what he had stumbled upon. Turning to his well-dressed guests, Turner, acting like he had tipped a few, bellowed a little too loudly: "This is Pete Babcock. Pete's going to win us a championship someday, or I'm going to fire his ass. I want a ring."

Embarrassed, Babcock looked at Turner and said, "Ted, led me introduce you to the New York media." Everyone laughed except Turner, who said seriously, "So which one of you is from *The New*

York Post?" It was an odd question, unless you knew that Turner and *Post* owner Rupert Murdoch had been engaged in an ugly feud for years. The eccentric Turner once said of his rival, "Murdoch is like the late fuhrer."

"That would be me," I said, raising my notebook, afraid he was ready to revoke my credential.

"Figures, the ugly one," Turner howled, and everyone laughed again. Before I could respond, Turner said, "I'm just kidding. Hey, I like *The Post."*

None of the reporters remembered to ask Turner about Mutombo's future.

■ ■ ■

The Knicks lost for the second straight time to the Hawks at Philips Arena. Mutombo snared 15 rebounds and blocked three shots. The turning point occurred after Childs committed three fouls on Atlanta point guard Matt Maloney during a two-minute span late in the third quarter. Sensing Childs was about to get a technical, Van Gundy hurriedly inserted Brunson. As Childs got to the bench, he kept yakking. The official stopped play, pointed at Childs and issued him a technical. Van Gundy shot Childs a long, icy glare, and benched him for the rest of the game.

In a spiel designed to soothe the bruised psyches of his players, Van Gundy took the blame for the loss, even though the players had missed open shots.

"I have to get them playing better on offense," Van Gundy said. "I have to do a better job teaching."

Two drives to the basket by Sprewell were rejected by Mount Mutombo, who giddily cracked after the game, "What does Sprewell think, I still have malaria?"

Sprewell and Rice stood outside the shower in their towels, whispering.

"We're so much better than that team," Rice told Sprewell.

"I know," Sprewell said, shaking his head. "I know."

But Sprewell was encouraged that he had driven to the basket, even if he missed his only dunk attempt against Mutombo. The pain from his back injury was finally disappearing.

"I don't think I've had a dunk all year," Sprewell said. "I haven't been able to attack the basket in some time because of the pain. Today was the first day I felt I had the bounce again."

If a loss to the Hawks wasn't bad enough, an ice storm hit Atlanta that night. The Cablevision charter sat on the runway for nearly three hours, waiting to be de-iced. The plane touched down at Westchester Airport at three a.m., forcing Van Gundy to cancel the next day's practice. The runway delay was a nightmare for the depressed Van Gundy, who wanted to tell the pilot to risk taking off, despite the ice.

"I was ready to hand out a few parachutes to those noteworthy individuals that deserved one and take our chances with the ice on the wings," Van Gundy said morbidly.

December 20

Losing breeds trade rumors, and *The Post* ran a back page story about the club shopping Rice. The date was significant because it marked the first day the Knicks were able to trade Rice. After signing a player, they had to wait 90 days under the Collective Bargaining Agreement before they could trade his contact.

Checketts wasn't pleased with the chemistry of the Gotham Guns and ordered Layden to gauge Rice's trade value, according to *The Post*. The three Guns had precious few nights when their games were in sync. But Layden had his work cut out for him. Rice, at age 33, had been struggling with his shot, had been lame for parts of the year and had three years remaining on a $36-million pact.

The Knicks' PR staff had a problem with *The Post*'s story, which made Checketts sound like he was ordering Layden around like a secretary. Politics always reigned supreme at 2 Penn Plaza.

December 21

Rick Pitino and his disgruntled band of Celtics came to town, with the ex-Knick coach's job hanging by a thread. Seemingly wanting to be put out of his misery, Pitino had recently told his players he'd quit in January if he didn't have them playing better defense. Celtics fans were ready to throw Pitino into Boston Harbor and save the tea.

When Pitino gave Van Gundy his first job as a Providence graduate assistant coach in 1986, he shook his hand and said, "Congratulations, Jim." Nonetheless, Van Gundy remained thankful for the chance. Before the game, Van Gundy staunchly defended Pitino.

Nobody expected anything less from Van Gundy, loyal to a fault to those who advanced his career.

"He is a great coach," Van Gundy said. "They are not ever going to get a better coach. If they don't win, I know one thing, it is not because of his lack of greatness as a coach."

Mike Vaccaro, the talented columnist from the *Star-Ledger,* asked Van Gundy if he puts the Knicks' troubles in perspective when he sees Pitino's mess. Van Gundy answered, "If you know anything about me, then you know I have no perspective on life. I don't have a clue about keeping things in perspective."

The remark was self-effacing and on the mark. In a *Sports Illustrated* article, Van Gundy talked about how he had rammed into his garage door, run a stoplight, hit another car and smacked into a gas pump because his mind was on basketball. He is a reputed bad driver. When Van Gundy drove the treacherous Pacific Coast Highway the prior summer, relatives were afraid he'd drive off the cliff into the ocean with his mind on the pick and roll. He and his assistant coaches and friends often discussed how he needed a hobby, a diversion from basketball. Chaney, for one, was afraid Van Gundy would burn out before he hit 45.

But Van Gundy is utterly focused on basketball, and an exchange with a magazine writer showed how out-of-touch he is with pop culture. The celebrities in the front row don't faze him because he doesn't know who they are.

"So what was the last CD you cranked up loud?" the writer asked.

"I don't own any CDs," Van Gundy said.

"So what music do you like?"

After a long pause, Van Gundy said, "One of my college roommates was into The Police and I got to like them. But I hear one of the guys left the band."

"Sting?"

"Yeah, that's it. I understand he's got a solo career, right?"

■ ■ ■

In the first quarter, Pitino was his usual animated self, berating an official for a foul call on Paul Pierce. Alertly, Jim O'Brien, his trusty assistant, seeing his boss in a prolonged argument with the official, took Pierce out of the game. Pitino turned to O'Brien, who had been his sidekick since they coached at the University of Kentucky, and shouted, "You don't ever do that again without consulting me!"

"You were talking to the officials," O'Brien answered meekly.

"Don't ever do that!" Pitino shouted.

It was an embarrassing moment for O'Brien. The Celtic players on the bench watched the scene and hid their smirks. When Pitino resigned the following month, those who saw the exchange at the Garden couldn't help but chuckle when they read O'Brien's quote after his first game as interim coach: "There really wasn't much difference to me going out there as head coach and going out there as Rick's associate because of how much he delegated to me."

Pitino's anger soon turned to joy as the Celtics won, breaking Pitino's 15-game Garden losing streak. Pierce and Antoine Walker, Boston's two young stars, combined for 54 points.

Houston scored 37 points in the Knicks' previous game against the Celtics. This time, he scored four. Although Johnson returned to the lineup, Camby got hurt again, straining his groin. The league-leading Sixers were up next the following night in Philly.

"Maybe that could be our turning point," Houston said glumly.

December 22-25

Van Gundy told the writers that the Sixers' game would be a major test of character. In the locker room, 30 minutes before tipoff, Van Gundy told his players, "We've got to fight, we've got to fight, we've got to fight, fight, fight!" He sounded a lot like a rah-rah college coach and the players dug the pure outburst of positive emotion. It was so out of character. They took the court for pre-game warmups as excited as a high school team gunning for the state championship, clapping and howling as they ran out of the tunnel.

Philadelphia's fans are among the most hostile in the NBA. They are notoriously tough on the home team, but the bile they direct at opponents can be relentless. In the second quarter, Thomas knocked down Sixers' forward George Lynch as he drove to the hoop. Lynch crashed to the floor after Thomas' high, hard foul, the kind of play that warms Van Gundy's heart. When Thomas came to the bench after a timeout, a group of fans started chanting, "Lazy, lazy, lazy."

"Mother fucker," a wild-eyed Thomas shouted back, pointing toward his hecklers. "Want to fuck with me?" The fans shut up quickly.

Nothing could distract the Knicks on this night, not the hecklers, not Iverson. After stinking out the Garden against the Celtics, the Knicks hammered the East's dominant team, 91-71, without Camby. Houston led the Knicks during a decisive 11-0 run in the third quarter. Thomas was dominant under the boards and Knight got five offensive rebounds in 16 minutes. The Knicks outrebounded the Sixers, 44-29.

The victory vaulted the Knicks into a four-day break that would take them through Christmas. Asked about the holiday, Van Gundy said, "It's going to be really enjoyable." When a couple of writers smirked at the apparent insincerity, Van Gundy said, "I'm serious. It's Christmas."

The victory temporarily took the heat and focus off of Van Gundy and his yellowed playbooks that *The Post's* Peter Vecsey recently referred to as "chiseled on a stone tablet."

"We don't need to change our offense," assistant coach Don Chaney said during the holidays. "We just have to get certain guys to play better. Guys were pressing. If we weren't getting wide-open shots, I'd be concerned that maybe it's the plays we're running. To me, it's not the plays. We're missing open shots and layups."

The players were thrilled to be home for Christmas, unlike last season, when NBC had them play the Pacers on Christmas Day and they spent Christmas Eve in an Indianapolis hotel. The staff at the hotel had been cut to bare bones for the holiday, so getting room service was difficult. Now the players could spend the holidays with their families after their best win of the season.

No player was happier than Camby, who drove to South Windsor, Connecticut to visit his mother, Janice, and his two younger sisters, Mia and Monica, for Christmas Day. Camby had been a father figure for Mia and Monica as they grew up in Hartford's Bellevue Square projects. Camby babysat them as their mother worked two jobs, including tracking down welfare checks. Janice bused Marcus to school in the suburbs for fear he would get involved with the North End gangs.

Camby's greatest fear was that his sisters would get involved with the wrong crowd, even now in the polished suburb of South Windsor. Camby knew how hard it was to break from the past. He was still friends with Tamia Murray, who had played a prominent role in a scandal involving Camby at UMass. During UMass games, Murray, who grew up with Camby in the projects, met agents or gofers for agents looking to attract his buddy as a client when he left college for the NBA. Murray accepted cash for Camby in bathroom stalls and set up rental car agreements and promises to provide prostitutes for him and his friends.

Murray had been a hustler his whole life. He had sold drugs, had two scars from bullet wounds and had always protected Marcus on Hartford's rough North End streets. Even after the scandal resulted in heavy sanctions against UMass, Camby remained close with Murray. Murray spent weeks at a time at Camby's home in Toronto and became a regular guest in Westchester after Camby was traded from the Raptors to the Knicks before the 1999 season.

"People say set loose from the past, but they really don't know," Camby told *The New York Times'* Selena Roberts in 1999. "Tamia is a guy who will always be in my corner."

Since Camby became a millionaire, Murray's life in Hartford had become even more dangerous. In 1997, Murray was hanging out on a street corner in the North End, talking to a woman, when, according to a *Times* account, a group of men jumped out of a car carrying chrome pipes and a revolver. They intended to kidnap Murray and shake Camby down for money. Murray was shot at, but escaped without injury.

"These people know me and Marcus were tight," Murray recalled in the *Times* story. "They put two and two together and knew if they got me, they'd get some free cash. They knew Marcus wouldn't go to the police. Around here, what goes on in the streets has to stay on the streets. Because of how tight I am with Marcus, I can't even stand on a street corner. If something happens to me, it happens to Marcus."

In four days, a career criminal named Troy Crooms, who grew up in the Bellevue Projects, would be released from prison after spending six months for passing counterfeit bills. In February, Crooms would start dating Monica without Marcus's knowledge. Marcus tried to keep track of Monica's friends, but he couldn't keep track of her boyfriends.

"She won't tell me anything about her love life," Marcus once said.

Unlike the thugs who attacked Murray, Crooms wasn't after Marcus's money. He was after Monica.

CHAPTER 11

A Kick in the Rear

December 27

The Knicks arrived in Washington to another Rod Strickland controversy. The native New Yorker, whose dream was to return to the Knicks, showed up two hours late for the Wizards' day-after-Christmas practice. It wasn't the first time he was late. He was home visiting his family in New York and didn't arrive back in Washington until eight a.m. He then took a nap, which turned into an extended sleep. "'Nod' Strickland," penned Peter Vecsey of *The Post*.

Michael Jordan had tried to ship the enigmatic Strickland for a year, but nobody was willing to give up value, including the Knicks. Still, Layden kept in the loop, monitoring the Strickland situation but offering Jordan players with contracts more insufferable than Strickland's: Johnson and Longley. In Jordan's mind, the whole point of shipping Strickland was to create cap space, not worsen the team's cap situation.

Jordan had become an irritant to some of the Wizards' established players. They believed he sold them out after a home loss to the Clippers in early December when he called his players "a disgrace to the fans in Washington" and said they had a "loser's mentality." Coming from an executive who attended a home game once in a blue moon and worked from his suburban Chicago home, the rip job left a bitter taste in the mouths of veterans Juwan Howard and Strickland.

"I don't think it was fair to the team," Strickland said.

Van Gundy tensed when he was asked about Jordan's ability as an NBA executive. In 1996, Van Gundy, appearing on a Chicago radio station, called Jordan "a con man." Van Gundy felt Jordan pretended to be your friend before tipoff to soften you up, then battered you once the game began. He felt Ewing and Oakley always got suckered in by Jordan's charm. They never fouled Jordan as hard as they fouled other players. The next time the Knicks faced the Bulls, Jordan scored 51 points, walked past Van Gundy in the corridor and shouted, "Calm down, you little fuck."

Van Gundy was more diplomatic when discussing Jordan the executive. "It just shows how strangulating the salary cap is," he said. "And another thing it does show..." Van Gundy stopped in mid-sentence. "Never mind," he said. If there was one topic Van Gundy had learned to be careful about, it was Jordan.

Strickland, unaware of what sanctions faced him for missing practice the day before, didn't smooth out the situation when he reiterated his desire to play for the Knicks. He figured he'd get fined, but he was wrong. Instead, he didn't start against his hometown team and played only 18 minutes. He felt humiliated, knowing the Knicks were one of the few teams eager to acquire him.

"I didn't think I deserved that," Strickland said, fuming afterward. "To do that, it was a bit much. I don't know if they're trying to put me out on Front Street or what."

The writers spent several minutes trying to decipher what Strickland meant by "Front Street." The best guess was that the Wizards were shopping him or making an example of him in front of everybody.

The unlikely tandem of Knight and Longley sparked the Knicks in the second half when the front line got into foul trouble. Longley and Knight defended and rebounded strongly, with Longley even making two sweet passes to help the Knicks win, 89-82. The Wizards were off to their worst start in franchise history, 5-24.

Meanwhile, big news came out of Orlando. Hill would miss the rest of the season because of lingering ankle problems.

December 28

The Knicks were on a two-game winning streak. They were 17-12 and some of the players were feeling good about where things were headed until they arrived at Purchase College and got hit by a 20-minute lecture from Van Gundy before practice.

The players did not have a very good feeling in their stomachs after Van Gundy got through with them. Van Gundy's message was that the club was heading down the wrong path. He said, "We're one loss away from middle-of-the-pack mediocrity"—a catch phrase Camby began to use jokingly with his teammates and out of the coach's earshot.

"I don't think so and most of the guys don't think so," Camby said after the Van Gundy lecture. "We didn't play a great game [against Washington], but the mentality around here was like we lost. Usually, we have those meetings downstairs after a loss."

The timing was indeed peculiar. When one of the veterans was asked if this was one of the weirder Van Gundy speeches, he said, "What speech of his isn't weird?"

After Van Gundy got done breaking down his players' spirit, he met with the writers and continued his gloom-and-doom message.

"I don't think we like where we're headed," Van Gundy said. "I'd think we'd be foolish if we liked where we're headed. We faced the easiest part of our schedule and we're 17-12. You look at the last two weeks. We had a miracle comeback against Milwaukee and a great second half against Philly. If you want to be honest about it, that's what we've done."

He was too honest for some players. "We could be better, we could be worse," Sprewell said. "I don't know. Jeff's kind of hard to please sometimes."

December 29

One perception Houston was unable to shake in New York was that he's a soft player and doesn't have the New York street-fighting mentality. That characterization is at odds with his ironman streak, which ended against the Bulls. Saddled with a stomach virus that rendered him unable to stand up, Houston did not make it to the Garden after having played in 258 straight regular-season games. Houston hadn't missed one since the 1996-97 season, also because of a stomach virus.

With Sprewell moved to shooting guard, his natural and favorite position, the Knicks easily beat the Bulls, 95-68. If Sprewell's eyes seemed wider, if his braids seemed to be dancing merrily around his head, it was no coincidence. With the Knicks up by 28 points, he dribbled hard to the hole and got battered by Corey Benjamin. The shot kissed in off the glass. Sprewell glared at the players on the Bulls' bench, swung his right arm at them and screamed, "Take that, motherfucker!" He relished playing his natural position and proving Van Gundy wrong about the club heading in the wrong direction. Sprewell had 24 points by halftime and finished with a season-high 32.

"They weren't double-teaming," he said. "I had to make them pay."

Houston met the team at the Westchester airport for their charter flight to Minneapolis that night. They would face the Wolves on NBC the next afternoon. After beating the Bulls by 27, they beat an onrushing blizzard by five hours.

December 30

In what Van Gundy thought was the Knicks' best game of the season, the Knicks won a defensive struggle at the loud Target Center, beating the Timberwolves despite not having Camby, Ward and Rice for the final three quarters. It was their fourth straight win following the Boston debacle.

The Knicks beat the playoff-contending Wolves by making life tough on Kevin Garnett. Johnson had his best defensive game of the season, holding the immensely talented power forward to 16 points. Sprewell and Houston each scored 27 points. Sprewell trash-talked with Wally Sczerbiak in the final seconds while dribbling out the clock. When asked afterwards if this was a big win, Sprewell needled the coach who just days ago had warned his team that it was heading in the wrong direction.

"You might want to ask Jeff," Sprewell said. "Today was one of our better wins thus far. I don't even think he can take that away from us."

The lone down note was Rice leaving the game with a sore left foot. He said after the game he had been bothered by it for two months but kept quiet and tried to play through the plantar fasciaitis, which is classified as a chronic injury.

■ ■ ■

A blizzard had clobbered the New York area the morning of the Minnesota game, canceling all flights out. Only two beat writers, Isola of *The Daily News* and Damon Hack of *Newsday,* made it out of New York. They had skipped the Bulls game and left the night before.

With the New York airports in chaos, Van Gundy was in such a good mood he allowed the two writers and sportscaster Spencer Ross on the charter flight back to New York the next morning. It was the first time in more than a decade that media members had been permitted onto the plush charter, which former Knick Scott Brooks once called "a Ritz-Carlton in the sky."

Hack and Isola were the beat writers who wrote most favorably about Van Gundy. "If it was any other combination of writers, hell would freeze over before I'd let you on," Van Gundy told them.

The plane contained five tables for playing cards, plus sofas. Van Gundy sat in the front with the coaching staff. The coaches had private VCRs in front of their seats and spent most flights watching game tapes and taking notes as the players slept or, with headphones on, listened to music on their Walkmans. Occasionally, the players played cards, but that was rare on late-night flights. Usually the five card tables remained empty.

Although the charter flights were convenient, they wiped out much of the social life players used to enjoy while on the road. Most teams left town immediately after a game. Gone were the days when players went out on the town afterward to socialize with teammates and friends from the particular city. The old-school Chaney missed those pre-charter days, when teams flew on commercial airlines and occasionally got stuck in airports during delays, just like everyone else. He believes it's the reason teammates aren't as close as they used to be. The old way allowed teams to bond. It forced teams to bond.

January 2

With the Celtics up next, I wrote a column for *The Post* that quoted Tom Heinsohn, the Celtics' radio commentator and former head coach during the team's glory days of the 1970s, as lamenting the era of RileyBall and Van GundyBall. Heinsohn, whose old Celtics ran the fast-break on every occasion, criticized the new NBA and its coaches who don't teach the art of transition basketball.

"All the years the Celtics won championships," Heinsohn said, "it was predicated on the offense scoring points and holding people below that. I won with the smallest team in the league. Dave Cowens was a six-nine center. Nobody's been a fastbreak coach for years in the NBA. The first guy who comes in and teaches how to run a fastbreak is going to win a championship. The current coaches think I don't understand. They think I'm old-school."

Directing his criticism toward Van Gundy, Heinsohn said, "They're playing big-man basketball with smaller players. That's tough to do. Jeff's a defensive guy from what I can see. Coaches tell me they want to run. They tell me the defense is bringing four people back and it's difficult. The first guy who figures out how to beat four guys retreating is going to win championships."

Van Gundy didn't appreciate old-timers waxing eloquent about how it used to be. He was amused when fans reminisced about the Knicks' great defensive teams that won championships in 1970 and 1973, the teams of Walt Frazier, Dave DeBusschere and Bill Bradley.

Van Gundy would never knock legendary coach Red Holzman, whom he respects dearly for his longevity and goodness. But Van Gundy is amazed by how rudimentary the defensive schemes were back then. When Van Gundy looks at old films of the championship Knicks, the lack of defensive sophistication is evident. That was before coaches used videotape, a breakthrough in plotting complex defensive strategies.

"They talk about the great team defense of the old Knicks," Van Gundy said after practice one afternoon. "If you look at their tapes, there were very little rotations or help. If a guy beat his man, it was a fucking layup."

While it's almost blasphemy in New York to knock the old Knicks and their legendary defense, Van Gundy was correct. The extent of rotations on defense that Riley introduced and Van Gundy honed has become commonplace in the NBA. It's safe to say that even the current Clippers played better team defense than Holzman's Knicks.

Soon after Heinsohn made his comments in *The Post,* Van Gundy faced the issue head-on. He said his distaste for running was a misconception. As much as players say they want to run more, they don't. The up-tempo style is too physically taxing.

"Everyone says I should run more," Van Gundy said. "I don't want to run more, I want to run more efficiently. Sometimes when players say they want to run, what players really mean is they want to jack up any fucking shot they get, and we're not going to do that. Running is very fatiguing and you play less minutes. We always think that's how players want to play. What they really want to do is shoot with freedom. Running is hard."

After his spiel with the writers that day, I noticed when he saw his point guard walking the ball up, Van Gundy swung his right arm wildly, trying to get him to push the ball up. He wasn't looking for a fast-break layup as much as trying to get the ball downcourt so the defense couldn't set up.

Van Gundy didn't think Heinsohn understood how the transition defense schemes had changed since the 1970's. Van Gundy, in fact, was proud that the Knicks were arguably the league's best transition defensive club. Nothing got him angrier than a game in which the Knicks allowed too many fastbreak points.

"One thing you can control as a team if you're committed to it is stopping the other team from scoring early in the clock," said Van Gundy. "You can send three back, or if that doesn't work, four back, or the whole house and get your defense set. There's been a much greater emphasis on transition defense the longer I've been in the league."

What also drove Van Gundy nuts was how the commissioner's office, reacting to complaints by fans and the media that the game was too boring and defensive, tried different measures to increase scoring such as allowing less contact between defender and offensive player.

"If you turned off the scoreboard and didn't chart the number of points in a game and how it's dropped dramatically, the fans would never know," Van Gundy said. "They would never judge a game by the final score. You're telling me four more baskets over 48 minutes really makes for a more exciting game? Four baskets? That's one more basket a quarter. That's going to bring the excitement back into it?

"The fans want to see competitive spirit between the two teams. They're not judging the game by, 'We hit 100, I'm having fun now!' That's where we make the mistake, judging the excitement and state of the league by the score. Just put up plus-one and cut out the aggregate score. 'What was the final score of the game? Plus-seven.' When we played Chicago or Miami in the playoffs, the score would be 77-76 and people would say, 'Helluva game.' What's the difference if it was 77-76 or 89-88?"

Van Gundy also disagreed that "isolation" plays, in which four guys stand away from the ball to allow a player to go one-on-one with a defender had made the game monotonous. He believes that argument is a conspiracy by white basketball writers who grew up playing suburban, pass-it-to-the-open-man basketball carping for the way they used to play.

"The fans I talk to, they want to see Iverson take it one-on-one against Sprewell," Van Gundy said.

Although Van Gundy normally does not enjoy his media chats when the subject is playing-time controversies or timetables for injured players, he relishes the chance to talk hardcore strategy. He wished the writers engaged him more on those topics.

■ ■ ■

The Knicks practiced the day after New Year's. They were coming off a two-day hiatus and the after-effects of their New Year's celebration were evident.

"It's never a good practice if you ask Jeff," Camby said. "But we were a little sluggish having two days off."

Ward was a surprise participant. He had always thought the eight-week timetable to rehab his knee after surgery was too long. Five weeks after surgery, Ward felt he was days away from returning to the lineup.

CHAPTER 12

Sprewell, Camby and The League

January 3

Grant Hill's season-ending injury brought about a minor controversy regarding his replacement in the starting lineup at forward for the All-Star Game. Hill had the second-most votes among forwards, earning him a starting slot. Commissioner David Stern would decide his replacement. Sprewell was third in the voting among forwards, but that assured him of nothing. After the coaches picked two or three reserve forwards, Stern would decide upon the final spot. Sprewell would likely need Stern's vote to get back to the All-Star Game, an achievement that would have allowed him to come full circle from the choking incident.

After the Knicks' morning shootaround at Boston's FleetCenter, Sprewell sat on a chair along the sidelines. When it was mentioned to him that Stern would make the call on his All-Star fate, he uttered "Uh-oh." Sprewell laughed, but he knew he probably could never trust Stern for the rest of his playing days. During the 1999-2000 season, Sprewell had been playing playing at an All-Star level for a championship contender, but the coaches shunned him and kept him out of the All-Star Game in Oakland. The coaches couldn't bring themselves to allow Sprewell to prance around that city as an All-Star just two months after Carlesimo had been fired. Houston was selected and Sprewell stayed home.

"I probably deserved to be on it considering where our team was," Sprewell said. "Usually a team with our record gets more than one."

Sprewell's statistics were nothing spectacular, but his selfless move to point guard had more than compensated for his shooting percentage.

"I'd like to go back," Sprewell said. "It would be nice, but I'm not banking on it."

. . .

Houston looked like an All-Star that night against the Celtics. He scored nine of his 25 points in the fourth quarter of a 100-91 victory. It was the Knicks' fifth straight victory and their twentieth win in 32 games. With Heinsohn broadcasting from courtside, the Knicks ran the fast-break more than they had all season.

"We want to see how long we can continue this streak and continue to recreate ourselves," Houston said in the loud locker room.

Childs, starting for the injured Rice, hit his first five shots, including three three-pointers. Shooting 39-percent from the field for the season, he needed this game. Opponents had gotten into the habit of doubling off him and daring him to make perimeter shots.

"I hope they keep doing that," Childs said.

Camby returned to the lineup after missing 11 days with a strained groin, and Celtics radio announcer Cedric Maxwell was overheard saying from his courtside seat, "Marcus Camby with that Chinese lettering on his arm, you know what that means. 'I'm soft.'" The two sets of tattoos of Chinese letters on Camby's arm actually translated to "Strive for your best" and "Love your family."

January 4

There was a Checketts sighting in the Garden locker room before the Orlando game. Making a rare appearance, Checketts schmoozed with some of the players for about 15 minutes during the reporters' access time. Unaware of their visitor, most of the Knicks lingered in the trainer's room or the back area that was off-limits to reporters. Checketts spent most of his time chatting with Travis Knight.

Then Checketts was approached by the writers. He agreed to talk on the record, although somewhat grudgingly. Checketts enjoyed speaking with the writers, but the order from the Dolans was to be quoted as infrequently as possible.

"I think you have to be a little bit patient," Checketts said regarding the possibility of another trade. "I think they can accomplish something very significant as they are currently constituted."

As currently constituted, the Knicks fell behind the Magic, 15-0, in the opening six minutes. Then Van Gundy replaced four of his starters en masse, with reserves Brunson, Longley, Thomas and Strickland entering together. Camby, in his second game back, walked to the bench, palms up, shooting an angry glare at Van Gundy. He was embarrassed by the deficit and Van Gundy's substitution heightened his humiliation.

That turned into the jolt Camby needed. When he got back in, he went high for rebounds and got loose for several dunks. He was the defensive stopper on his old Toronto teammate, Tracy McGrady, forcing him to miss his final three shots and drawing a key charge.

Van Gundy's decision to go with Camby on the swingman McGrady showed how little he trusted the team's perimeter defense. The Knicks prevailed, 95-92, in overtime for their sixth straight win. Suddenly, there wasn't much talk in New York about Patrick Ewing.

January 5

On their day off, the Knicks made a minor transaction that affected only the players inside the locker room. They waived second-round pick Pete Mickeal, who had spent the season on the injured list with a phantom lower back injury. The NBA can be a cruel business, and this transaction was dirty. Mickeal was released on the day his minimum $317,000 contract would have become guaranteed for the rest of the season. Mickeal's release reminded players that when coaches talk about teams being family, it's gibberish. The NBA is a cold business. A defensive specialist, Mickeal was a good practice player with a fine attitude, liked by his teammates. But the Knicks didn't think he shot the ball well enough to be activated in a pinch. The players would miss having him around.

January 6

With Ward ready to return to the lineup, Van Gundy warned the players that playing time was going to be harder to come by. With Ward and, most recently, Rice out of the lineup, the players' grumblings about minutes had lessened. Now a playing-time crisis was on the verge of resurfacing.

Ward went through a full practice and deemed himself ready for the next night's game against Washington, but the timing of his return was suspect. Childs had recently moved into the starting lineup and was playing his best ball of the season. Even if Rice hadn't been injured, Van Gundy had planned to scrap the big backcourt alignment when Ward returned. With the team going well, Ward told Van Gundy he didn't have to start. Van Gundy would hear none of it. He felt the Knicks functioned better with a point guard, whether it was Ward or Childs.

"Minutes are going to be a problem," Childs told the writers.

Van Gundy said "We know the questions that are coming up. Whoever doesn't play that game, you'll hover around him and say, 'Are you upset?' He'll say the politically correct thing or he won't. We all know the real answer. Hopefully, he won't be tempted into saying how he really feels."

The minutes crunch wouldn't start fully until Rice got back from his foot injury. And as he rolled a frozen bottle of Gatorade over his aching heel, Rice admitted he wasn't ready to return for another few days.

January 7

A celebration for new New York Senator Hillary Clinton and Bill Clinton was held at the Theater of Madison Square Garden, the building attached to the main arena. The party ended just as the Knicks players were arriving for the Wizards game. Secret Service would not allow anyone into the building as the Clintons roamed through the bowels of the Garden and headed for the exits. For 20 minutes, several players, including Sprewell, Thomas and Strickland, sat in traffic, unable to pull their vehicles into the Garden's garage. Half the team was late. Meanwhile, Garden employees, the concessionaires and the clean-up crew, waited for 45 minutes outside the Garden's employee entrance. An hour before tipoff, nobody was able to get in.

Rod Strickland didn't show up at all. The Wizards left Strickland home as he nursed a bruised shoulder, not to mention a bruised psyche.

After sitting out 21 games, Ward regained his spot as starting point guard in a 103-87 victory over the Wizards. Brunson was placed on the injured list to open a roster spot. Sprewell didn't have to handle the ball and was delighted that the big backcourt experiment was over. He never felt he had the timing down for the position.

The Knicks' seventh consecutive win was their longest winning streak of the Van Gundy era. The Knicks also tied an obscure post-shot-clock defensive record. The Wizards became the 28th consecutive opponent the Knicks had held under 100 points.

"This is the best team I have ever been associated with," Sprewell said in a contented locker room. "I've never been on a seven-game winning. This is uncharted territory for me, but it's fun."

The Knicks had three days off to savor their good fate. One more victory, over the Rockets, and their eight-game winning streak would match the longest since Riley's 1994-95 team.

January 9

The mood around the Knicks had become light and airy. Van Gundy, in a relaxed frame of mind after practice, rapped with the writers for longer than usual. Van Gundy on this day was a man few saw: chatty, inquisitive and joking. No scowl, no furrowed brow, no words dripped in negativity, his face a picture of darkness. Everything was positive.

Anyone who has been around Van Gundy for long knows about his fascination with the media. Van Gundy has a lot of opinions about journalism, most of them bad, and often is inquisitive about the business. The chitchat on this day ranged from the role of a newspaper copy editor to Van Gundy quizzing the writers on whom their favorite columnists were. Van Gundy asked, "What makes a good sports columnist anyway?"

One of Van Gundy's pet peeves with sportswriters is that they never admit in print when their predictions and theories go wrong. In Van Gundy's view, they demand accountability from the people they cover but none from themselves. Another concern is with radio talk show hosts and columnists who claim to be know-it-alls about every sport. Van Gundy has enough problems taking seriously the beat writers who talk to the players every day, watch every single minute of every single Knicks game and cast judgments on the state of the club. He doesn't understand how a columnist can burst onto the scene after not being around for weeks and pass judgment.

"I have enough trouble being an expert in one sport," Van Gundy said.

Despite his distaste for the media, he admits that for $1 million a year, he would host a radio sports talk show. "But not for a penny less," he said.

Van Gundy is savvy enough to know that the headlines placed above writers' stories are written by editors, not by reporters. But he was unaware that copy editors occasionally made alterations to the writers' stories.

"The copy editors get to change your stuff?" Van Gundy said. "I'd love that fucking job."

January 10

The Knicks were allowing a league-low 83.9 points per game and had surprised themselves by being strong defensively without Ewing. But Van Gundy didn't think the team had started playing its best defense.

"This team has great defensive pride, and we think we're capable of being the best defensive team in the league," Van Gundy said. "Everyone says that because you've won seven in a row, you're playing your best basketball of the year. We're not."

Van Gundy was impressed by how the team had embraced his defensive philosophies and rotations and played hard to the last tick of the 24-second clock. But he was not ready to compare this club to the Knicks team that reached The Finals in 1994 and featured Oakley, Ewing and Mason. He wished his group would take on the nastiness of those old Riley teams.

"That was physical, imposing, intimidating," Van Gundy said. "People didn't come into the paint because they risked injury. We've been good in a different way, with less size."

The Houston Rockets, their opponent the next night, would pose a keen challenge to their seven-game winning streak and their 28-game, record-tying streak of holding teams under 100 points. One of the best offensive teams in the league, they were led by the explosive point guard Stevie Francis and swingman Cuttino Mobley, two guys Van Gundy feared because of their ability to penetrate defenses.

January 11

Rice's plantar fasciaitis forced him to miss his fourth straight game. Nevertheless, he was in a cheery, talkative mood in the locker room before the game. He felt vindicated by reports that Kobe Bryant and Shaquille O'Neal were feuding in L.A. and the Lakers were sinking without him.

Throughout most of the season, Rice had kept his bitterness about his Lakers' ordeal to himself. Agent David Falk had said that he never had a client treated as poorly as the Lakers treated Rice, but Rice wouldn't comment further. Even though his own road with the Knicks had been rocky and his foot problems were not going away, Rice took solace that the Lakers were fizzling without him.

"When they lose a game or two, it brings a big smile to my face," he said. "When you see them going through problems, you do get a little satisfaction. I'm not going to sit here and lie to you."

Well, most pro athletes would. Most athletes would sit there and tell you they felt badly for the Lakers and their players. Most pro athletes would say they took no great satisfaction in their old team's troubles. Rice wasn't like that. He spoke with candor.

Despite his troubled season, Rice had become the most approachable player in the room. Somewhere along the ride, Rice had decided there was no reason to be grumpy to anybody. There were worse things in life than making $36 million on a new contract to live the charmed NBA life, even if things weren't going his way on the court.

Rice read the New York tabloids, scouring them on his chauffeured ride to practice, and had sensed from recent articles that the Knicks didn't miss him. Ribbing a couple of writers, he asked, with a big smile, "How come you never talk about how much better we're going to be when I get back?"

■ ■ ■

The Knicks set the under-100 defensive record against the Rockets, holding them to 76 points, but lost the game by one point. Scoreless for the final 3:19, the Knicks choked on a six-point lead in the final two minutes. Sprewell and Houston couldn't have put the ball in the Hudson River, shooting a combined six-for-28. This time, the Knicks needed Rice's shooting.

The play that haunted Van Gundy occurred with nine seconds remaining. Cuttino Mobley isolated Sprewell at the right of the key and easily swept past him for a layup. Mobley had gone past Sprewell like he was standing still, but no Knick had helped out. Van Gundy was horrified.

Johnson took the desperation last shot, a forced one-handed leaner from 20 feet out that grazed off the front rim. The play was set up for Houston, but he couldn't shake free. The winning streak was over. A new NBA defensive record had been set, but none of the Knicks cared to discuss it.

January 12

The Knicks felt they would be defending the Eastern Conference's honor in their nationally-televised game against Portland the next day. Most NBA observers considered the Western Conference vastly superior to the East. The Blazers, the most talent-rich club in the NBA, had won 10 straight games and were 27-10. Four days earlier, they had destroyed the East's elite club, the Sixers, by 17 points in Philadelphia. They possessed an incredible amount of depth on a front line led by Rasheed Wallace.

"We want to make a statement whenever we face a Western team," Houston said. "We're not buying into the hype."

Rice, who last faced the Blazers in the Western Conference Finals the prior spring, declared himself ready to play after missing four straight games.

"There is going to be pain the rest of the year," he said. "I'll just have to deal with it."

January 13

With tipoff slated for 5:30 p.m. to suit NBC, Van Gundy could not fit in a morning shootaround. Instead, he held another walk-through at the Garden, again cutting into reporter's access time. Van Gundy arrived for his pre-game session with the writers 25 minutes late.

"Fuck you, fuck you, fuck you," Van Gundy said when reminded that he had again violated the access period. "I'm trying to win a game, not answer the same old questions."

Van Gundy was in an edgy mood partly because Rice missed the pre-game walk-through. Rice hadn't played in two weeks, and Van Gundy had wanted him there. Rice had been stuck in traffic on the West Side Highway.

"There was an accident and you know how it is, everyone wants to be a spectator," Rice said after he arrived and met with Van Gundy.

During his pre-game chat with the writers, Van Gundy was asked about the Lakers' struggles and Shaq and Kobe's feud.

"All I know is they keep winning and it doesn't matter," Van Gundy said. "They know in the end they're going to be there. All that other stuff, everybody loves it. Everybody loves to write about it and read about it because they can't stand two people to be successful."

■ ■ ■

Camby brought the Blazers down to size. He flew through the thicket of Portland skyscrapers and led the Knicks to a 91-78 win. Camby had 16 points and 15 rebounds in 25 minutes as the Knicks flogged Portland from start to finish. It was their loudest statement yet about their improvement without Ewing.

"If we did anything today, we opened people's eyes to how good we can play defensively," Sprewell said. "If we continue that type of success defensively, people will have to start considering us one of the elite teams."

As was becoming habit, Camby spoke to the media while sitting at Strickland's cubicle, which was located by the entrance to the locker room. Camby had a corner locker, up against a wall. Space was tight around Camby's locker and made it impossible for reporters to surround his cubicle without also being in Childs' space. When Strickland came out of the shower in his towel, he became ticked at the scene in front of him.

"He's going to have to start paying rent," Strickland said. He walked back to the trainer's room to put on his clothes. Having not played that evening might have had something to do with his foul mood.

January 14
Van Gundy asked the players to treat the Spurs' game the next day like it was the playoffs.

"I think tomorrow is like Game 2 of a playoff series, when you had a great win in the first game, a day off, a one o'clock start," Van Gundy said. "So I'm really interested to see if we've matured to the point where we can come out tomorrow and be energized by that Portland performance."

Camby's hustle and dynamic play had energized the club. The respect he was gaining in the locker room grew by the day. Van Gundy was now calling him "our best player" without hesitation.

"I think he realizes how good he is now, but I hope he realizes how good he can be," Houston said.

January 15

The Knicks were well on the way to their most dominant victory of the season during their annual Martin Luther King Day matinee. They were on the verge of posting back-to-back blowout wins against the West's two elite teams not named the Lakers. Camby was dominating the Spurs' David Robinson with 11 rebounds and six blocks.

Late in the fourth quarter, Camby wasn't letting up, even though the Knicks were ahead by 20 points. He charged toward the rim, looking to pounce on an offensive rebound, when Spurs forward Danny Ferry blocked him out and threw up his right arm. Ferry's forearm slid across Camby's face and Ferry's finger penetrated Camby's left eye.

Camby and Ferry had battled fiercely all game. In the third quarter, Ferry had elbowed Camby in the face during a battle underneath the basket. Camby felt Ferry was a dirty player who used his elbows illegally. After getting poked in the eye, Camby wasn't in the mood to talk things out. He charged at Ferry, but didn't get within 10 feet of him. Childs and Kurt Thomas intercepted him before referee Bob Delaney bearhugged Camby.

Chaney ran out to midcourt and held Camby, who continued to argue with referee Derrick Stafford about Ferry's persistent elbowing. If this was one of the Knicks' more excitable players, such as Childs or Thomas, Chaney would've grabbed Camby and pulled him off the court. But this was Camby, as mild-mannered a guy as there was in the league.

The assistant coach was confident peace had been restored. "Everything's okay, I'm fine," Camby told Chaney. But Camby kept jawing with Stafford. When he wiped his eye and saw two drops of blood on his finger, he screamed at Stafford, "I'm fucking bleeding." Over the past two years, Camby had suffered from a form of pink-eye disease, requiring several visits to ophthalmologists.

Ferry, who had been thrown out of the game, was several yards away from Camby and in front of the press table, exiting the court with his back turned to Camby. Camby pulled away from Chaney and sprinted toward Ferry as one of the Spurs screamed, "Danny!"

Van Gundy had been standing on the sideline at midcourt. The moment he saw Camby break for Ferry, he sprang like a cat down the sideline. Ferry ducked as Camby charged him. As Van Gundy tried to get between the two, Camby uncorked a wild roundhouse swing with his right arm. Camby and Van Gundy's heads crashed together and the punch missed Ferry by several feet.

Van Gundy crumpled to the ground, clutching his forehead, blood spurting from a gash above his left eye. A Spurs assistant coach handed Van Gundy a towel. The Knicks trainers dashed over from the bench. Van Gundy, on his knees, applied a white towel to his head and said over and over, "I'm all right, I'm all right," as blood spurted.

Within a minute Van Gundy got up, leaving behind a puddle of blood on the blue sidelines. Thinking he would coach the final minutes, he began walking to the Knicks' bench. Assistant trainer Said Hamdan grabbed Van Gundy and led him to the locker room. Van Gundy didn't argue as he made a right turn into the tunnel.

Camby remained on the court, bewildered, as if he had just been in a car accident. He did not realize that he had head-butted Van Gundy. When he left the court, he picked up a metal folding chair and carried it a few steps before putting it down.

With order restored, Chaney was left in charge. Before sending his stunned players back onto the court, Chaney told them, "Just finish the game. Forget about the situation. We don't need anyone else to get suspended."

As the last minutes played out, Van Gundy had his eye X-rayed in a small room
near his office. When the game ended, Van Gundy made a brief appearance in the locker room.

"Great game. See you Tuesday," he said, without mentioning the incident.

The players tried to make light of the situation, with one Knicks veteran piping up loud enough for Camby to hear, "I'll fight either of them because now I know they're both bleeders."

Camby didn't laugh. He was in no mood for jokes. He dressed quickly and left the locker room through a side exit without speaking to anyone. To a man, his teammates were ticked off that after superior wins over Portland and San Antonio, the fans and the media would be talking only about the Camby-Ferry-Van Gundy incident.

Wearing a menacing look, Camby stood quietly against a wall at the end of a hallway five yards from the Spurs' locker room door, making eye contact with nobody. The Spurs players would have to walk past him to get to their bus.

Knicks officials panicked over Camby loitering in the hallway. They figured Camby was waiting to ambush Ferry again. Chaney told a Spurs official to keep Ferry in the locker room until Camby was gone. Spurs head coach Gregg Popovich, an assistant with Golden State during Sprewell's early years there, popped into the Knicks' locker room and whispered in Sprewell's ear, "Listen, Marcus is out there and he still looks very upset. Can you make sure nothing happens?"

"I'll take care of it," Sprewell said.

Sprewell told Camby not to do anything stupid. Camby told Sprewell he was waiting for friends. Meanwhile, Layden and Knicks operations manager Ed Oliva stood yards away from Camby in the hallway, watching his every move. Oliva approached Camby and pleaded with him to stay cool. Camby interrupted and shouted, "I know, I know!" But he wouldn't budge.

Chaney, who felt bad about letting Camby loose, was ready to take every precaution to prevent another incident. He asked Johnson to speak with Camby.

"C'mon Marcus, let's get out of here," Johnson said. Camby didn't move. He didn't like being treated like a child.

"Why is everyone looking at me like this?" he thought. He hated that people were staring at him. He wasn't going to change what he was doing just because others feared he was out for revenge. He would stand in that spot until his friends came out. He wanted to make sure they didn't cause trouble, either.

Camby's friends finally arrived. Camby, business manager Rick Kaplan, housemate Percell, Camby's girlfriend Eva, a cousin and two other friends from Hartford walked toward the freight elevator. Layden, Checketts, Oliva, Mills and a Garden security guard escorted them. But the freight elevator got stuck on the second floor. The group waited for nearly 10 minutes. Tensions were rising. Checketts, who rarely sweats, was sweating. When the elevator was fixed, the group descended to the ground floor. As luck would have it, Camby's Black Lincoln Navigator was blocked by a Garden flatbed truck, which had a flat tire.

Camby walked to the security office to get his keys, passing by the Spurs' bus. Camby saw Robinson and the two exchanged hellos. Ferry was still in the Spurs' locker room waiting for a police escort to the bus. Wearing suits, Checketts and Layden spent five minutes grunting, sweating and pushing the disabled truck out of the way of Camby's Navigator.

When Camby got into his Navigator with Kaplan, there was little conversation.

"You know, Jeff got hit pretty bad." Kaplan said.

"I didn't even know that until I got to the locker room," Camby said. "I have to call him later. I'm just pissed I'm not going to get to play the next game."

"Prepare to miss at least three," Kaplan said.

Meanwhile, upstairs, 15 stitches had been laced into Van Gundy's eyebrow. When he met the media, he wore a white bandage diagonally across his brow. His left eye was black and nearly closed.

"He got in the shot that every one of our players would like to do to me," Van Gundy cracked. "He just got a free one."

January 17

Camby and Van Gundy exchanged phone messages the prior night, but did not talk to each other. Camby arrived early at Purchase College to meet with Van Gundy in his office. Camby was a little uneasy about speaking with his coach and wasn't sure what to expect. Van Gundy told him he wasn't concerned about his own eye injury. He was concerned about the impending suspension and told Camby that his reckless behavior directly affected the team.

Van Gundy quickly changed the subject to Camby's performance prior to the fight.

"Despite everything, the defense you played on Robinson was the best I'd ever seen," Van Gundy said. Camby was genuinely touched by the remark. Despite all of the tabloid headlines and pictures depicting the Garden bloodbath, with every SportsCenter highlight showing only the brawl, Van Gundy's most vivid memory of the game was Camby's defense on Robinson.

Sporting a cut above his left eye, Camby then met with the media and apologized to everyone except Ferry. He felt badly for the children who had to witness the incident on a holiday that commemorates peace between all races (Ferry is white). Camby announced he would make a donation of $20,000 to the Martin Luther King Center in Atlanta. Framed Martin Luther King posters were on the walls in Camby's home. Camby hoped the league would see the fight as the aberration it was.

Both Checketts and Mills had worked in the NBA offices before joining the Knicks and had strong relationships with Stern. They each called Stern and lobbied for leniency with Camby. He would be automatically suspended for one game for throwing a punch. If the league felt the incident was premeditated, Camby could be suspended for four games. His seemingly threatening behavior outside the locker rooms and an erroneous Associated Press report about him lingering by the Spurs bus would not help.

Mills and Checketts asked Stern to look at the other recent suspensions for throwing punches, noting Oakley got three games, and he connected. The Knicks' brass feared that the league office would be swayed by the front-page headlines and pictures in the tabloids. The NBA's office was in Manhattan. A picture of the fight even made the front cover of the staid *New York Times*.

January 17

The NBA suspended Camby for five games and fined him $25,000. When Kaplan called to give him the news, Camby was speechless. The incident would cost him $375,000 in lost salary alone. The suspension assured that he would miss the Knicks' game against the Lakers on Super Bowl Sunday.

Van Gundy felt the media swayed the league office into the suspension, even though the disciplinarian was Stu Jackson, one of his closest friends. The media had harped on the notion that Stern would give Camby less than five games, not wanting to lessen the appeal of the Lakers-Knicks showdown on national TV.

Van Gundy viewed the severity of the suspension as a New York thing. If the same incident had happened on a Thursday night in Vancouver in a game involving the Cavaliers and Grizzlies, he said, the suspension would have been two games. Now Van Gundy had lost his most consistent player when the club was peaking and Camby was thriving.

"I wonder what he would have gotten if he actually hit the guy," Van Gundy said sarcastically.

On the afternoon his suspension was levied, Camby had a promotional event to attend at the Garden's club lounge. The Chase Corporation had donated money to the Cambyland Foundation. In turn,

Camby had agreed to host an event for Chase's sponsors in which he would answer questions from kids and their parents.

"I guess you want me to cancel it?" Kaplan asked Camby.

"No, I'm comfortable doing it," Camby said.

For an hour, Camby answered questions from the audience. Nobody asked Camby about the Ferry fight, even though the wounds could be seen on his forehead and above his eye.

"Which team do you like playing for the best, Toronto or the Knicks," an 11-year-old named Jessie asked Camby. The Knicks center smiled for the first time in days.

"That's the easiest question I've heard in a while," Camby said. "The Knicks."

CHAPTER 13

Bibles, Bucks
and Buffett

January 18-19

Since taking over as Seattle's coach following Paul Westphal's dismissal in late November, Nate McMillan had reduced Ewing's playing time to 20 minutes per game. Ewing's shooting percentage was down to 40.6 percent, and his scoring average and rebounding averages had dropped to career lows of 9.3 and 7.8, respectively. In two games in January, Ewing went scoreless for the first two times in his career.

McMillan kept Ewing in the starting lineup but wouldn't play Vin Baker and Ewing together. He felt the club was too slow with the two heavyweights on the floor.

Ewing managed to fit in with his teammates better than he had during his final two years with the Knicks. The Sonics nicknamed him "beast." Brent Barry had dumped a bucket of ice water over Ewing's head in the locker room bathroom after a road game two weeks ago. A few days later, Ewing got back at Barry, dumping water on Barry on the team bus after a game in Washington. Those shenanigans never went on between Ewing and his teammates in his last days in New York.

But his play was not improving, and a quote attributed to McMillan was as harsh an indictment of Ewing's skills as any coach had uttered since Don Nelson in 1995.

"Officials understand he's not getting past players and he's looking for a bailout," McMillan said. "They're seeing exactly what we are, that the guy has slowed down a little."

More than a few eyebrows were raised when the Knicks saw McMillan's quote. Certainly, Van Gundy wouldn't have been as harsh, although after a recent practice, he revealed that he had watched Ewing on television the other night. "I wanted to call him up on the phone and say, 'Play some fucking defense," Van Gundy said. During Ewing's last season with the Knicks, Van Gundy occasionally slipped in a remark about Ewing's transition defense being a problem. Weighed against all of Van Gundy's compliments and his campaign to have officials continue give Ewing "star calls," that critique wasn't even newsworthy.

Had McMillan's remark been made by Van Gundy the prior season in New York, it would have made back page headlines. Instead, in Seattle, the statement barely caused a ripple. It was the stark truth that Seattle fans had feared. Ewing was on his last legs. At least he hadn't missed a game.

January 19

Rice rejoined the Knicks at the Palace of Auburn Hills, 20 miles outside Detroit, for the morning shootaround. He had just flown in from Toronto, where he spent two and a half days, undergoing electric shockwave therapy on his left foot in a desperate attempt to wipe out the pain. The therapy was illegal in the U.S.

The contraption that delivered the shockwaves looked like an X-Ray machine found in a dentist's office. Rice sat on a table while gel was rubbed onto his foot. The X-ray machine's arm had a soft, cushioned ball at its end. It was lowered directly onto Rice's heel. The pain was immense at the beginning, and Rice winced. Dr. Grant Lum asked Rice to tell him when the pain lessened and was nearly gone. At that point, Lum moved the cushioned ball to another spot on the foot. The session lasted 20 minutes and exhausted Rice.

After landing in Detroit, Rice was driving to the arena when a pickup truck pulled up beside him. The man driving the truck did a double take when he saw Rice, then reached over and placed an eight-by-ten photo of Rice against the window. In the photo, Rice was wearing his University of Michigan uniform. Rice, who had won a national championship at Michigan and was born in Flint, laughed as hard as he had all season. Maybe it was a good omen for that night.

When he arrived at the arena, Rice attempted to run, but felt a sharp pain in his foot. Dr. Lum had told Rice that during the first 24-to-48 hours, the foot would throb from the treatments. Rice sat out the shootaround and wasn't sure he would be ready for the Pistons.

"How do you want me to describe the pain?" Rice asked a writer. "When I try to run on it, the inside of the foot feels like somebody has a ball of pins and is sticking it."

■ ■ ■

Camby, serving the first game of his suspension, joined the club on the trip. He was allowed to go to the Palace for the shootaround but not to the arena that night. He said he would watch the game from his hotel room.

Camby claimed he took the trip because he wanted to be with his teammates, but he had no choice. Van Gundy made all suspended players travel with the team. At the very worst, Camby could benefit from participating in shootarounds.

■ ■ ■

A radio man from a Detroit station stuck his microphone in Van Gundy's face before the game and blurted, "How's the shiner?" Van Gundy shook his head and shot him a smile that said, "You're-an-idiot."

The bandage was off, revealing Van Gundy's discolored left eye, a hideous mixture of purple and black. Van Gundy, ready to coach his first game since the headbutt, told the writers, "If I saved Marcus an additional game, the black eye was definitely worth it."

Van Gundy was still annoyed at the length of the suspension but refrained from calling Stu Jackson to complain.

"I don't talk to him about his job," Van Gundy said. "If we talked about things like that, we wouldn't have a friendship."

In the locker room two hours before the game, Rice still wasn't sure he could play. He decided to give it a go, then had one of his best shooting games of the season. He scored 18 points, hitting eight of 13 shots, and the Knicks beat the Pistons, 97-91.

Houston, back in the arena where he once hated to play, scored 34 points. Pistons fans had treated him harshly during the first couple of years after he bolted Detroit in 1996 and became a Knick. His nerves became jangled whenever he faced the Pistons. Houston felt his former Pistons teammates went out of their way to lessen his production, even at the expense of overall team defense.

Houston still had ties to the area. His wife, Tonja, whom he met when he played in Detroit, was from the affluent suburb of Bloomfield Hills.

"I used to put too much pressure on myself," Houston said. "That's over with."

January 21-24

Reggie Miller was one of the most loathed opponents in New York sports, an athlete who frequently broke the hearts of New York fans. Miller's Pacers were making their first Garden appearance since shooting down the Knicks' season in Game Six of the 1999-2000 Eastern Conference Finals. The Pacers, trying to remake their team on the run after losing starters Dale Davis, Mark Jackson and Rik Smits, had fallen on hard times. They were two games under .500.

The lack of defensive spirit Van Gundy witnessed in Detroit was obvious against the Pacers, who made like old times and battered the Knicks, 89-74. Miller got in a jab at the Knicks, saying, "I think the rivalry between the two teams is over. When they first got rid of Patrick, I considered it over. To me, there is no more rivalry."

Miller forgot one point: Perhaps the rivalry wasn't the same because the Pacers weren't the power they had once been.

■ ■ ■

Following the morning shootaround in Milwaukee, Eric Konigsberg, a freelancer for *The New York Times'* Sunday Magazine, was invited to a bible study group run by Ward in Houston's hotel room. Konigsberg had been around the team off and on since December, working on a long feature on the players' off-the-court lives. Konigsberg, distinguishable by the fake sheepskin beige coat he always wore in the locker room, had grown frustrated by the players' insistence on shielding their personal lives.

Two years earlier, Konigsberg, then working for *New York* magazine, wrote a feature on Sprewell in which the most interesting anecdote wasn't about Sprewell. Johnson played a locker room game in which he tried to flash PR director Lori Hamamoto after he came out of the shower. Hamamoto denied the story, but the piece caused a great deal of embarrassment to the Knicks. Konigsberg didn't figure his upcoming article would embarrass anyone.

As Houston, Ward and Thomas read from the scriptures, Konigsberg listened intently on a couch. The conversation moved to Konigsberg's religion, Judaism. Ward asked Konigsberg questions about the Jewish holidays. Soon, they were debating about whether the Jews killed Christ, with both Ward and Houston quoting passages from the Bible in defense of their argument.

At first, Konigsberg enjoyed the give and take. It had been difficult to engage other players in a conversation on subjects beyond basketball. But as Ward kept talking, Konigsberg became uneasy.

The debate lasted only a couple of minutes. Neither Ward, Houston nor Thomas sensed they had insulted Konigsberg. In fact, when Konigsberg left Houston's room, he thanked them profusely and praised them for their bible-study sessions on the road. It fkew against the image of the philandering NBA player. But Konigsberg was flustered by the debate, unsure whether it would be included in his story.

Down in the lobby of the hotel, Konigsberg bumped into Knicks PR assistant Jonathan Supranowitz. Konigsberg expressed his frustration about the players being unwilling to open up about their off-court lives. Supranowitz bought him a Scotch at the hotel bar. Konigsberg never mentioned the debate he had with the players, even though Supranowitz was Jewish.

■ ■ ■

After his team's spotty defensive effort against the Pacers, Van Gundy knew the Knicks' record streak of keeping teams under 100 points was in jeopardy against Milwaukee. The Bucks were averaging 99.7 points per game. The Knicks had held 33 straight opponents under 100. Milwaukee had scored over 100 in eight of its last nine games. Something had to give.

Two weeks earlier, Van Gundy had minimized the significance of the defensive streak. He believed a more authentic barometer for a great defensive team was holding teams under 90 points. Still, he was sorry to see the record-setting streak end at the Bradley Center and sorrier to see the Knicks play lazy defense for the third straight game.

The Knicks failed to defend the three-point line and Bradley Center turned into a madhouse as the Bucks closed in on 100 points. The

Knicks' defensive streak had started to get national attention, and the Bucks' players had talked about putting a stop to the run. When guard Lindsay Hunter hit a three-point shot from the deep left corner for the Bucks' 101st point, the noise in the arena became deafening. Hunter finished the game with five three-pointers and the Bucks with a franchise-record 14.

Seething after the game, Van Gundy said, "It's one thing if Mark Pope is making threes. But this guy came in with 11-of-18 three-pointers against us this year and we act like we have no idea of what he does well."

It was another gratifying moment for Grunfeld, who again did not speak with Van Gundy despite being in the same hallway. Grunfeld also didn't see Camby, who was back at the hotel serving his suspension. But when writers quizzed Grunfeld about Camby's resurgent year, Grunfeld said "I've always believed in Marcus."

The defense did not improve in Charlotte the next night and the Knicks lost their third straight, 81-67. Van Gundy knew how vital Camby had been, but he never imagined their dependence would result in a 1-3 record since the suspension. They had one game left to play until the suspension ended: on Super Bowl Sunday against the Lakers. They had arrived at the midpoint of their season with a record of 25-16 and were playing ugly basketball.

"We've got to get back that fire," Sprewell said, wincing in the locker room after bruising his ribs. "We're not out there competing."

The issue over Rice's playing time came up again during the two-game road trip. In Milwaukee, Rice hit six of his eight shots in the first half, then took only three shots in the second half while getting limited playing time.

"I wish there was an easy solution for three guys at two positions," Van Gundy said.

January 26
All of the New York papers contained the same story. Rice, two days away from facing the Lakers, had spouted off about his old team and old coach.

"Rice: Jax had me at boiling point," screamed *The Post*'s headline.

"L.A. Story still steams Rice," blared *The News*.

"A stifled Rice fires away at Jackson," trumpeted the *Times*.

In the visitors' locker room in Charlotte after the defeat to the Hornets, Rice knew the rapid-fire questions from the beat writers were coming about his feud with Jackson. Rice still carried a grudge against Jackson that dated back to the finals the previous spring. Their relationship had been uneasy all season. When, after a loss in Game 4, Rice remarked about being underutilized in the fourth quarter with Bryant injured, whatever was left of their connection became irreparably severed. Rice's wife, Christina Fernandez, added her two cents, blasting Jackson for mistreating her husband in what the national media dubbed "The Cuban Mrs. Crisis." Christina is Cuban.

"I don't think Phil wanted me there from day one," Rice told the New York writers. "The moment he got there, he was talking about how he wanted Scottie [Pippen], how he wanted [Toni] Kukoc. He never came out and said he wanted Glen Rice. It led me to believe he never wanted me there in the first place."

Rice mockingly called Jackson "God." He admitted he had to control himself from getting physical with the so-called Zen Master. "It took a whole lot not to," Rice said. "I would go home, carry it home with me, have discussions with my wife. It was getting to me. A lot of times it was hard to go out there and play basketball."

When the session was over and Rice walked to the team bus, he felt he had gotten a lot off of his chest. As refreshingly candid as Rice had been this season, his honesty this time surprised the writers. It's one thing to rip the Lakers one month from the showdown, but to raise a fuss days before their nationally-televised battle showed guts.

January 26-27

When Rice's quotes were read to him, Jackson was in no mood to fire his own salvo. He admitted to courting Pippen, but insisted he never kept Rice in the dark.

"Glen and I had nothing emotionally against each other," Jackson said.

When Rice found out the next day that Jackson had claimed they had an open line of communication, his anger resurfaced.

"He addressed that in the papers," Rice said. "He never came to me one-on-one to talk about it."

The media's focus on the Rice-Jackson feud overshadowed the bleak situation facing the Knicks. They had lost three straight games, Sprewell's ribs were bruised, Camby was ready to serve the last game of his suspension and Thomas, the backup center who had injured himself crashing to the floor in Charlotte, was not expected to play against the Lakers because of a sprained ankle. Longley would be forced into making his first start as a Knick against Shaquille O'Neal.

Van Gundy knew his team had plenty of excuses to fall back on and challenged his players to keep from thinking a victory over the Lakers was impossible. Even though it seemed that way.

■ ■ ■

An hour before tipoff, Rice and Jackson passed each other in the hallway connecting the two locker rooms. They exchanged nods and lukewarm hellos. When Jackson met the media, he said "I have no problem talking to Glen, just not his wife."

Christina attended the game and sat in her usual seat in the third row behind where the celebrities sat, across from the Knicks' bench. She wore a white blouse with "R-I-C-E" in rhinestone letters on the back. Rice and Christina had met when he played for the Heat and lived in Miami. They were a good-looking couple, having once posed for *Sports Illustrated's* swimsuit issue, but her soft good looks belied the fact that she was the boss of the Rice household, a domineering wife very much involved in her husband's bassketball career, as Jackson found out during the finals. Christina had a say in all of Glen's business decisions.

But on the day Rice faced the Lakers, she didn't want to stir the pot any more than she had and claimed the remarks she made during The Finals had been twisted by the media.

The Lakers left O'Neal behind in the locker room when they walked out for the pre-game warmups. He was nursing a sore foot and officially scratched from the lineup 20 minutes before tipoff, giving Van Gundy little time to adjust. During player introductions, the fans cheered loudly to the announcement that O'Neal would not play, a curious reaction considering that many fans had bought tickets to see the superstar.

Without Shaq, the Lakers looked like an average team and the Knicks pocketed an easy 91-81 victory to stop their three-game slide. Rice appeared overexcited in his first game against the Lakers and shot three-for-eight from the field but he ripped down 10 rebounds.

Two of Rice's kids played around by his locker afterward. Rice's smile had never been brighter.

"I was nervous in the beginning but it's great to beat those guys," Rice said.

Despite the hype, the game was dull. The wry Jackson found a way to keep himself entertained. He argued with the referees about the green religious wristbands Ward and Houston were wearing, claiming they were illegal. Players are not allowed to wear jewelry. The wristbands were made of cloth.

"How come they're allowed to play with those hospital bracelets?" Jackson screamed at referee Greg Willard. On the next play stoppage, Willard looked at Ward's wrist and, seeing nothing wrong, gave him the ball for the inbounds pass.

Ward and Houston had proudly worn those knitted bands for four years. The band's inscription used to contain the initials WWJD for "What Would Jesus do?" The new lettering read, "Our God Reigns."

"It's my tattoos," Ward said after the game. "It's not jewelry. It serves a purpose." Both Ward and Houston thought Jackson must have been fooling around.

The bigger controversy had Jackson allegedly conspiring with Shaq to keep him out of the game for the purpose of showing up Bryant on national TV and proving what the Lakers were like without their monster center. Indeed, witnesses had seen O'Neal walk into the locker room without a limp two hours before tipoff. The theory sounded good, but it was wrong. O'Neal would miss the next three games with a form of plantar fasciaitis.

January 30

For the second straight year, the coaches snubbed Sprewell when they selected the reserves for the All-Star Game. Sprewell's statistics weren't overwhelming. His shooting percentage was 42.8 percent and he was averaging 17.3 points-per-game. But he had shifted to point guard for part of the season, putting himself in less of a position to take shots, and his leadership on the team with the second-best record in the East seemed like enough to merit a berth. Houston, not Sprewell, was selected.

That left filling the final spot, the one vacated by Hill's injury, in the hands of Commissioner David Stern, who would make the decision the following day. Sprewell figured to be in contention with Brian Grant, Antoine Walker, Jalen Rose, Reggie Miller, and Jamal Mashburn.

"Frankly, I never gave it a thought he would not make it," Van Gundy said.

"At this point, I'm just taking it as I didn't make it and I'm getting ready to go home," said Sprewell, who seemed unusually downcast.

■ ■ ■

That night, the players gathered at Chelsea Piers in Manhattan for a mandatory charity bowling event benefiting the Red Holzman Foundation. Strickland was one of the first players to arrive. While he was in the game room playing a video golf game, Ed Oliva of the operations staff walked up to him and said, "Jeff wants to talk to you."

"Does it have to be right now?" Strickland asked.

"Yeah, right now," Oliva said.

Strickland knew the news couldn't be good, especially when Van Gundy asked him to step outside.

"I have to tell you you've been traded to Vancouver for Othella Harrington," Van GUndy said. I want to thank you for your hard work."

Strickland smiled weakly. The meeting lasted a minute. What was there to say? He had finally accepted his minor role on the club. Staying in New York meant getting into the playoffs for the first time in his career. Now he was headed to the woeful Grizzlies. But he couldn't blame the Knicks for trading him for Harrington. They were getting a power-forward/center to help address their size issue. The deal made perfect sense.

Strickland hugged some of his teammates and left the bowling alley. Most of the players hadn't arrived. Camby would arrive late. When he got to the bowling alley, his teammates asked him if he knew about the trade. Camby panicked, thinking they were talking about him.

After the bowl-a-thon, Camby went straight to Strickland's place and helped him pack. Most of the players had enjoyed the sincere, friendly Strickland. They wished he had gotten more of a chance to play.

At about the same time, on the Grizzlies' charter flight from Vancouver to Phoenix, assistant general manager Billy Knight walked to the back row and told Harrington about the trade. Harrington had become disliked in Vancouver for complaining about the rainy climate and the high Canadian tax rate. Canadians didn't appreciate the knocks by an American basketball player.

Harrington also was tired of playing for a perennial loser. He suppressed his smile during the rest of the flight. He didn't want his teammates to see how happy he was to be a Knick.

January 31

When practice ended, neither Sprewell nor the Knicks had heard from the league office. With Camby surrounded by reporters seeking his reaction to the Harrington trade, Sprewell leaned into the media scrum, held his fist under Camby's chin as if it were a radio microphone, and asked, in a deep radio voice, "Are you worried that the trade for Othella Harrington will cut down your playing time?"

Sprewell made the reporters laugh and Camby smile. He was concerned for his friend, who had worked hard to become the team's dominant frontcourt player. Sprewell hoped neither the five-game suspension nor the addition of Harrington would affect Camby's mind.

"I don't know if we're better," Sprewell said. "I don't know if Othella is going to play a whole lot."

■ ■ ■

The Knicks got the good news an hour after practice. Stern had named Sprewell to the All-Star Team. The same man who tried to end his NBA career had now picked him to be an All-Star.

The Knicks' staff was unable to reach Sprewell, who never answers his home phone. They wanted to inform him before he got the news from television or radio. Van Gundy drove to Sprewell's house, located a few blocks from Purchase College, and rang the doorbell at his player's mansion. Sprewell, holding his baby daughter in his arms, opened the door and saw Van Gundy, who had never been to his house before. Sprewell's stomach turned. He thought Van Gundy was going to tell him he'd been traded.

But when Van Gundy informed him that he had been named to the All-Star team, Sprewell smiled widely. Van Gundy was glad he had delivered the news in person. He would've missed that smile over the telephone.

February 1

The Sixers came to town with Allen Iverson embroiled in controversy. Four days earlier in Indiana, the notoriously obnoxious fans at Conseco Field House had, according to Iverson, called him "monkey, nigger and jailbird." Iverson yelled back at a heckler, "Go home, faggot."

Iverson's word choice was suspect, considering his lyrics from the gangsta rap CD that had been viewed as demeaning to gays.

In his pre-game chat with the writers, Van Gundy supported Iverson while condemning the Pacers' fans whom he considered racially insensitive. For years during the Knicks' playoff wars in Indiana, Van Gundy had heard fans behind the bench holler racial comments at Ewing and John Starks.

"Indiana is very bad," Van Gundy said. "We've been there a lot. I'm not trying to weigh in on right and wrong in that situation, but definitely Indiana is as bad as any crowd."

Van Gundy's defense of Iverson was the best "D" Iverson saw all night. He ripped the Knicks in the third quarter, hitting three consecutive three-pointers. When the Sixers' 87-80 victory ended, Iverson talked about how much he loved playing at the Garden. He finished with 31 points and eight assists. Even Camby's return to the lineup wasn't enough of a jolt for the Knicks.

"The whole difference is that Philly is a consistent team and we're inconsistent," Van Gundy said.

The Knicks' had the second-best record in the East at 26-17, but they still hadn't beaten the first-place Sixers at the Garden.

February 2

With the pain in his left foot intensifying, Rice scored two points against the Sixers. The shockwave therapy eased his discomfort only temporarily. He hadn't decided if he'd play that night against the Nets at The Meadowlands. For the first time, Rice mentioned surgery as an option, which would put him out until before the playoffs. He also said he would consider not playing for an extended period to see if rest would alleviate the pain.

He made these comments two hours before the Nets' game. As had become commonplace during his first season in New York, Rice looked revitalized just when his situation looked the bleakest. He singed the Nets for 16 points, hitting seven of 12 shots.

With Thomas missing his third straight game because of a sprained ankle and Camby sitting out the second half with the flu, Harrington made his first meaningful contribution as a Knick. In 29 minutes, Harrington showed a stylish game in the low post, with an array of dunks and an unorthodox lefty jump hook shot. He finished with eight points and nine rebounds.

February 4

Earlier in the week, Houston received an honor that, in his eyes, surpassed making the All-Star Game. The results of the History Channel's poll on the Knicks' greatest moments were released. Houston's shot that bounced off the rim and glass before going in at the buzzer to beat the Heat in the deciding game of the first-round playoff series in 1999 had earned the top spot in the voting.

Houston's shot beat out Willis Reed hobbling through the tunnel before Game 7 of the 1969 Finals against the Lakers and the Knicks winning their last championship in 1973. The voting results showed that 30-something fans had taken over the Garden. Houston and his wife, Tonja, agreed it was the highest honor he had ever received. He was given a painting that depicted the shot and placed the portrait in a prominent spot in their Connecticut home.

Houston's historic shot, which bounced off the front iron, kissed the glass and hung in the air before dropping through the twine, had occurred blocks away at Miami Arena, the Heat's old home. Had the ball caromed off the iron and glass slightly differently, Van Gundy would have been fired and Phil Jackson would have become the Knicks' coach.

■ ■ ■

Remembering his post-game tirade following the Knicks' last game against the Heat in November, Sprewell felt obligated to ensure the club was mentally prepared this time for Miami. He had told reporters before the flight to Miami, "I'm going to do everything in my power to make sure that the players who weren't here understand the significance of this game, what it means to win against Miami."

In the visitors' locker room at Miami's AmericanAirlines Arena an hour before tipoff, Sprewell sensed a seriousness he hadn't felt before the last Heat game. The guys were ready. He decided not to speak up. He hoped they had listened to his words last time and remembered his anger.

The electric atmosphere of Miami Arena carried over to the new building, hard by picturesque Biscayne Bay, but still in the same seedy downtown Miami neighborhood. The Knicks-Heat games felt more important here than they did at the Garden. Miami fans, relatively quiet during the rest of the season, desperately tried to outshout the transplanted New Yorkers, who filled a third of the seats. The result was a harsh, relentless attack on the ears, as every basket, every play, was met with a loud reaction from the fans.

Even the Heat's in-game entertainment staff stepped up its production for these games. Last season, during a timeout in a Knicks-Heat playoff game, a video was aired of the Heat's red mascot Burnie prancing through New York City. The mascot hung posters of the Heat logo all over Manhattan, at the Statue of Liberty, the Empire State Building, and even on a yellow cab. The skit climaxed when the Heat's marketing camera crew, during a Garden tour, snuck into the Knicks' empty locker room and filmed the mascot plastering the logo above Ewing's cubicle. The Knicks were not in on the joke. The Heat had pulled a fast one over their rivals.

■ ■ ■

Singer Jimmy Buffett, a Palm Beach resident, had been a Heat season-ticket holder since the franchise's inception 10 years ago. The fans who sat near him behind the baseline alongside the Heat bench didn't view him as a guy who sang about drinking margaritas. They saw him as a quiet, subdued fan. He was no Spike Lee, the rambunctious, towel-waving film producer whose trash-talking battle with Reggie Miller once cost the Knicks a playoff game.

But there is something about Knicks-Heat that makes fans go crazy. Late in the fourth quarter, as another classic headed to the wire in a frenzy, Buffett's voice got louder. He was angry at the officials as he watched Miami choke away another game against the Knicks. His language was worsening. Buffett watched Eddie Jones miss both of his free throws in the final minute and Bruce Bowen miss the second of his pair. When Camby shoved his way in for the rebound of a missed shot by Sprewell, Buffett screamed, "This is bullshit! This is bullshit!"

Referee Joe Forte didn't know the identity of the man shouting, only that he was sitting next to a boy who looked like he was about 10 years old. Forte didn't know it, but the boy was Buffett's son. Forte stopped the game and ordered Buffett to leave his seat.

Stunned, Buffett wouldn't budge. Forte asked for security. "I don't want him in the first row," Forte said. Riley was both amused and affronted. He screamed at Forte, "Do you know who that is? Do you mean to tell me you've never been a Parrothead in your life?"

Forte still had no idea that he was ejecting Mr. Margaritaville and had no idea what Riley was talking about. Forte thought Riley was trying to insult him by calling him a Parrothead and threatened to give Riley a technical if he said anything else.

The Heat's head of security summoned Andy Elisburg, the Heat's senior vice president of basketball operations. Heat management didn't want to do anything to further annoy the officiating crew in a close game. Elisburg walked to Buffett's seat and told him his kid could stay but he had to be moved out of the front row.

"You've got to be kidding," Buffett said.

The fans behind Buffett were enraged. "Don't go, Jimmy," several of them yelled.

Elisburg and security escorted Buffett from his seat. At first, they planted him in a plastic folding chair behind the Heat bench, but Buffett, uncomfortable, decided to watch the rest of the game from the tunnel players and coaches used to get to the locker room.

With Rice finding his shooting touch, sinking post-ups and bombs, the Knicks captured the thriller, 103-100, in overtime. But the win was not sealed before Johnson and Anthony Mason, the two players involved in the 1996 swap between Charlotte and the Knicks, squabbled in the final seconds, exchanging heated words and nearly coming to blows. Mason started the flare-up of tempers by pushing Johnson after he took an inbounds pass with two seconds remaining. Johnson, a former amateur boxer, charged Mason, who backed away. Don Chaney got between the two, so punches and suspensions were avoided.

As the jubilant and exhausted Knicks got to the locker room, Sprewell shouted to his teammates, "That's playoff intensity. That's a playoff-type game. That's the way it should be." This time, there was no need for a post-game lecture on the importance of playing the Heat.

Johnson was unwilling to discuss his late-game fracas with Mason. When beat writer John Brennan of *The Bergen Record* tried to ask the question a second time but in a different manner, Johnson snapped,

"I already said no comment. Now you fucked it up for everyone." Johnson stormed off, not realizing the writers didn't care to talk to him about anything but the fight.

Over in the Heat's locker room, Tim Hardaway was still astounded that Buffett got ejected. "How are you going to kick out Jimmy Buffett?" Hardaway asked. "He's a mild-mannered guy. They would never throw Spike Lee out."

As Ward walked to the bus, someone asked what he thought about Buffett's ejection. Ward, who doesn't drink margaritas and listens only to gospel, said, "Jimmy Buffett? What was he doing here?"

February 5

As it was, two games against the Heat and Rockets figured to be a bruising back-to-back set. But even if they weren't emotionally spent from the Heat game, the Knicks would not have kept up with the Rockets on a night Hakeem Olajuwon turned back the sundial.

Olajuwon, who had single-handedly prevented Ewing's Knicks from winning the 1994 championship, had asked for his release the week before in order to sign with another club, preferably Miami to fill Mourning's void. Against the Knicks, Olajuwon made a convincing statement that he should stick around a while. He scored 16 of his 18 points in the second half with his patented "Dream Shake" move. Olajuwon often resembles a bobble doll as he does his low-post feints. The "Dream Shake" consisted of a fake to the baseline, a fake into the middle and then a fallaway 10-foot jumper.

To a man, the Knicks were stunned by Olajuwon's renaissance performance in the 100-86 blowout loss. Their gameplan wasn't about stopping Hakeem. "I didn't think he had it in him," Sprewell said.

CHAPTER 14

The Homecoming: Part I

February 7

ESPN magazine ran a cover story on Chris Webber, who was not bashful about listing his choice destinations. The Knicks were on his list, along with Indiana, Detroit and Houston.

"I'm bored to death here everyday," Webber said of Sacramento. "It would be sweet to win a championship with Spree in a major market just because it hasn't worked out with friends before."

■ ■ ■

Mark Cuban, the Mavericks' eccentric owner, shot baskets with his players two hours before game time at the Garden. He wore blue jeans, sneakers and a blue, long-sleeved polo shirt. There was no owner like him in the NBA. Though he had a flock of critics, he had unmistakably brought refreshing exuberance to the NBA.

But his interview with *Penthouse* magazine brought a few red faces to the powers-that-be in the league office and another reprimanding phone call. Cuban, unmarried but dating a steady girlfriend, spoke of his infatuation with Courtney Love and Elizabeth Hurley. Asked, "What was the best pickup line a woman ever used on you?" Cuban responded, "Wanna fuck?" Talking about his first kiss, Cuban said, "I think I came twice, but at that age, it was the same as reloading."

The same powers that had made a habit of fining him for his public critiques of officials decided against another slap on the wrist for his sexually explicit marks in *Penthouse*. After all, it would just give more publicity to the *Penthouse* story.

■ ■ ■

The Knicks carried a 28-18 record into their final game before the All-Star break. Cuban sat behind the Mavs' bench, alongside the press table. Throughout the game, he asked a couple of the writers near him what they thought about various calls. Cuban leaned over periodically to look at the replays on the monitors. "Let me see that!" Cuban said. The Internet billionaire had gotten his way throughout his business life. If he seemed obsessed with the officiating. it was because he wasn't used to having an arbitrary ruling go against him.

The wildness at the Garden began when Michael Finley connected on a fallaway desperation 10-foot jumper over Sprewell at the buzzer, sending the game into overtime. When the ball went through the hoop, Cuban climbed onto the press table, kicked up his heels and twirled around on his backside, treating the table like it was the oak bar at McSorley's Ale House.

The madness continued when Dallas's Howard Eisley banged in a three-point shot at the buzzer to force a second overtime. Cuban stayed off the press table this time. The second overtime quieted Cuban down as the Knicks pulled out a 96-93 victory to go 29-18 entering the All-Star break.

During his pre-game chat with the writers, Van Gundy, had raved about Rice's heart in playing hurt and his ability to shoot well despite not practicing because of his aching foot. Van Gundy said he'd spend the All-Star break thinking of ways to get Rice more minutes.

The trading deadline was just two weeks away. Even if Van Gundy believed what he was saying, his remarks seemed like an attempt to pump up Rice's trade value with Mutombo still available.

■ ■ ■

Raptors general manager Glen Grunwald was caught by surprise. He received a phone call from Scott Layden, who told him he was interested in their point guard, former Knick Mark Jackson. This was the first inquiry about Jackson that Grunwald had received since his contract became tradable in mid-December. The previous summer, Toronto had signed him as a free agent to a four-year, $16 million deal. At 35, Jackson had slowed down on defense but was still considered one of the elite playmakers ever.

Grunwald told Layden he'd be interested in talking. The Raptors had a younger backup point guard in Alvin Williams who seemed ready to start. With payroll budgets always a concern, Grunwald didn't mind seeing if he could get back a contract less burdensome than Jackson's and a player of comparable value.

All-Star Break

For the first time, Sixers' coach Larry Brown could visualize Mutombo in a Sixers' uniform. The trading deadline was 11 days away. Theo Ratliff was out with a fractured wrist. In a classic All-Star Game, Brown saw something in the fourth quarter in Washington as he was coaching from the sidelines.

Mutombo ripped down 22 rebounds in 28 minutes. For one night, he was not involved in a meaningless regular-season game for the woeful Hawks. He was playing on a big stage, on national TV. Brown knew his Sixers would be playing on a bigger stage come May and June. "What would the team be like with Mutombo?" Brown thought.

■ ■ ■

During the All-Star Break, George Kalinsky, the Garden's official photographer for 30 years, flew to Orlando to receive an award at Disney World. Kalinsky was honored as the Photo Imaging and Manufacturers and Distributors' 2000 Photographer of the Year.

Kalinsky's most famous Knick photograph, and one of the most famous in sports, is of Willis Reed limping out of the Garden tunnel before Game 7 of the 1970 Finals. But snapping shots of the Knicks was just a small part of his resume. One of his photos of the Pope sits on a desk in the Vatican. In the early 1970's, he taught Frank Sinatra how to use a camera and took classic photos of the singer.

At the start of the 2000-2001 season, Kalinsky's photos were spotlighted in an exhibition at the National Arts Club in Manhattan to benefit the Lustgarten Foundation for Pancreatic Cancer. Mark Lustgarten, former chairman of the Garden, had died of pancreatic cancer in 1999. One of the photos, blown up to poster size, was of a nude Phil Jackson when he played for the Knicks during their glory days of the early '70s. As a lark, Kalinsky had snapped the picture of Jackson sitting in a twisted position on the carpet in the Knicks' locker room. The photo didn't show Jackson's privates.

Kalinsky thought he'd give the photo to Jackson as a gag, but Jackson loved the nude shot so much, he still calls it his favorite basketball shot. Jackson encouraged Kalinsky to use the nude shot in exhibits and commercially. During the Lustgarten exhibition, Kalinsky was asked by one of the gossip columnists if there was any Knick he'd like to photograph nude. Never one to disappoint an inquisitive scribe, Kalinsky said he would like to shoot Sprewell in the buff.

"He has a charisma and a showmanship that very few of the players have," Kalinsky explained when I saw the gossip item. "It's not necessarily the kind of body the person has. It's the personality and he's got it."

Kalinsky never pursued the Sprewell nude, but seconds after a game in November, he took a shot of Sprewell's eyes as he walked off the court, perspiration dripping. Using digital-age technology, Kalinsky did a repetition of Sprewell's eyes four times. The shot turned into a keeper, a dramatic portrait of four sets of Sprewell's eyes in the threatening glare that opponents feared. Sprewell hung the photo up in his house.

After being shown the image of Sprewell's eyes, Houston asked Kalinsky if he could do something offbeat for him. Instead of recreating the repeating eye shot, Kalinsky worked on a photo depicting a series of Houston's jump shots. After spending several games training his lens on Houston's jumper, Kalinsky noticed something interesting about Houston's technique: every shot he took was identical. He jumped to the same height, his release point was the same height and he was always six inches above the defender's hand. Kalinsky told Houston about this.

"I know. My father taught me to do that," Houston said.

Of all the requests players have made, Kalinsky remembers most vividly Ewing's final one. The summer before his last season with the Knicks, before anyone sensed that Ewing's time in New York was winding down, Ewing asked Kalinsky to make him a photo album of his career in New York.

"Wouldn't it be incomplete?" Kalinsky asked Ewing.

Ewing shrugged.

Every other week during his last season with the Knicks, Ewing asked Kalinsky for an update on the photo album. Before the playoffs,

Kalinsky had it ready: 250 pictures of Ewing in chronological order. The last page had no picture, but Kalinsky had inscribed, in a calligraphy pen, "The Best is Yet to Come." When Ewing saw it, his eyes watered. More than anyone, Kalinsky looked forward to photographing Ewing's return to the Garden in two and a half weeks.

February 13-15

Instead of going to Toronto for more electric-shock treatments on his foot, Rice spent the break in the Bahamas, sipping Pina Coladas on the beach with his wife. Rice iced his sore left foot on the white sand of the Caribbean. The problem was, the ice melted as quickly as the cubes in his drinks.

Van Gundy's solution for expanding Rice's role was to get him onto the court in the final minutes of close games. He admitted that to do so, he might have to finish games with the big backcourt alignment he had discarded.

Sprewell and Houston returned to the club fatigued from the All-Star break functions, parties, media sessions and meetings. Certainly, they were not tired from the scant minutes Brown played them. Houston could have used the time away from basketball, having spent his summer playing for the Olympic team.

After the Nuggets routed the Knicks, 96-77, at the Pepsi Center, some players used Denver's high altitude as an excuse. Sprewell and Houston both admitted to being tired. The Knicks' transition defense was an embarrassment, as they were repeatedly beaten downcourt for layups. The Knicks allowed 22 fastbreak points while getting only two of their own.

"Transition defense is very simple: get your butt back before they get the ball down," Van Gundy raged afterward.

The next night during his pre-game chat with writers before the Knicks played Utah, Van Gundy was asked about the altitude being a factor in Denver. He had read the newspaper clips in his hotel room, and the altitude theory raised his ire.

"The air?" Van Gundy said. "We'll go with the air. I'm glad I didn't say it was the air. You'd have a fucking field day with that. I just don't know why we can't ever say as a group what we didn't do instead of us making excuses."

The Knicks didn't put up much of a fight against the Jazz, either, except in the locker room after the loss. Some players questioned the special treatment Utah's Karl Malone received at the Delta Center. Malone shot 16 free throws in the 106-90 wipeout.

"Why do you think they got to the line more?" Childs asked. Told that they attacked the basket, Childs scoffed, "Who attacked the basket? Malone? He didn't attack the basket. All he did was turn, elbow the guy who was guarding him and get the call. Where we at? Utah. Okay."

Sprewell wasn't about to complain. He realized Malone was going to get favorable calls at the Delta Center no matter what. The idea was to overcome the disadvantage. Sprewell again fretted about the Knicks' intensity level.

"We don't have the fire right now as a team," Sprewell said.

Van Gundy believed the team had lacked defensive intensity since beating San Antonio on Martin Luther King Day. Their malaise had started when they beat the Pistons despite a sloppy defensive performance in the first game of Camby's suspension. They were 5-7 since beating Portland and the Spurs back-to-back. The trading deadline was a week away, and the Knicks were in slippage mode.

February 16-18

After beating the horrid Nets at the Garden, despite giving up 104 points, the Knicks headed for Orlando still trying to find the defense that had gained national acclaim only last month for setting an NBA record. The Knicks were routinely letting teams either reach the century mark or come close. Van Gundy was dejected after the 114-104 shootout win over the Nets, knowing the team's defensive pressure and rebounding were nowhere close to where it needed to be for a long playoff run.

In the locker room before the Magic game, the writers informed the players of a quote by McGrady in that day's Orlando Sentinel. McGrady, who had torn apart the Knicks' defense this season, said he wasn't "intimidated" by them and wanted to play them in the playoffs. The mild-mannered Houston took a jab at McGrady, who had played for the Raptors last spring when the Knicks swept them in three games.

"If I got swept in the playoffs, I'd want to play that team, too," Houston cracked.

■ ■ ■

Daytona Speedway is an hour from Orlando, smack-dab in the heart of NASCAR country. The Daytona 500, the premier event on the NASCAR circuit, had just finished as fans began entering the TD Waterhouse Arena. Dale Earnhardt, the most famous NASCAR driver in the country, had been involved in a grisly crash in the final laps. America awaited word on the severity of Earnhardt's injuries.

When Magic officials learned that Earnhardt had died, they debated whether they should inform the crowd before the game, since the tragedy was so fresh and close to home. Orlando GM John Gabriel decided telling the crowd was proper. P.A. announcer Paul Porter was apprehensive, too. He knew the announcement in these parts was akin to telling NBA fans in another city that Michael Jordan had been killed in a plane crash.

"Ladies and gentlemen," Porter said. "Before we begin tonight, please observe a moment of silence for the tragedy that occurred this afternoon at Daytona Speedway that claimed the life of NASCAR driver Dale Earnhardt."

The reaction by the 16,000 fans made it abundantly clear the vast majority was unaware of Earnhardt's death. A collective gasp resonated from the crowd, making for an eerie few moments. Everyone in the arena would remember where they were when they learned the news of Earnhardt's death.

■ ■ ■

The game allowed the fans to escape the tragedy for two-plus hours. McGrady's brilliance had the Orlando crowd juiced up. He scored 32 points, blistering the Knicks on penetrations and jump shots. He scored 15 points in the fourth quarter and single-handedly won the game for the Magic, 96-88.

With a sizable coterie of Knicks fans in the building, the Magic patrons were eager to celebrate the triumph. The noise reached a crescendo in the final seconds. Hill, on his crutches, hopped joyfully off the court with a huge smile when it was over. Rivers raced onto the court to hug his players, then sprinted off, jubilantly clapping and laughing while high-fiving the fans leaning over the guard rails by their seats next to the tunnel.

■ ■ ■

While the Knicks were in Florida, the Heat were in New York, spending three days off before their showdown at the Garden on February 20. That gave one of the Heat players time to stir up the pot. Tim Hardaway, the outspoken point guard, was asked by Fort Lauderdale *Sun-Sentinel* writer Ira Winderman what it was like spending three days off in Manhattan.

"New York fans are assholes and they're going to continue to be assholes," Hardaway said. "But I go out, hell, yeah, I take it, I give it right back to them. Hell with them. They're real people just like I am."

■ ■ ■

Phone lines sizzled across general managers' offices across the country. With the deadline three days away, Layden resumed his talks with Atlanta about Mutombo. A new team had entered the fray, the first-place Sixers, but Layden didn't know much about it. Babcock had kept a lid on the Sixers' sudden interest since the All-Star Game.

The Knicks were still monitoring point-guard situations around the league, looking for an upgrade. The newspapers reported on their talks for Strickland, Vancouver's Mike Bibby and Golden State's Mookie Blaylock. None of those talks ever became serious. Layden was proud. He had managed to keep his inquiries with Toronto about Jackson out of the papers. With three days to go, the Jackson deal looked promising. The only problem was making the deal work mathematically under the salary cap by adding throw-in players.

February 20

The Mutombo rumors were searing, and Camby was named prominently as trade bait. Referring to Camby in a story, Isola of The News referred to him as "a six-foot-11 walking trade rumor." After the morning shootaround before the Heat game, Camby confided, "I don't want to play anywhere else. But that really isn't in my hands now. When I wake up Friday morning, I want to wake up as a Knick."

The players, from Camby to Houston to Sprewell, were feeling the heat from the trade rumors. Sprewell did not want to lose his friend and thought the Knicks did not need Mutombo. Truth is, the Knicks had taken Camby off the table in late December and offered Rice once his contract became tradable.

"It's fair to say we'll all feel better once the deadline passes," Sprewell said. "Once we know where everybody stands, who's here, who's not, who's in, who's out, things can get back to normal."

Van Gundy did nothing to cool the fires when he said, "I don't think any of us like the direction the team has been headed the last month. Scott has to decide if this is a bad stretch or is this who we are."

Van Gundy liked to lump personnel decisions on Layden. He didn't want the players to think he was involved in trading them. Behind the scenes, however, he had as much input as anyone in the organization. And yes, he liked the idea of bringing in Jackson at the point.

■ ■ ■

That night, the Garden throng chanted the A-word at Hardaway with 10 seconds remaining in the game. Not "asshole," but "Air-ball!" Hardaway tossed an airball from the left wing with his club down by one point and 10 seconds remaining, but he got another chance to quiet the crowd. With the Heat down by two after Ward hit a free throw, Hardaway squared up at the three-point line as time wound down. He pump-faked Childs to get open, but his shot glanced off the left side of the rim at the buzzer.

Childs, who had hounded Hardaway on both shots, looked at the Miami bench and pounded his wrists together before walking off the court. "That's the lockdown," he said. "I was letting him know I put the handcuffs on him."

A Raptors official scouted the game and watched Childs intently. Meanwhile, Pete Vecsey was about to report in the next day's Post that the Sixers were going to win the Mutombo sweepstakes. Kukoc, Theo Ratliff and Nazr Mohammed would head to Atlanta for Mutombo. Layden had steadfastly refused to give up Camby in the deal right up until the time he made his last offer of Rice and Longley for Mutombo. When Layden learned that Babcock was going to acquire Ratliff, he asked if he'd be willing to deal the younger center. "No thank you," Babcock said. Layden had struck out on Mutombo.

February 21
Standing in the visitors' locker room at the Palace of Auburn Hills, Sprewell shrugged his shoulders when asked about the Sixers acquiring

Mutombo. In his mind, the Sixers were going to be tough to beat because of Iverson, not Mutombo. Sprewell believed Ratliff and Mutombo were similar players with the same strengths.

Layden stayed back at his office on the fourteenth floor of 2 Penn Plaza, hammering out the details for a Jackson trade and trying to make it work under the salary cap. At halftime at Auburn Hills, Hamamoto led the beat writers upstairs to the Pistons' public-relations office for a conference call with Layden.

"Sitting here tonight, there's very little activity," Layden said over the speaker phone. "I don't anticipate anything happening. It goes back to how we feel about the team. We believe in this group."

This was a major departure from his recent comments about how hard he was working the phones to try to improve the club. But Layden was trying to lead the writers off the scent. The last thing he wanted was another team finding out that Jackson was available. Only a handful of teams knew it. Layden had been burned in the first Ewing deal when the Pistons pulled out after the trade became public. That cost him Vin Baker.

In the locker room, the players were relieved to hear Layden's remarks . . . except Houston. "What else is he going to say?" Houston asked.

The approaching trading deadline did not spark the Knicks' play. They got hammered by the Pistons, 90-85.

February 22

Jackson was devastated and shocked when he was traded from the Knicks to the lowly Clippers after the 1991-92 season. He thought the Knicks were on the verge of contending for a title. He didn't believe the trade made them a better team.

But Riley had wanted to get bigger along the front line. Jackson was dealt for Charles Smith and Doc Rivers. The frontline now boasted Ewing, Oakley and Smith, with Mason coming off the bench. Rivers became plagued by bad knees and played just one full season. The Knicks went through point guards like a family of eight goes through toilet paper. Jackson always wondered what would have been if they hadn't made the trade. So did Checketts, whose stomach churned watching Jackson's Pacers twice eliminate the Knicks in the playoffs with the former St. John's star right at the center of the execution.

The Knicks announced the Jackson-for-Childs swap at six p.m., right on the deadline. Muggsy Bogues, the five-foot-four guard who had been on the injured list all season, also was dealt to the Knicks to help them fulfill the salary-cap requirements: salaries transferred in the trade must be equal on both sides if both clubs are over the salary cap.

Jackson, who had kept his home in Saddle River, New Jersey, phoned his buddy and former Pacers teammate Reggie Miller. When Jackson told Miller that he had been traded to the Knicks, Miller screamed, "Liar!" and hung up. Jackson called Miller back and begged him to believe it. Miller prayed Jackson was lying.

"Now how can I play against the Knicks with the same fire?" Miller told his buddy. "How could I hate them now?"

Of the several phone calls Jackson made that night, one was to Longley. They barely knew each other, but Jackson boldly asked if there was any chance of getting to wear No. 13, the number he wore with the Knicks and Pacers. Longley, startled, told Jackson he couldn't give it up. It had been his father's number. Jackson, whose dad had died two years before, understood, though the rejection was the first sign that none of the Knicks were nostalgic about Jackson's return to his hometown after seven years.

The deal received instant positive reaction. The hometown kid, the Brooklyn-born, St. John's star was back. The Knicks had shopped Childs for two years with little success. Jackson was the best playmaking point guard the Knicks had since Jackson. Van Gundy immediately called him "one of the best decision-makers in the NBA. He gets it to people on time and on target."

But there were drawbacks. Jackson had never been regarded as a strong defender. He lacked great lateral movement. At 35 years old, he had slowed down. He also had three years left on his contract. Childs had just one year left. Financially, the Raptors had done well in the deal.

The Knicks, though, thought they had found the playmaking point guard that would make Sprewell, Houston and Rice more effective. "It has the makings of a great story," Layden said. "He'll be excited to come back home and complete the cycle."

February 23

Childs found out about the deal while getting a haircut. His first thought was that at least he wouldn't have to hear the trade rumors anymore. He had grown sick of them.

The day after the trade, Childs delayed his flight to Toronto, perhaps as a parting shot. Childs didn't get on the flight until late afternoon, which meant he likely wouldn't take his physical until the evening. The Knicks faced the Suns at the Garden that night. Jackson would not be able to suit up until Childs passed his physical. An hour before tipoff, word reached the Garden that Jackson could play. Childs had passed. Jackson wore No. 31, flipping the digits of his old number. In the locker room, Van Gundy handed him a sheet on which a couple of offensive sets were written. Jackson studied them while sitting on the bench during the first quarter.

The roar from the fans was sweet and loud when Jackson entered the game in the second quarter. The entire Garden crowd stood up and welcomed him back. With Ward starting for perhaps the final time, Jackson played 13 minutes in an 88-84 loss to the Suns, but the defeat didn't faze the Knicks. They finally had their playmaker.

February 24

Jackson spent the morning before his first practice learning the playbook. He recognized most of the sets from playing against the Knicks as a Pacer. "The Phoenix game was basically take off my clothes, suit up and do whatever. I didn't have a clue," Jackson said.

Rice and Ward figured to be the two players most adversely affected by the trade. After the All-Star break, Van Gundy had decided he wanted to finish games with the big backcourt, having Sprewell at point guard with Houston and Rice on the wings. The trade changed that. Van Gundy thought he was finally done with the gimmicky point-guardless alignment.

The coach truly felt badly for Rice, who couldn't catch a break. Van Gundy went out of his way to show his concern for the three-time All-Star. He spoke with Rice about playing time more than with any other player. He did not want to lose Rice like Phil Jackson had last season. Rice had shown Van Gundy a constant willingness to play hurt.

"He's a starter who's not starting and I don't want it to grow to where frustration affects his performance," Van Gundy said.

February 25

The countdown to Ewing's grand return was down to two days. In his pre-game chat, Van Gundy wondered how the fans would react to Ewing. He had always been disappointed at how fickle the Garden fans were regarding Ewing. Although Ewing would never admit it, Van Gundy figured the fans' fickleness was a factor in his decision to request a trade.

While almost everyone else seemed certain Ewing would get a standing ovation, Van Gundy wasn't sure. "I have no idea what reaction he's going to elicit," Van Gundy said, "which I think is unfortunate."

■ ■ ■

The Kings, without Webber, were in town for a Sunday matinee. Their star power forward was nursing an ankle injury, but he did not join the club to New York to avoid the media's questions about his desire to be a Knick.

Ward's reign as the Knicks' starting point guard ended against the Kings. Jackson started, but Ward gave the team a lift in the second half by playing one of his best games of the season. He snuck around Vlade Divac's back to steal the ball and trigger a fastbreak basket for Allan Houston late in the fourth quarter to seal the win. If Ward was sparked by his new, diminished role, he wasn't saying. Van Gundy had recently told him that he wasn't as active and daring defensively as usual. The pivotal steal against Divac was the perfect example of the aggressive plays Ward was capable of making.

"If it weren't for the Holy Sprit guiding me, I probably would've handled this totally different," Ward said.

In truth, Jackson and Ward were handling the awkward situation quite well, thanks to their religious beliefs. When the trade happened, one of Ward's first remarks was that he had another person with which to attend his bible study and pre-game chapel.

Van Gundy, too, was proud of how Ward had handled the Jackson trade. Maybe Ward's pride was wounded, but he would not let that stop him from playing hard. In fact, for one day, Ward had played with more reckless abandon than he had all season.

■ ■ ■

After the Sonics practiced at the Celtics' practice facility in Waltham, Massachusetts, several members of the New York media greeted Ewing.

The Sonics would face the Celtics that night, then play the Knicks the next. Ewing sat on a chair with ice bags wrapped around his knees and wrist – a familiar sight for New York reporters. Without being asked, he reflected about his early years with the Knicks when he was in his prime and did not have teammates talented enough to win a title. The usually guarded Ewing had never addressed this issue. At the time, he had allowed the media to opine about his weak supporting cast.

"There are some things I wish the Knicks organization could have done to make the team better when I was young than when I was older and hopefully we could have gotten a ring," Ewing said, adding that he had approached his agent, David Fal, early in his career about trying to swing a deal for another one of his clients, such as Jordan. "It never happened," Ewing said. "That's life."

Ewing never could have admitted such things when he was still with the Knicks.

The fans would have accused him of blaming others for not winning a ring.

CHAPTER 15

The Homecoming: Part II

February 26

Walt Frazier returned to New York as a Cleveland Cavalier. Pitcher Tom Seaver returned to New York as a Cincinnati Red. Reggie Jackson came back as a California Angel, Eddie Giacomin as a Detroit Red Wing, Mark Messier as a Vancouver Canuck and Pat Riley as coach of the Heat. Ewing's return had the potential to zoom to the top of the list of emotional New York homecomings. As sentimentality swam over the Purchase facility after the final practice before the game, Jackson revealed that he had spoken to Ewing two nights earlier. Jackson and Ewing had remained close friends. It was a cruel irony that Jackson's return to the Knicks coincided with their first season without Ewing.

"I'm going to dunk on you," Jackson told Ewing over the phone.

"I'll be waiting for you at the basket," Ewing responded.

With Ewing's Garden return imminent, stories abounded in the newspapers about how New York had not seen the true Patrick, that he put on a mask for 15 years to shield his outgoing personality. Jackson says he even bought into the hype of Ewing being a stone-cold character.

"I remember being afraid of him because everybody thought he was just some angry man who didn't know how to talk," Jackson said. "And then when I got to know him, it was like, 'Wow, he's nothing like this. It would be an embarrassment to the city if they don't give him his just due."

The contrasts of Ewing were rehashed in the newspapers—his infamous autograph snub of terminally-ill children at a Thanksgiving Day party balanced by his late-night visits to children at hospitals and his one request: "Don't tell the media about it."

Sonics general manager Wally Walker had wondered since the trade where Ewing got his bad reputation. Even during a trying season in which the coach who recruited him got fired four weeks into the season, Ewing never once complained to management or new coach Nate McMillan, who reduced his playing time.

Mike Saunders, the trainer who had handled Ewing's injuries for all 15 years, told *Newsday* of meeting Ewing for the first time when the center played for Georgetown. The Hoyas were playing a matinee against St. John's at the Garden, and Saunders was there early preparing for the Knicks' game that night. After the game, Ewing was hanging out in the locker room lounge, and Saunders offered him orange juice and a snack. Ewing and Saunders didn't see each other again until after the Knicks drafted him, but Ewing's first words when they were reintroduced were, "I remember you, Mike. You tried to recruit me with that orange juice."

The week after he got head-butted by Camby, Van Gundy spoke to Ewing on the phone.

"Why can't you stay off the floor during fights," Ewing said.

Van Gundy responded, "How about you get down the floor a little quicker before the shots gets taken while you're still at the top of the key."

"Why don't you just shave your head since you're already bald," Ewing rang back.

The relationship between the two wasn't always as fluffy, despite the widely held perception that they got along famously. Ewing had made plenty of unannounced, unreported trips to Van Gundy's office to bargain for more playing time and shots.

"Everyone painted us as bosom buddies, but there were disagreements," Van Gundy said.

Van Gundy was not going to let his homecoming pass without defending Ewing's lack of an NBA championship.

"I've long believed you can't define players by whether they won or didn't win a championship," Van Gundy said. "To me, he was a championship player because he did everything in his power to help the Knicks win a championship. Nobody will be able to convince me that those players who played with Jordan are more of a champion because they played with greatness more than someone like Patrick.

"In Ewing's prime, unfortunately, he ran into Jordan in his prime and Olajuwon in his prime and he ran into an injury the other time he had a chance. Through no fault of his own, we didn't win, but I don't think that diminished what he did here at all. That's what bothers me so much about the media. Doesn't come up big in big spots? That's a joke."

Camby was ready for his second battle against Ewing. Having taken Round One in Seattle and been regularly called by Van Gundy the team's "most consistent and best player," he felt more secure talking about the match-up this time.

As a teenager in Hartford, Camby wore Ewing's brand of orange and blue sneakers that pictured the city's skyline on the back and the number 33.

"I remember those days walking around with those sneakers," Camby said.

"What happened to them?" Kernan of *The Post* asked.

"I outgrew them," Camby said.

■ ■ ■

Ewing's father, Carl, still living in Cambridge, Massachusetts, near where Patrick attended high school, fainted from heat exhaustion after the Sonics-Celtics game. He had been waiting in the hot, steamy bowels of the FleetCenter for his son to come out of the locker room, wanting to wish him luck one more time before he went to New York.

Ewing didn't see his father when he came out and thought nothing of it. He casually boarded the bus when a Sonics official came rushing on. "Your father fainted, Patrick," the official told him. When the ambulance came, Ewing told Wally Walker, "I'm going to stay here with Pop."

"Stay as long as you need to," Walker said.

As the Sonics' bus pulled out of the FleetCenter, Ewing stepped into the back of the ambulance with his father, bound for the hospital.

Ewing despised flying commercial airlines because of the lack of leg room, but if he was going to face the Knicks at the Garden, he'd have no choice. The Sonics left for their short charter flight to New York, unsure when they'd see Ewing again.

Ewing watched over his father at the hospital all night and got little sleep. With his father in stable condition, he took a morning flight to New York and arrived at the team's hotel in Manhattan at one p.m., missing the morning shootaround at the Garden. He visited his house in New Jersey to see his kids and drove to the Garden, just as he had on so many other nights.

Most Knicks' players parked their cars at the bottom of a winding ramp, then had to walk up the ramp to get to the locker room. As the Knicks' franchise player, Ewing had the privilege of pulling his car up to the top of the ramp, saving his bad knees from the rigors of the climb. He was not going to change that ritual just because he had changed teams. Ewing pulled up to the Garden ramp in his white Mercedes CL-600 at 5:54 p.m. and handed the keys to an attendant. He got out of his car beaming, wearing a gray button-down shirt and gray slacks, and slapped hands with two Garden security guards.

In the locker room, Ewing sat by his cubicle dressed in his green and red Sonics uniform and rust-colored warmup top. About 25 reporters moved toward him in the small room.

"Why are there so many cameras here today?" Ewing asked, grinning. "I feel like the president. I don't talk before games, man. You know that ain't ever going to change."

Minutes later, he walked toward the Knicks' side of the hallway. Ewing and a handful of his former teammates, including Sprewell, Houston and Jackson, sat down in the Rangers' locker room and reminisced. Van Gundy joined in, too. When it was time to go out for pre-game warmups, Ewing stood last in line in the tunnel behind his Seattle teammates. As his frame came into view, the fans jumped out of their seats and a chilling roar went up through the Garden, which was only half full 20 minutes before tipoff. Ewing turned left, instead of right as he had for years, and headed for the visitors' basket. The fans cheered. Ewing drove for a layup and the Garden exploded as if a key basket had been made in a playoff game.

Ewing smiled broadly when he spotted Star Jones sitting under the basket wearing her jeweled Ewing jersey. He went over and gave her a kiss. John Thompson, his college coach, was broadcasting the game for TNT. Thompson clapped for Ewing during pre-game warmups. A fan held high a sign that read, "33 Thanks For 15."

Before lining up with his own teammates for the National Anthem, Ewing hugged Sprewell, Thomas and Houston. "We love you, Patrick," a fan screamed during the anthem, and the crowd cheered. "You're the man, Patrick," another fan yelled.

After the anthem, Ewing stood in front of the Sonics' bench as the lights dimmed. Knicks P.A. announcer Mike Walczeski boomed, "We're proud to have an all-time great with us tonight. We welcome back our No. 33, Patrick Ewing." The music to Natalie Merchant's "Thank You" beat out of the sound system as a one-minute video lit up the scoreboard. The opening scene showed a younger, thinner, less-gray David Stern at the podium at the 1985 Draft announcing, "The New York Knicks with the first pick select Patrick Ewing."

Fifteen years were encapsulated in one minute, from Ewing dunking in a rebound against Indiana that sent the Knicks to the '94 Finals to his late basket against Miami the prior spring that clinched Game 7. The last snippet was of Ewing speaking gently to a five-year-old girl during a school visit. The scoreboard then flashed, "Welcome home, Patrick."

When the video ended, the fans who had already been on their feet cheering roared louder. Ewing looked up into the crowd and raised both arms. He wore a slight grin. His face was glistening with sweat and his eyes were moist as he fought back tears. A wave of noise cascaded down to the court. Ewing had told reporters he hoped he wouldn't cry, but now it looked as if he would.

Ewing rocked from foot to foot as he looked up into the crowd and waved his right hand. The fans chanted, "Pat-rick Ew-ing." All of the Knicks and Sonics players were clapping, including the coaching staffs. Everyone except Van Gundy. Van Gundy stayed seated, looking down, a blank expression on his face. He had been openly cheering Ewing for years. He didn't have to start now.

Ewing successfully held back the tears. Hopping up and down, he looked like he was starting to feel a little embarrassed by the length of the ovation. Maybe that's what the P.A. announcer Mike Walcezski was thinking when he interrupted the ovation to say, "Now let's meet the starting lineup." The standing ovation had lasted nearly three minutes.

Walcezski announced Ewing first instead of last. The crowd cheered louder than it had before for another 40 seconds. The outpouring of emotion was overwhelming. Who knows how long the cheering would have lasted had Walczeski not decided to get on with the show again and introduce Seattle guard Shammond Williams.

Checketts cheered Ewing from his luxury box in the Garden sky. He felt the fans weren't cheering him because they wanted him back as a Knick. They were cheering him for his 15 years. When the ovation ended, Ewing was an opponent at the Garden for the first time since he played center for Georgetown against St. John's in the 1985 Big East semifinals. The Knicks had played 55 games without him and had won 32 of them, but as Ewing walked onto the court for the opening tap, the divorce seemed absolutely final.

Ewing and Jackson were the first to take the floor. They met inside the mid-court circle and hugged, whispering in each other's ears. McMillan was going to call the first play away from Ewing, figuring the pressure would be too great and Ewing might still be feeling emotional. After the ovation, the Sonics coach scratched the play he had drawn up and drew a new one for Ewing. On the Sonics' first possession, Ewing got the ball on the low left post. Camby, smirking, guarded him. Reaching into a time machine to steal a move from his past, Ewing spun past Camby along the left baseline and ducked in for a layup. The Garden crowd howled, but that was the last time they'd loudly cheer one of his baskets. He was a Sonic now.

Minutes later, Ewing worked a high pick and roll with Payton and put in another layup. In his most spectacular moment, Ewing violently jammed in the rebound of a missed shot by Baker. The fans gasped. Some applauded. Ewing tipped in his own miss with seven minutes remaining in the first quarter. He had come into the night averaging nine points-per-game, but he had scored eight of his team's first 14 points in the first five minutes.

If this were a storybook, the night would've ended there. But age and cold reality grasped the rest of the evening. Camby got rolling and Ewing, perhaps feeling the fatigue of a long night in the hospital, appeared winded. At times, he did not join the offensive set because he was walking down the court while the Sonics pushed the ball up. The Sonics clearly were a better team when Ewing was not on the floor. In the first half, the Knicks outscored Seattle by 18 points when Ewing was in the game. Seattle outscored the Knicks by 11 during the nine minutes Ewing sat on the bench.

During a timeout in the third quarter, Ewing sat on the edge of the press table as rivulets of sweat dripped near the writers' computers. A mosquito buzzed in Ewing's sweaty hair, but he was unaware. A couple of writers along press row saw the bug feeding off Ewing's perspiring head but didn't have the guts to shoo the bug away or let Ewing know about it. The mosquito remained on Ewing's head his next two trips down the court. Symbolic, perhaps.

During another timeout, fans behind the bench kept yelling, "Patrick, Patrick, Patrick." Ewing turned around and a fan yelled, "Thank you, Patrick." Ewing nodded his head and winked.

Ewing was scoreless in the second half until he hit a meaningless jumper with 12 seconds remaining. He was again looking like a declining 38-year-old center with mosquitoes buzzing around his old bones. Leaping past Ewing as he had done in Seattle, Camby finished with 21 points, 17 rebounds and five blocks as the Knicks prevailed, 101-92. Ewing had 12 points and five rebounds.

As the final 12 seconds ticked down, deafening chants of "Pa-trick Ew-ing" echoed in the half-empty arena. Van Gundy later said the pre-game ovation had not touched him as much as the one at the end. The final, booming serenade for Ewing made the night for Van Gundy.

"The spontaneity of the crowd chanting his name [at the end] was about the best thing I have seen during my time at the Garden," Van Gundy said. "Other than getting to the two Finals, that's the best memory I am going to have about being here."

Ewing did not have a good game, except for the first five minutes, but he couldn't remember feeling any happier after a regular-season defeat.

"I thought it was great what the fans did," Ewing said. "Many times we had a love-hate relationship. But I think they appreciated what I brought to the table every night. They did a great job showing their appreciation to me. I was like, damn, all right, let's get the game started before the tears come out."

Ewing was smiling widely when Van Gundy saw him in the hallway later. Van Gundy knew at that moment how much the ovation had meant to him. But for Camby, this game had removed any doubt that the Knicks had made the right move by going with him as their center.

"The emotion of the night was about Patrick returning," Camby said. "But the game was about us. I was ready for this tonight. Oh, man, I was ready for this one."

CHAPTER 16

A Childs' Revenge

March 1

Layden's luck had run as dry as scorched earth. Not only had he failed to outbid the Sixers for Mutombo, but just a week after the Knicks landed Jackson, the point guard they craved more became available. Rod Strickland, whom the Knicks attempted to acquire from the Wizards for more than a year, had his contract bought out by Washington. Strickland was a free agent, eligible to sign with any club.

Layden called Strickland's agent, David Falk, to see if Stickland had any interest in coming to New York. The Knicks still had their $2.25 million salary-cap exception available. Falk said Strickland didn't want to reunite with Jackson. The two had had their fills of point-guard controversies in the late 1980's, when they awkwardly shared the Knicks' job. Strickland got traded from the Knicks during his second season in New York.

■ ■ ■

After a routine victory over the Celtics, the Knicks were visited in the locker room by Giants quarterback Kerry Collins, who had just led his team to the Super Bowl.

"You had a great run this year," Camby told Collins. Camby was having a great run, too. He scored 27, his most as a Knick, and added 17 rebounds and three blocked shots against the Celtics.

The victory moved Van Gundy into third place among Knicks coaches in wins with 224, ahead of Riley. Van Gundy saw no significance in the achievement, having needed 48 more games to pass Riley, whom he still called the greatest basketball coach who ever lived. Van Gundy's .594 winning percentage, too, paled in comparison to Riley's .680 clip. Holzman remained first on the all-time list with 613. Van Gundy knew he wasn't going to last long enough in New York to come close to matching Holzman's mark. In fact, Van Gundy, always a worrier, was certain he wouldn't be around to see his current contract expire after the 2002-03 season.

March 2

Clutching a heating pad, Camby laid on the trainer's table in the back of the visitors' locker room at Chicago's United Center. Back spasms had immobilized him just as he was on the best roll of his career. In the last six games, Camby had been everything a team wants in a dominant center, hogging rebounds, blocking shots and even developing a rainbow jump shot that had disappeared from his repertoire since he got traded from Toronto before the 1999 lockout. Camby was averaging 16.6 points and 16.2 rebounds the past six games, but now he was in pain. Again.

Thirty minutes before tipoff, Camby decided he couldn't play, making the thirteenth time, including five games due to the suspension, he was not in the lineup. For all of Ewing's lack of production, he had missed just one game for Seattle.

Again, the Knicks turned into a low-energy team without Camby. Facing the worst team in the league, the Knicks saw their three-game winning streak crash. At the final buzzer, white streamers poured onto the court to hail an extremely rare Bulls' win, 81-72.

"This game kind of tells you what the Knicks have been all year," Sprewell said. "We've just been up and down."

Having lost six straight road games, the Knicks flew to Toronto for a nationally-televised Sunday matinee, their first meeting against an old friend. Not Oakley. Childs.

March 3-4

During the 1997-98 season, Van Gundy had promoted Ward to starting point guard, replacing Childs. At the time, Van Gundy's spin was that Childs "volunteered" to come off the bench. Childs campaigning to be a backup seemed odd considering his large ego and seemed stranger when Childs later said he wanted more playing time. Nobody believed the story, although Childs went along with it.

After getting traded to the Raptors, Childs circled March 4 on his calendar. He wasn't merely anxious. He was jumping out of his skin in anticipation of battling his old teammates. He had even dreamt about the game. Childs didn't discuss his feelings about being a Knick immediately after the trade. But the day before the game, he couldn't stay silent any longer.

"I won't sleep, I won't eat, I might even eat a bucket of onions before the game and breathe on those guys and make their eyes water," Childs said. "I just want to be real nasty. It's more fun being a Raptor. It got to the point where I wasn't having any fun. I don't know if they saw that and that was the reason they pulled the trigger. When you wake up in the morning and you're going to practice for the game and you're not excited about it? I mean, I enjoy playing, but the excitement wasn't there with the way things were going, the playing time. I'm yelling at guys. That's not me."

A number of Knicks occasionally had problems with Van Gundy's slowball offense and his frequent negative remarks but knew that airing complaints to the press was career suicide. Both Houston and Longley had approached Van Gundy privately in January to say that his negativity was turning off the players. Now Childs was free to say what he wanted about Van Gundy.

Childs felt Van Gundy had stunted his creativity as a point guard. In Toronto, he could make a turnover without receiving the Van Gundy death glare. He played tightly for Van Gundy, as if his next turnover might lead to him being yanked.

While Childs had a burning desire to destroy the Knicks, Jackson seemed nonplused by the game. He wasn't angry at the Raptors. By signing him as a free agent last summer, the Raptors' ultimately gave him the opportunity to return to the team which he wished he had never left.

"What about the matchup with Chris Childs?" someone asked.

"Chris who?" Jackson deadpanned.

■ ■ ■

Childs darted through the lane, squeezed by Jackson and tossed in a lefthanded layup off the glass. Then he turned to the Knicks' bench, his chest puffed out, and smirked at his former teammates. He glowered at the Knicks again after making an 18-foot jump shot in the fourth quarter of the Raptors' 98-88 win.

Childs played magnificent defense against Jackson, bumping and grinding and leaving no space between the two. Jackson, who received a smattering of applause during the introductions, made the mistake of treating the game as if it was nothing special while Childs fought like it was the biggest game of his life. Late in the fourth quarter, Childs chest-bumped and high-fived with his teammates, giggling like a boy. The Air Canada Centre crowd was in full throttle, taking immense pleasure in their new point-guard's revenge.

While Childs was a buzzard all game, the Knicks played with the life of a mosquito-infested carcass. They rallied from 17 points down and cut their deficit to six in the final minute, but then faded to their seventh straight road loss. In the locker room, Sprewell again had a few choice words for his teammates. He talked about rediscovering the passion from earlier in the season and asked them to get on slacking teammates. Sprewell had hoped when they entered the room after the game, Houston or Johnson, the co-captains, would say something to the group, but again he was the one doing the talking.

In the shower, Sprewell expressed disappointment to Rice and Johnson that when the club made their big run at the end, there was little enthusiasm. When Sprewell is at his best, he is a vision of gyrations and scowls. Sprewell wished some of the guys would be that way, especially Houston.

Van Gundy wasn't sure what he was more livid about, Childs' showboating or that his team let him get away with it. The loss would have been a little more tolerable if one of the players had gotten in Childs' face and told him to pipe down. Even before the game, when Van Gundy and Childs passed each other in the hallway, Van Gundy wouldn't acknowledge his former point guard, not after the scathing remarks he read in the paper.

"We just don't have a passion about ourselves," Van Gundy said. "We're a sleepy type of group."

Childs finished with 12 points and three assists in 26 minutes. He settled down in the dressing room until someone asked him about possibly facing the Knicks in the first round of the playoffs, a distinct possibility. His face lit up.

"It would be like having Christmas all over again," he said. "It would be something to play them when it's all on the line."

March 5

Ewing sent the New York papers an open letter to the New York fans, thanking them for their ovation on February 27. The letter read:

> To the great fans of New York: I was truly overwhelmed by the heartfelt reception you gave me last Tuesday night at the Garden. It is definitely one of the highlights of my career. And I know it is an experience I will cherish for the rest of my life. I honestly didn't know what to expect when I returned to New York to play before you. But I do know that for the 15 years I proudly wore a New York Knicks uniform, I tried to give you everything I had every night. For sure, there were disappointments along the way but the love and appreciation which you shared with me Tuesday more than made up for them. Make no mistake. I miss the great fans of New York, but I know whenever I play I will always have a special place in my heart for you. Thanks, Patrick Ewing.

■ ■ ■

Van Gundy likes to call himself "old school." He doesn't like the new-school tradition of post-game prayers at midcourt, with players from both clubs huddling. He doesn't like fraternizing with opponents before a game. He doesn't want his players to get too friendly with the opponents because he believes it affects their competitive fire. When Van Gundy called Jordan "a con man" years ago, the reference was to Jordan's ability to make some of his opponents feel like they were his friends before he stomped on them.

So if none of his players were going to speak out against Childs' bratty behavior, the coach would defend his team's honor. Sprewell, for one, said after the game that he didn't blame Childs for his antics, and that he did the same thing against Golden State. That wasn't what Van Gundy wanted to hear.

"Every dog has his day," Van Gundy said after practice. "So the barking dog had his day yesterday. And he's talking and everybody's rushing to judgment, saying, 'Now look who's got the better deal.' You know what? I will be happy to put Mark on the floor."

Van Gundy felt it was important to stick up for Jackson, whose ego had to have been bruised by Childs outplaying him. Now Jackson was getting ready to face another one of his former teams. The Pacers were up next in a home-and-home, back-to-back set. Though he had faced the Pacers while with Toronto, this was the first time he'd do so as a Knick. He knew Reggie Miller would be sickened at the sight of him in a Knicks' jersey.

March 6-7

Anti-inflammatory medications had become a bad word in the NBA, especially since Mourning's illness. Of the many rumors regarding Mourning's kidney illness, the most alarming had the disease caused by his constant use of anti-inflammatories. After he was diagnosed, Mourning warned other players to watch their intake of pills, even though his doctors assured him the anti-inflammatory medicine did not cause the illness. Nevertheless, medical opinions stated excessive use of the pills dissolved the stomach lining.

Popping two anti-inflammatories a day was as natural to Johnson as a morning cup of coffee is to most people. He needed the pills—"meds," he called them—to lessen the distressing ache in the disk of his back. Otherwise he couldn't play. Lately, the back had felt good. Now Johnson's stomach was the problem. Nausea engulfed him on most days and he vomited frequently. Thinking the pills were causing his stomach to rebel, he had stopped taking them a week ago.

■ ■ ■

Miller didn't hit much Garden net all game, but his aim proved true at the end. With 1:58 remaining, as he took a seat on the Pacers' bench with the fans chanting "Reggie Sucks" and the Knicks on their way to a 97-83 victory, Miller reached into his mouth, removed his gum and fired it onto the court. Maybe he wasn't purposely aiming at referee Eddie Rush, but he connected off the back of Rush's head.

Rush thought a fan had clocked him. As he turned toward the Pacers' bench, the fans behind the bench chanted, "Reggie did it!" Thinking they were kidding, Rush ignored them.

Miller finished with 14 points. He figured he'd get the Knicks the next night at home.

Johnson sat out the second half. His back hurt like it hadn't all season. He wasn't surprised, not after going off the pills. Before the game,

Longley was placed on the injured list. He, too, had stopped taking anti-inflammatories at the same time Johnson had. Longley was beset by a chronic injured left ankle because of a deformity in his bone structure. He had suffered from diarrhea for weeks and blamed the pills. Longley knew he couldn't play without the pills, but it wasn't worth the suffering if Van Gundy wasn't going to play him.

The next evening, Miller arrived at Conseco Field House at five p.m. for the rematch. He was shooting jumpers when a Pacers official came up to him and said, "The league called and you're out." Miller had been suspended for one game and fined $10,000 for his gum-hurling. Furious, Miller punted a ball 40 rows into the stands.

MSG Network had caught the gum-throwing incident and provided the league with the tape. Pacers' coach Isiah Thomas was ticked at the league for needing all day to determine the punishment. The delay in announcing Miller's suspension placed the Pacers in a sticky situation. They didn't have time to prepare for Miller's absence.

Over in the Knicks' locker room, wisecracks were tossed around like Miller's Trident.

"I guess he didn't like the gum anymore," Rice said.

Jackson spoke to his old buddy in the afternoon before Miller knew the MSG Network footage had caught him red-handed.

"He's like O.J.," Jackson said. "He said he didn't do it."

■ ■ ■

Sprewell, like Iverson and Van Gundy, regarded the Indiana fans as racially insensitive. Sprewell had heard a stream of "choke" taunts from fans in almost every arena, but in Indiana it grated on his nerves more because of the tone.

The Pacers' crowd was in rare form on this night. Though the fans didn't call him a monkey, they called Sprewell and his teammates just about every other profanity. Sprewell had a busy night. In the third quarter, he shouted at Sam Perkins for setting illegal picks. When Jermaine O'Neal interceded, Sprewell went ballistic and tried to get at Indiana's young center. The officials restrained him.

The game ended with Sprewell hitting the game-winning basket and going on a wild victory dash. He tore down the left sideline like an Olympic sprinter, staring down almost every customer in the front row and spitting out words, his face twisted in a menacing scowl.

"That was my time to give it back to them," Sprewell said. "I'm not going to let them say certain things without responding."

Johnson missed his first full game because of back pain and Van Gundy predicted his starting power forward could miss several more.

March 9-10
Instead of using the Nets as a launch pad to their showdown against the Heat at the Garden, the Knicks got humiliated at The Meadowlands. Nets rookie forward Kenyon Martin tore through the Knicks' defense, which offered no resistance. The brilliant Stephon Marbury sprinted out on fastbreaks and the Knicks were turtle-slow in retreat. The Knicks didn't bang a body all night.

Adding to the horror was a scene in the final seconds that cut to the core of Van Gundy's concerns about his club. Marbury began shouting profanities at Ward as the two players walked off the court. "Fucking bitch," Marbury screamed. Only two years ago, he had said the Knicks would never win a championship with Ward and Childs as their point guards. The dig struck of envy. The Brooklyn-born Marbury wanted to be a Knick and had revealed his dream to Sprewell during the All-Star Game when they shared the same locker room.

Van Gundy was not surprised that the devoutly religious Ward took the abuse without saying anything back. But he was disgusted that one of Ward's teammates let Marbury get away with it.

Afterward, when asked the precise words Marbury used, Ward said, "I don't speak that language. It's not the language of Christians. Quack, quack, quack, it rolls off my back."

At practice the following day, Van Gundy could no longer hide his feelings of disgust about his team's cowardly reaction to Marbury five days after letting Childs embarrass them with his taunts on NBC.

"You let Childs off the hook after he taunts you and that's okay," Van Gundy said. "Another guy goes at your point guard and you don't have anybody even think about saying something. Where's the team pride? Seriously, where's the pride? There should've been an altercation right there. I'm not talking fight, but goddarn."

Van Gundy had thrown his dart and hit a bullseye. More than one veteran regarded the team as a fractured group with too many cliques and nobody standing up for anyone else. If anyone had the right to question a team's lack of toughness in these situations, it was Van

Gundy. Despite his diminutive frame, Van Gundy had shown on two famous occasions that he was willing to put his body on the line to save his players.

Reminded that his supposedly warrior-like team of four years ago did not do anything when Jordan screamed profanities at him, Van Gundy retorted, "If you don't want to stand up for your coach and mess with God, that's fine. But come on now. How many teams are going to come in, talk shit about us before the game, talk shit about us during the game, talk shit about us after the game and we say it's okay? No team pride."

One player privately agreed, saying, "We've had a fractured locker room all season. We haven't become a team yet. We haven't found an identity. Too many guys going in too many different directions."

■ ■ ■

Johnson, who had missed two straight games, did not practice. He went to a room across from the Purchase gym, picked up a black marker and signed hundreds of miniature basketballs for Ayala Donchin, the community relations director. The autographed balls were being given to fans who purchased a commemorative Madison Square Garden brick for a children's charity.

As he signed ball after ball, Johnson, who rarely gives interviews, admitted his season was in jeopardy. He had started acupuncture and tried yoga.

"I'm looking for something just to relieve some pain," he said. "I've been playing eight years with this. The meds were getting me over the hump, taking the edge off some pain. It didn't completely take the pain away. Now maybe I have to adjust to playing with whatever amount of pain."

Johnson had taken blood tests and his liver readings were normal. But he had no idea when he'd be back onto the court. The more Johnson spoke, the more it seemed evident he was worried about his career.

■ ■ ■

That morning, Sprewell spoke on the phone to an NBA security official about taunting the fans in Indiana. At first, when he learned that the NBA wanted to talk to him, he thought he was in trouble again. Not so. The league was investigating the Indiana fans' behavior.

"They're the worst fans in the league," Sprewell told the NBA security man. "But you already know that."

March 11

The fans at the Garden gasped, then booed. Miami's A.C. Green swished an 18-foot jump shot from the right wing, launching Miami into a 21-point lead with 23.8 seconds left in the first quarter. At that bleakest of moments, nobody figured the game would come down to a desperation three-point heave by Hardaway at the buzzer that missed the net, giving the Knicks the win. But when the Knicks and Heat play, it's safe to miss the first 59 minutes and still catch the drama.

Thomas was the Knicks' hero. The rumblings were getting louder that Thomas deserved to remain the Knicks' starting power forward the rest of the season, no matter what happened to Johnson. Before the game, Van Gundy admitted that Johnson and Longley had career decisions to make.

Thomas was making Van Gundy's decision easy. With five minutes left, he collided in mid-air with Anthony Mason. Thomas came down grimacing, clutching his groin, then staggered to the bench. It was fitting. Thomas had played a ballsy game, finishing with 16 points and 14 rebounds.

This was a sweet victory for the Knicks, who were battling Miami for the third seed in the East. Finishing the regular season in the No. 3 spot was important as that club would avoid the dominant Sixers until the Eastern Conference Finals. Van Gundy thought his club, for the first time in weeks, had shown heart.

March 13-14

On his 32nd birthday, Johnson flew to Charlotte to get a second opinion on his back, just as Van Gundy said he expected Johnson to return as a starter if and when he was ready. Johnson's game had slipped badly, both offensively and defensively, but as a co-captain, he was an influential leader. The problem was, his on-court struggles rendered him quieter than usual. When he wasn't playing because of back pain, Johnson found it difficult to put on a happy, gung-ho face and inspire others.

In Johnson's absence, Van Gundy hoped Sprewell and Camby would continue to emerge as leaders. He spoke privately with Camby about the responsibility of picking up the other guys now that he had become their most consistent performer. Van Gundy had all but given up hope that Houston would suddenly change his tranquil personality and meta-morphasize into a vibrant force in the locker room.

This was a difficult time for Houston, whose play had slipped since the All-Star break. His lack of energy was obvious in some games and his jump shot had dulled. He thought he could be more vocal, but he wasn't about to do so now with his own game in disarray.

"If the guys know I'm going to be there on the court, they know they're going to get a pass from me," Houston said. "I'd rather do that than scream at somebody. That's just my personality. But maybe I could raise it and do both. Sometimes a fault of mine is not showing emotion. That's how I've always been."

The Knicks suited up nine players against the Cavaliers at the Garden. Sprewell was home sick with an upper respiratory infection, Johnson was in Charlotte and Spencer, who had been taken off the injured list when Longley was put on it, was sick, too. That gave Postell a chance to play meaningful minutes for the first time since November. He played a career-high 18 minutes and scored a career-high seven points in a 98-79 victory.

The former St. John's star had become a Garden favorite. He always got a nice ovation when he entered games in the final minutes of blowouts. The Garden fans had a fascination with the end of Van Gundy's bench, probably because he gave the fans so little opportunity to see his lesser-used players.

March 14-15

Johnson returned to practice as the bearer of good news. The anti-inflammatory drugs had not damaged his stomach lining and he could go back on them without permanent risk. He had no bleeding ulcers.

A Johnson interview wouldn't be complete if there wasn't a tense, angry moment. When a writer brought up the speculation about his retirement, Johnson said, "Speculation? Whose speculation?" When the writer said Van Gundy had mentioned it, Johnson abruptly ended the interview and walked away in a huff. Welcome back, Larry.

■ ■ ■

Childs was coming back to town for his first game at the Garden in a Raptors' uniform. As Isola of *The News* wrote, "There will be no video tribute."

Jackson realized this was his time to silence those who had questioned the trade. Childs had shown him up on national television and Jackson had quietly accepted his medicine that afternoon. But since then, Jackson had become miffed at the general sentiment that the trade wasn't working out. After Jackson helped beat the Pacers, he took a stab at his new rival, saying, "I'm not going to be Chris Childs and be a jerk because I won a basketball game."

It was not in Jackson's nature to keep quiet. He was the most candid player on the Pacers. Since moving to New York, he had become too politically correct, on and off the court. Jackson and Miller were the leaders of the Pacers' locker room, but Jackson had stepped back since he got to the Knicks. He knew some of the Knicks' veterans still viewed him as a Pacer.

"I'm sure deep down Chris has to know if he was the GM, he'd have pulled the trigger, too," said Jackson, feeding the hungry notebooks of the writers. "Film doesn't lie. I don't have time to concern myself with Chris Childs."

The stage was set for Jackson vs. Childs: The Rematch.

Childs, never one to back down from controversy, said before the game he wished Jackson had the guts to say such things to his face. "Be a man about it if you got something to say," Childs said. As a peace offering, Childs walked over to the Knicks' locker room carrying a box of Cuban cigars, legal in Canada but contraband at the Garden. The high-quality cigars were for the new dad, Brunson, whose wife had given birth to a baby boy the day before, and a birthday present for Johnson.

"I don't think I have the personality to be a villain," Childs said.

Uh, wrong. With 5:48 left in the first quarter, Childs entered the game and was loudly booed and taunted. That was expected. The surprise was that the booing never stopped. Every time Childs touched the ball, the fans vilified him. No one could remember a former Knick getting such a hostile reception.

Childs could have worn the hostile reaction as a badge of honor had his stay with the Knicks been more successful. But the fans never believed Childs had fulfilled the expectations he carried when he signed a six-year, $24 million contract. The point-guard position had been viewed as the Knicks' weak spot for years, and he had failed to be the solution. For Childs to have the audacity to taunt his former team after one good game rankled the fans.

In the third quarter, Jackson got the ball in the low post. Jackson dribbled and backed his way closer to the basket, bumping and grinding against an overpowered Childs, who couldn't stand his ground. Jackson then unleashed a spectacular behind-the-back pass to an open Thomas, who laid it in. The Garden exploded in noise. Half of the fans rose from their seats and applauded. On the night Childs was booed out to Broadway, Jackson officially was welcomed home as a Knick.

Childs finished with no taunts, no staredowns, no victory and no points as the Knicks slaughtered Toronto, 88-72. The Knicks ended a streak of six straight regular-season losses to the Raptors, who were a strong candidate to be their first-round opponent.

The Knicks players hadn't expected Childs to be cheered, but they were surprised by the belligerent reaction he received.

"I guess you can't talk bad about the Knicks," Sprewell said.

"I guess they all watched how he acted in Toronto on NBC," Camby chimed in.

To Jackson, his glorious behind-the-back dish to Thomas was a defining moment. The pass showed the beginnings of attaining a chemistry with his new teammates. Thomas had cut toward the basket when he saw Jackson back Childs down to the basket. Thomas' own defender took a step toward Jackson, ready to double-team him.

"I've been here three weeks. Kurt finally understood," Jackson said. "He finally got it down and ducked in."

Said Thomas: "We've known Jackson can make that pass. He's been making it against us for a good number of years. That was the first time he hit it with one of us." Meanwhile, Childs was bewildered by the nightlong boos. "Maybe I looked like Reggie Miller to them," he said.

CHAPTER 17

West Coast Blues

March 17

The Knicks looked bored in blowing out the Bulls. They led by 28 points after 18 minutes and won, 101-80, but Van Gundy wasn't happy.

"We played great from the six-minute mark in the first quarter to the four-minute mark of the second quarter," Van Gundy said. "Those 14 minutes were great. Then we got careless like most teams get with leads."

Houston's scoring slump had become alarming. Since the All-Star break, he had not been the same player. His output in the second half of games had dropped. Van Gundy and Houston did not see eye-to-eye on the reason for the drop-off and met to talk things over. Houston didn't think he was getting enough shots or plays run for him. He was not going to force shots that didn't present themselves in the normal flow of the offense.

"A lot of it is on me, a lot of it isn't," Houston said.

Believing Houston's energy level was too low, Van Gundy contended Houston controlled his own destiny. He wanted him to play more forcefully to get open and create his own space.

"I worry about him when he starts thinking things are out of his control," Van Gundy said. "This is all in his control. We need him. Badly."

Houston was shooting just 41.8 percent from the field and 27.1 percent from the three-point line since the break. His scoring average was 16.2 since the break compared to 20.3 before the break.

"The only thing that's changed is he's become less efficient," Van Gundy stated. "He may be looking toward me not calling him plays, but he's got a great passing point guard in Mark Jackson who's always looking for him."

March 20

With Cleveland on tap, the Knicks' braintrust finally decided to rest Rice temporarily. When the Knicks were in Toronto, Rice had visited the electric-shock therapy clinic for another series of treatments on his foot. This time, the procedure aggravated the pain.

Rice missed the blowout victory over Chicago with a stomach virus. Now the Knicks, with a light schedule ahead, wanted to see if at least a week off would make a difference. Normally, plantar fasciaitis requires two months of rest.

Rice hadn't practiced with the team since the All-Star break and rode an exercise cycle to stay in shape. "If you can't practice, you can't get rhythm or confidence," Van Gundy said.

Rice's season had turned into a cruel irony. Checketts and Layden had traded the injury-beleaguered Ewing partly to become more durable as a team. While Ewing had remained healthy, if unproductive, in Seattle, Rice had taken over the Big Fella's role as the aging superstar whose status often was a game-time decision.

"Well, at least the foot is still attached," Rice said, clinging to the positive.

■ ■ ■

Nobody would have blamed Van Gundy had he taken a bow after the Knicks' 110-75 victory over the Cavaliers. The New York papers had written a lot about Van Gundy's challenge to Houston. Even if Van Gundy had hoped he would motivate Houston out of his funk, he could never have expected the kind of night Houston had in Cleveland's Gund Arena.

His textbook jump shot looked truer than it had all season, featuring the perfect lift that Kalinsky had admired. He fired them up without hesitancy, no matter how closely he was guarded, as if his slump had never existed. In the third quarter, Houston cut a swath through the paint, soared and threw down a resounding right-handed dunk over the outstretched arms of seven-foot center Chris Mihm. After the dunk, he continued to kill the Cavs from the perimeter and finished with a career-high 39 points.

As he got dressed, Houston had a series of red scratches on his chest from the pawing of helpless Cleveland defenders.

"It was unbelievable," Jackson said. "It wasn't fair for a moment."

The players were perfectly giddy and felt great for the well-liked Houston. Trainer Saunders seized the moment. Houston was surrounded by writers waiting for him to get dressed. The modest Houston likes to be fully clothed for post-game interviews. Saunders burst through the milling crowd and thrust a white cardboard cake box in front of the star of the evening. Saunders held the white cakebox as Houston warily opened it up, revealing only Saunders' middle finger sticking through a hole in the bottom.

A mighty burden had been lifted off Houston's shoulders and a touch of his old bravado resurfaced.

"I heard Muggsy [Bogues] say 'I didn't know he could dunk,'" Houston said. "Sometimes you do it just to let guys know you could do it."

March 21-24

When Harrington found out that he had been traded to the Knicks, he figured he would no longer be a starter. But he never imagined Van Gundy's rotation would be so tight that there would be games he wouldn't play in at all.

Before Johnson's back gave out, Harrington endured a stretch of seven of eight games in late February and early March in which "DNP—did not play—was next to his name in the boxscore. Van Gundy religiously stuck to an eight-man rotation, and Harrington was ninth.

A shy guy who went out about his business with quiet professionalism, Harrington was the last person to create a stir in the press. He knew Van Gundy took exception to players whining about playing time.

Johnson's absence created a role for Harrington, who found his niche with his nifty, left-handed jump hook shot in the low post and with his overall tenacious approach. The Knicks expected Johnson to come back for the West Coast trip next week against Golden State. In the seven games Johnson missed, Harrington shot 58 percent from the field and averaged eight points in 21 minutes.

When Van Gundy was asked if he would expand his eight-man rotation to keep the productive Harrington in the flow, he smiled weakly and said he'd be more inclined to contract the rotation to six or seven rather than expanding it to nine or 10.

"He's got his eight-man rotation and he likes to stick with that," Harrington said. "I'm not the coach. Ultimately, it's his decision. I just have to play well and show him what I can do."

But the fans and large segments of the media felt Harrington should be kept in the rotation and that Thomas should be installed permanently into the starting lineup. Unswayed, Van Gundy believed a couple of the writers on the beat had an agenda and unfairly picked on Johnson's shortcomings. He told them so.

■ ■ ■

With the Nets up next, Ward knew he'd be asked about Marbury. Maybe Van Gundy wanted Ward to say he was ready for payback after Marbury's unsportsmanlike display, but those words weren't coming from Ward's lips.

"If they have to vent those frustrations that way, they're frustrated in some other areas," Ward said. "The best man always comes out on top and that's the person who goes about his business quietly and doesn't taunt other people. I don't have a problem listening to people like that because I'm Christian and in the Bible Jesus got taunted all the time during his death and didn't say a word. He went about his business."

Ward did not subscribe to Van Gundy's belief that the team lacked pride. He had learned from an incident in Miami in the second round of the 1996 playoffs. P.J. Brown had flipped Ward while boxing out for a rebound after a free throw, touching off a brawl in which key players such as Ewing were suspended. The Knicks lost control of the series, prematurely ending a season in which they appeared ready to dethrone Jordan's Bulls.

"Pride comes before every fall, and that's what's wrong with a lot of men today," Ward said. "People always want to fight back. That's the natural instinct for a male. The one thing about me is when confrontations come, I'm walking away."

As it happened, the Knicks shied away from all confrontations and competition against the Nets. In their last game before a pivotal five-game West Coast trip, they lost for the second straight time to the Nets, one of the worst teams in the NBA. This time, Marbury let his playing do the talking. His 22 points and seven assists buried the Knicks. At the final buzzer, he hugged Ward. It was Marbury's first win at the Garden since Lincoln captured the city's high school championship.

"We don't have the maturity to handle winning right now," Van Gundy said glumly.

March 24

A ranting Van Gundy repeated three dates over and over: the dates of their three most humiliating losses of the season, to Chicago and twice to the injury-riddled Nets.

"March 2, March 9, March 23," Van Gundy said. "There's a reality about those games for our team. Our approach obviously doesn't work. How we go about our business does not work. What are we, 41-27? You could say it's working. But March 2, March 9 and March 23 will tell you that our approach as a group does not work."

The Knicks left for the West Coast staring at the dates March 26 through April 1, a trip that would prove Van Gundy either right or wrong. Golden State, Sacramento, Vancouver, Portland and the Lakers lied ahead.

■ ■ ■

Sprewell did not expect his second visit to the new arena in Oakland to be as theatrical as his first on November 20, 1999, when he was fined $10,000 for cursing out his hecklers. The madness had begun during pre-game warmups when a fan yelled, "Who are you going to sue next?"

"Shut the fuck up," Sprewell yelled back.

When the game began, three season-ticket holders sitting in the last three seats of the first row along the sideline were relentless. One of the fans, Marc Anthony Jones, screamed "Pootytang" at Sprewell virtually every time downcourt. Several times, Sprewell turned to the group and yelled profanities. The three hecklers seemed to be having a glorious time, but the NBA didn't think it was so much fun and fined Sprewell.

"I'll just laugh and smile at the fans now," Sprewell said the day before the Golden State game in Oakland. "The majority will really be on my back. Maybe it won't be as bad as last year. But I don't expect to be cheered. If that's the case, I'd be very, very surprised."

Van Gundy believed the fans' abuse of players was out of control and couldn't accept the concept that athletes were paid sufficiently to accept verbal taunts.

"The answer is always that you're paid a lot of money so you should have no pride and just take your flogging," Van Gundy said. "I guess if you were paid $4.50 an hour, you could go in there and take care of business. I think we've set this thing where they've paid their money for tickets, they can say whatever, which I think is wrong. Everybody thinks they're the first one to say, 'Hey Sprewell, you choked anybody lately?' These are professionals with money, too, the people in the front row. They must have misery in their jobs."

March 25

The Knicks held their morning shootaround at a childhood haunt of Van Gundy's, the University of San Francisco. Van Gundy was raised in the Bay Area, in Martinez, California, before moving to Rochester, New York as a sophomore in high school.

Bill Van Gundy, Jeff's father, coached at St. Mary's, which, like USF, was in the West Coast Athletic Conference. As a 10-year-old, Jeff would sit in the USF gym and watch games. "I was a little guy sitting up there in the bleachers fake scouting," Van Gundy said.

Checketts, who joined the Knicks for the trip, attended the shootaround wearing a black leather jacket with the Knicks' logo on the back. As MSG Network filmed the final stages of the shootaround, Checketts, never camera shy, bounded onto the court to have what appeared to be a pensive talk with Sprewell. A nice photo-op for the bosses back home.

One of USF's players, wearing his school warmups, watched the end of the Knicks' shootaround. As Van Gundy left the gym, he spotted the player.

"What's your name?" Van Gundy asked him.

"Andre Brewer."

"What year are you?"

"I'm a sophomore."

"How was your season?" Van Gundy asked.

"I had a pretty good year, 10 points—"

"No, I didn't mean your season," Van Gundy said loudly, so everybody within earshot could hear. "I meant the team's. See, I'm a coach. I care about the team concept, not individual performances. You should want to talk about how the team did."

Brewer smiled sheepishly.

■ ■ ■

The Golden State crowd's reception for Sprewell was decidedly warmer than it had been the last time. Many fans booed loudly, but a few thousand fans gave Sprewell a standing ovation. Several of them wore Sprewell jerseys.

The same three hecklers were sitting in the front row. Marc Anthony Jones wore a microphone for FOX TV, but even he didn't think Sprewell deserved to be fined for what happened last time.

"Absolutely not," Jones said. "It was fun."

Sprewell spat his venom solely at the Warriors this time. After the Knicks took a 20-point lead at half-time, Golden State's rookie forward Chris Porter scored eight unanswered points in the third quarter.

"You guys can't stop me," Porter said to Sprewell.

Sprewell, booed each time he got his hands on the ball, talked smack right back at Porter later in the quarter. He posted up Porter or drove past him on three straight possessions. Standing at the free throw line after Porter fouled him on a drive to the hole, Sprewell jabbered at Porter and Blaylock between each foul shot.

The Knicks blew a seven-point lead midway through the fourth quarter and the game went down to the wire. Antawn Jamison, who finished with 41 points, scored on a runner in the lane with 9.7 seconds left to put the Warriors up by three. The Knicks were finished. Or so everyone thought.

That afternoon, Rice laid in bed in his hotel room and watched the 1997 All-Star Game on ESPN Classic Sports. In that game, he wore a Charlotte Hornets uniform, repeatedly scored on long shots, finished with 26 points and earned the game's MVP. As he embarked on another comeback in his turbulent first season with the Knicks, Rice thought it was a good omen to see a replay of the game in which he built his reputation as one of history's greatest long-range shooters.

In the dying seconds against Golden State, with the Knicks trailing by three, Ward tossed up a desperation 33-footer that hit the rim and bounced off. Houston kept the ball alive by tapping it to Rice, who was playing his first game in 11 days. Standing in the right corner behind the three-point arc, Rice went up for a shot as if it were the 1997 All-Star Game again. The shot dropped through the hoop as the buzzer sounded, forcing overtime. The Knicks went on to win, 89-87, as Blaylock missed a three-pointer at the buzzer. Sprewell tossed the ball towards the ceiling.

"We need some miracles in the season," Van Gundy said. "We certainly caught a miracle tonight."

Sprewell was still incensed at Porter's "can't stop-me" boast. "He started talking to the wrong person," Sprewell said. "Honestly, I think he got me going because I was having an awful game up to that point."

Nobody was more relieved than Sprewell. He approached Rice in the locker room, slapped him on the back and said, "Gee, thanks for hitting that three. I definitely didn't want to lose to these guys." Slowly but surely, as the months rolled by, Sprewell had grown to admire Rice's guts in playing through pain and being effective.

March 27

The rumors had sizzled for more than a month, ever since Mourning began practicing with the Heat. But the suddenness of the news was shocking. Not only did Mourning hold a press conference to say he was returning, he announced he was going to play that night against the Raptors.

Doctors had told Mourning his condition was not expected to worsen in the next six months. Mourning, sounding like a man running out of time, said, "If I wait, I might lose that opportunity. The future is definitely not promised to me."

The league-wide sentiment was that Mourning would return at some point during the season. Riley had done a masterful job shooting down the rumors. When, a few weeks earlier, he had said he would put Mourning on the playoff roster, he called the move symbolic and said speculation about Mourning's return was "ridiculous."

In fact, three hours before the Mourning press conference, Riley had received a call from *New York* magazine writer Chris Smith, who was doing a piece on Van Gundy. When Smith casually asked Riley about Mourning's status, Riley told him, "No, he's not coming back."

When they heard the news, the Knicks were in the visitors' locker room at Sacramento's ARCO Arena getting ready for Webber's Kings. They seemed ambivalent. Several players had a gut feeling Mourning was coming back. Sprewell knew it when he heard about Riley leaving a playoff roster spot for him. Yet, the players wondered how effective Mourning would be after sitting out so long.

"You're always going to question yourself after being out for a while," Sprewell said. "You never know how he's going to come out and play."

■ ■ ■

Most NBA superstars do not talk to writers before games. Sprewell is a notable exception. Many hide in the trainer's room or simply deny requests to talk. But Webber graciously answered all questions from the New York writers and revealed he had spent the last two summers living in New York, bouncing from one friend's home to another's.

Asked if Sprewell would play a role in deciding whether he signed with the Knicks in the summer, Webber said, "Everybody knows how I feel about him as a person. I don't think that could be overstated. He's not just a basketball friend, but a friend. I'm sure that will weigh into my decision. I think the Knicks play hard and with a lot of pride, East Coast style."

■ ■ ■

ARCO Arena is located smack dab in the middle of farmland. When Webber first joined the Kings after getting traded by Washington, he started crying on the plane when he saw where the arena was situated. Located in the least-urban city in the league, ARCO contains the most raucous fans in the league. Complemented by an ear-splitting cowbell and fans wearing cowboy hats, the atmosphere for Kings' games is as good as it gets, even if your eardrums will pay the price. The hecklers behind the Knicks' bench in Sacramento easily rival the Pacers' fans.

When the game began, one fan kept yelling at Sprewell, "I'm over here. Come over here and kick my ass." He must've shouted the same taunt with different variations of his creative theme 50 times throughout the game. The man seemed like he genuinely wanted to fight Sprewell.

"Jeff, give Latrell a gun," the man bellowed during the fourth quarter.

The fans even got on Marv Albert, the legendary voice of the Knicks. Legal troubles stemming from an alleged kinky incident in which sexual assault charges were filed had threatened his career in 1996. "Marv, I'm wearing ladies' underwear," another fan shouted repeatedly. Albert was wearing his headphones and was oblivious to the taunts.

The Knicks built an 18-point lead in the first half, but it vanished quickly. Webber dominated. He obtained great low-post position and either made a little spin move or backed his defender in, resulting in easy flip shots. He made it look too easy.

Johnson, who had returned from his eight-game absence the night before in Oakland, got ejected in the first quarter after fouling Webber and getting two quick technicals for muttering to the official, "Fuck you, bitch." The Knicks missed Johnson's defensive grit against Webber. Thomas and Camby were no match for him.

As the Kings gained control in the final two minutes, another fan kept hollering, "This is the West Coast, Jeff. You're going to lose. This is the West Coast."

But, in another West Coast miracle, the Knicks forced overtime for the second straight night. With the Knicks down by three and 12 seconds remaining, Jackson stole an inbounds pass and got the ball to Sprewell. Double-teamed, Sprewell swung the ball into the left corner, thinking he was feeding the ball to Rice. Instead, the man all alone in the corner was Thomas.

Thomas, who entered the game one-for-nine in his career from behind the three-point line, caught Sprewell's pass and went right up to unleash the shot. The ball rattled in. As his teammates mobbed him, Thomas kept a straight face, acting like he was the least surprised of anyone. The game-tying shot forced overtime, but the Knicks ran out of magic. Focused on double-teaming Webber, who finished with 39 points, the spent Knicks got bludgeoned from the perimeter by Peja Stojakovic. He scored 12 points in overtime to lift Sacramento to a 124-117 win.

Afterward, Sprewell challenged himself to stop being Mr. Nice Guy on the court, not that anyone had mistaken him for that after the fiery words he had with Porter in Oakland and his trash-talking duel with the Kings' Doug Christie.

"I have to get back to being myself," Sprewell said. "I've been too nice. I'm going to play with a lot of passion and really finish this season off strong as well as getting my teammates into it. Especially Marcus and Glen. Charlie and Allan are a little more laid back. But the guys who will get fired up are Marcus, Glen and LJ, too. I'm going to be in their ear, hype them up."

Although Sprewell was talking about himself, the message was clear: he wanted his teammates to follow his example, particularly emotional guys like Camby, Rice and Johnson. He felt the club needed to ratchet up its emotions. The Knicks' captain-in-spirit had come calling again with a loud message, while their incumbent co-captains remained silent.

■ ■ ■

Sprewell and Camby left the ARCO Arena locker room together and were met by Bob Gist, Sprewell's agent.

"I'm worn out," Gist said to the guys. "This back-to-back stuff. I'm just watching it. I can't imagine how you guys feel playing."

Gist was trying to recruit Webber, who had fired his long-time agent, Fallasha Erwin. Gist had met Webber when Webber and Sprewell were teammates with Golden State. Gist figured it couldn't hurt for Sprewell to introduce him to Webber again. Four percent of a $120 million contract—Webber's expected new salary—wasn't chump change.

Sprewell, Gist and Camby stumbled upon Webber as he was on the court, signing autographs and taking pictures. Sprewell waited patiently for about 10 minutes. For once, Sprewell, wearing teal-tinted Cartier sunglasses, wasn't recognized by any of the kids. Gist spoke briefly with Webber, telling him, "I look forward to speaking to you after the season." Sprewell and Webber hung out in the tunnel. They had only a few minutes to talk before the Knicks' bus pulled out for the airport for the flight to Vancouver.

"Good luck in the playoffs," Sprewell told Webber. "You guys have a shot."

March 28-30

Harrington woke up in his Vancouver hotel room and looked out the window. Light rain was falling and fog obscured his view. Vancouver was just as he remembered it. The Mississippi native had been called "The Rain Man" in these parts because of his publicly-stated distaste for the Pacific Northwest climate. Ironically for Harrington, the Grizzlies were in the final stages of finalizing a move to Memphis.

In Vancouver, Harrington had been more tired of losing than he was of the rain and burdensome Canadian taxes. But the combination of the three made him thankful to be a Knick, even with the Grizzlies' pending move to his native South. Harrington expected the fans to give him, as he called it, "the Stevie Francis treatment." After he got drafted, Francis had refused to play for the Grizzlies and forced a trade. Upon his return, the Vancouver fans booed Francis lustily and threw garbage at him.

By afternoon, the sun broke through the haze. Checketts, Garden PR chief Barry Watkins, Layden and two members of the Knicks' PR staff took the beat writers and team broadcasters for a boat ride on the picturesque bays surrounding Vancouver, arguably the loveliest city in the NBA.

Earlier in the road trip, Checketts had given a state-of-the-Knicks address in which he answered a wide range of questions about the status of the club.

"I do think, as currently constituted, this is a club good enough to get out of the East," Checketts said. "There shouldn't be any questions about how it's structured. The trade deadline has passed. The time for inconsistency has passed. We have 13 games left and it's time to see what this group can do together."

Checketts did not give any such speech to the players on the trip. When asked why Checketts was here, Van Gundy cracked, "I thought it was to take you guys on a boat. We do these things to curry favor and all we get is a big bill."

No expense was spared as Checketts rented a yacht from the docks at majestic Stanley Park. Hors d'oeurves and drinks were served by waitresses. A buffet lunch featured Alaskan king crab legs and lobster ravioli and crème brulee for dessert. The yacht had two decks, the lower one containing a plush dining room and living room area. The upper deck was outdoors and sported a panoramic view. The yacht sailed for three hours through the straits of Vancouver with a view of the famous snowy Grouse Mountain on one side. On the other side was the Vancouver skyline with its office towers and high-rise apartments, many of which glittered with glacier-blue-tinted windows.

Toward the end of the meal, with everyone seated in the dining room, the discussion turned to half-time acts at the Garden. Radio play-by-play man Mike Breen campaigned for Checketts to hire a unicycle show performed by an Oriental couple we had seen eight days ago in Cleveland. The spectacle featured a Japanese woman riding a unicycle 30 feet in the air. She attempted to flip a stack of dishes and cups with her feet into midair and onto her head. When the plates landed properly on top of her head, she received the loudest ovation heard all night.

Breen mentioned he had spoken to the Japanese couple after their act in Cleveland. They told him Madison Square Garden was the only NBA arena in the country they hadn't been to. They said it was their dream to play in New York.

"That doesn't mean it will play in New York," Watkins said skeptically. Checketts agreed to take a vote among the assembled on whether the Garden should hire them for a night.

"I want to see how Dave votes first," Layden cracked. Everyone laughed. Layden had indeed grown tired of the perception that he doesn't go to the bathroom without Checketts' permission. The vote was a landslide in favor of the Oriental unicycle show.

During dessert, everyone sang "Happy Birthday" to Walt Frazier. "It's his 40th," Checketts announced. The Knicks legend and current wordsmith of the MSG Network had just penned a vocabulary book for kids called *Word Jam*. Frazier, 56, gave a brief speech in which he thanked the Knicks for all they had done for him. He was truly a perfect fit in the Knicks' broadcast booth. Nobody ever had a bad word to say about "Clyde," who was still as laid-back cool as they come, disappearing to St. Croix in the summer.

After the Ewing trade, Checketts had talked about one day bringing Ewing back in a broadcasting role similar to Frazier's. It was difficult to imagine this scenario unfolding, considering Ewing's limited gift for gab. If Ewing was trying to win friends at the MSG Network during his return to the Garden in February, he had failed miserably. After doing an on-court interview with TNT seconds after the final buzzer, he blew off the MSG Network's Al Trautwig, telling him, "I've got to ice my knees."

Outside on the windswept top deck of the yacht, Checketts seemed relaxed as he chatted about the past. There was no sign that Checketts was in heated talks with the Dolans about a contract extension. Nobody even knew Checketts' contract was up. He had kept it a secret. One of the holdups to a new deal was that the Dolans wanted to scale back

Checketts' responsibilities. Not only did he oversee the Knicks and Rangers, but he also ran the WNBA's Liberty, MSG Network, Radio City Music Hall, The Theatre at Madison Square Garden, the boxing division and assorted movie-theatre properties.

Checketts talked about how opinions about a trade change over time. The Johnson-for-Mason deal in 1996 was a perfect example. Mason had just played in his first All-Star Game. Johnson's season—and career—were in jeopardy because of his back. The Mason-for-Johnson trade had nearly been scrapped at the last moment. After the two sides had agreed to the trade, Checketts received a frantic call from Hornets owner George Schinn who said, "I spoke to Don Nelson and he said Mason gets on these steroid rages on the coaches. Is that true?"

"He could be tough on coaches," Checketts told Schinn.

Mason's late-night tangos with the law in which he got arrested for disorderly conduct were one of the chief reasons the Knicks wanted to trade him. But the deal had not gone down as one of Checketts' finer moments because of Johnson's back. Now Johnson was at a career crossroads with $28 million left on his contract. Checketts shook his head wistfully. "If only Larry was healthy," he said.

■ ■ ■

The Knicks stayed at the Sutton Place Hotel four blocks from the water. The Knicks' PR staff had tried to convince Van Gundy to stay at the Pan Pacific Hotel on the bay.

"It's beautiful," PR assistant Jonathan Supranowitz told Van Gundy. "You look out the window and you could see the water, the snow-capped mountains."

Van Gundy was unmoved. All he wanted to do was watch films on the VCR.

"You could also see the waterplanes landing on the bay," Supranowitz persisted.

"Waterplanes? Now that's cool," Van Gundy said.

■ ■ ■

Erick Strickland's new apartment was three blocks from the hotel. He had been placed on the injured list days earlier because of a strained left knee and his season was probably over. Strickland had dearly wished he could play this one game, if only because Knick fans never got to see what he could do.

With a rare day off on the road, Sprewell, Thomas and Johnson were invited to Strickland's apartment for dinner and round-robin chess. The four had become avid chess players. They had started to play on flights against each other and sometimes by themselves on their pocket computers. The players even trash-talked to each other during their chess battles.

Sprewell was the best of the bunch and proved to be the master again that night. Johnson had only picked up the game last summer and loved it. Chess was a game Johnson, with his bad back, could play sitting down. Dominos had been his prior passion. He considered chess a relaxing escape from worrying about the big game the next day.

Getting away from their hotel rooms and hanging out at a friend's apartment was a treat for the players. Their schedule had been grueling with 23 sets of two games in two nights. They had practically no leisure time on the road, going in and out of cities in less than 24 hours. Most of their time had been spent at the arenas or in hotel rooms.

■ ■ ■

Vancouver coach Sidney Lowe surprised Van Gundy by starting a big lineup, sending out six-foot-nine Shareef Abdur-Rahim at small forward instead of power forward. The matchup was delectable for the Grizzlies because Abdur-Rahim got to post up the six-foot-five Sprewell. This was a situation in which the structural flaw of the team with Sprewell at small forward was magnified.

Forced to double-team Abdur-Rahim in the post, the Knicks left the Grizzlies open for perimeter shots. Bryant Country Reeves, who had been a big dud in the NBA, rained in jump shots all night in an 89-68 rout that broke the Grizzlies' nine-game losing streak.

The fourth quarter was interesting only because Harrington made his first appearance of the game. He was booed viciously, worse than Sprewell had been booed in Oakland. The jeers echoed every time he touched the ball. Harrington wore a sheepish grin.

The rout dropped the Knicks to 1-2 on the trip, and questions about Van Gundy's defensive philosophy surfaced in the locker room. Sprewell believed the coaching staff should make personnel adjustments when he was severely outsized at small forward in the post, or even use the big backcourt and go without a true point guard. Doubling for him in the post and leaving the perimeter open was suicide, Sprewell thought. If necessary, he felt Van Gundy should spare egos and take out Houston, or even himself if he was struggling, and have the taller Rice or Johnson play small forward.

"If I'm on the box, there's nothing I can really do other than expect guys to double-team, but that's what's hurting us," Sprewell said. "If it calls for it, we've got to do things so we don't have to double-team as much. If that calls for taking myself or Allan out or taking Jackson out and going big, then that's maybe something we should start thinking about because teams are hurting us because we're having to double for me."

When Camby was asked about Reeves' having a great game from the outside, he said, "It's not on us. We're just following the game plan."

Something else was brewing in the locker room. Some of the Knicks sensed that Houston and Sprewell were drifting apart. They had never been close off the court, but each greatly respected the other's game and value to the team. Houston had picked up on Sprewell's recent innuendos. Sprewell's appeal for more trash-talking and emotion seemed like a direct hit on the reserved and righteous Bible boys, Houston and Ward.

"You hear I'm one of the quiet guys," Houston said. "Well, talking doesn't do anything. We've been talking all of these games. It's not doing anything. We need to just sit back and think about what our purpose is. Are we just talking? Because I don't know what we're thinking about. What are we really trying to accomplish?"

Houston had no use for verbally assaulting an opponent on the court. His distaste for trash talking went against his religious faith and quiet nature. But Houston wasn't against emotion on the court. He'd rather the talking was done between his teammates, pumping each other up and complimenting a good pass.

Houston also was not ready to embrace Sprewell's criticism of the double-teaming strategy in the post. "I can't question a game plan," the coach's son said. "That's the coaching staff's job."

The next night, the Knicks played in Portland at the Rose Garden. Van Gundy had reviewed the clips faxed from New York and again saw an avalanche of excuse-making, similar to what had happened on the previous West Coast trip. Back then, the three Gotham Guns

217

had talked about the difficulty of adjusting to fewer minutes and shots with three players sharing two positions.

Van Gundy did not buy into the latest squealing. He felt a team playing with enough energy can get away with double-teaming the post. The Sixers were the best example. To blame the strategy was not owning up to their lack of hustle in rotations. In his chat with the writers before the Blazers' game, Van Gundy had planned to let his club off the hook and not air his feelings publicly like he had on the last West Coast trip. It was a fragile group. When asked about the Knicks' structurally flawed alignment, Van Gundy started to praise the Grizzlies before he stopped himself in mid-sentence.

"You know what?" he said. "I'm just trying to bullshit you. I'm not even going to answer the question. It's not even worth it to answer. I can't even come up with a good excuse for them. That lineup is fine."

Nothing was fine against the Blazers, who punished the Knicks with even more ferocity than the Grizzlies had. A 16-0 run by Portland in the third quarter put the Knicks out of their misery. The Knicks committed 21 turnovers and were destroyed on the glass, 43-29. Another power forward, Rasheed Wallace, smoked them inside, racking up 30 points.

The Lakers were up next, and Kobe Bryant was set to return after missing the last five games with a sprained ankle. The Knicks, losers of three straight games, were a Hollywood disaster movie unfolding. Van Gundy spoke to the players, preaching, "You can either jump ship or stay in there and try to save this thing." Houston even suggested a team meeting might be in order to air out dirty laundry.

"This is when you see what guys are made of," Sprewell said. "We're scraping the bottom of the barrel. I'm not down on anyone. I love these guys. I know they're fighters. We have to keep working together with no one going off on their own. I'm in it for the long haul."

March 31-April 1

When Rice declined the Lakers' invitation to have a ring ceremony at center court when the Knicks were in town, he did so because he didn't want to draw unnecessary attention.

"If they're going to boo me, I'm not going to go on center stage and let them," Rice told the Lakers' official. Rice figured he'd hear the same kind of boos Sprewell and Harrington had already heard on this trip. After all, if Clipper fans booed him here in November, what might the Lakers' fans do?

"Let's hope I'll do a lot of shutting them up," Rice said.

In rare form before the Lakers' game, Van Gundy talked to the players about doubt. From reading their quotes in the papers, he had sensed that doubt had crept into their minds.

"Doubt is a bad thing," Van Gundy told them. "Latrell, you weren't too small a forward when we went to The Finals or Eastern Conference finals. We've been labeled as too small, too undersized. But we're the No. 1 defensive team in the league for a reason. We can guard when we go all out."

■ ■ ■

Bill Clinton watched the game from a luxury suite at the Staples Center. Like Van Gundy, the former president and basketball fanatic lived in Chappaqua. He still hadn't been invited to the Garden for a Knicks' game. Considering the Knicks were always on the lookout for models and celebrities, this snub was mysterious. Garden officials remained mum on the topic.

■ ■ ■

Bryant didn't last the first quarter. His ankle was too sore, and he came out. The Knicks used a tag team on Shaquille O'Neal, utilizing every personal foul at their disposal. The game came down to the final 5.9 seconds. With the Knicks clinging to a one-point lead, they formed a human wall around O'Neal, preventing him from getting the ball. Forced to go left along the perimeter, Derek Fisher tossed up an off-balanced 15-footer that missed badly. Thomas snatched the rebound. Sprewell punched the air. Camby pointed to his Knicks jersey. Spike Lee ran onto the court to hug Sprewell and Camby. Team Turmoil had gotten through another crisis and would head home with a 2-3 record on the trip.

Checketts didn't know what to make of his club. "We could win a championship or go down in the first round," he said. "That's no news flash."

Rice had a gritty performance against his old team. The boos weren't nearly as severe as he had expected them to be. In fact, he heard some cheers when he entered the game.

"One thing this organization [the Lakers] has never said is how much I've been missed," Rice said. "If I get a chance to put it back in their face each time, I'll do it."

The charter wasn't leaving until the next morning. The Knicks had a night out on the town in L.A. A handful of the players were going to a promotional party for Sprewell Racing, the high-performance wheel accessory Internet firm based in L.A and owned by Sprewell. Sprewell, who normally wears brightly colored sweaters, had on a gray business suit for the occasion. He looked too corporate.

CHAPTER 18

Unanswered Prayers

April 2-5

The win over the Lakers did not erase all the issues festering within the club. Sprewell continued to feel that double-teaming the post was an awkward strategy, even though it worked against the Lakers.

"We'll see," Sprewell said. "It all will be evident really soon. We'll continue to stick to the game plan. If that's what beats us, it's not on us as players."

In their first game back home, the Knicks proved little in a victory over Orlando. Knicks killer McGrady left the game early in the second quarter with a strained quad. The reserves keyed the victory as Thomas, coming off the bench since Johnson's return, Ward, who had been outplaying Jackson for two weeks, and Rice supplied the spark in a 94-82 victory. Van Gundy was angry with the starters because of their inability to play hard at the start of the third quarter—a season-long problem.

"I am done talking to the starting group about their responsibilities," Van Gundy said. "They have to get loose, get into a sweat and they have to play well. If they don't, they are coming out. It's too late in the year to beg them."

■ ■ ■

The Knicks PR staff received the excerpts of an upcoming *New York* magazine story by Chris Smith, who, like Konigsberg, had tracked the team for a couple of months. The story created a buzz because Van Gundy was quoted as taking issue with the access Knicks' pastor John Love was granted in their locker room. He also took to task the pre-game chapel involving both teams.

Van Gundy had always been concerned about fraternization between opposing players, but he had never linked it with religion. He told Smith that the worst thing to hit basketball was God and golf. When Harrington first joined the team, Pastor Love had tried recruit to him for chapel while the player was in the locker room studying Van Gundy's playbook.

"I'll tell you what I do have a problem with: We have it in our situation here," Van Gundy said. "We let a preacher into our locker room who spends as much time as he wants with our players before games. Do people in offices have preachers coming into their place of business interrupting their work? No. They have to do it before and after work. They don't get to do it during work. That's the problem I have. As a team and an organization, you've got to try to minimize those distractions. It used to be alcohol and women more. I think we're giving this guy, this pastor, too much freedom and I think the interaction between people before games, opposing sides, the fraternization is wrong for the league. It's wrong for competition. Everybody's hugging before games, praying together."

Van Gundy knew he had a lot of damage control to do with chapel regulars Ward, Houston and Jackson. Before they could read the quotes or be asked about them, Van Gundy spoke to the players in his office two hours before the Knicks faced Washington. "I want you guys to know that the remarks weren't directed at you personally and I shouldn't have said them," Van Gundy told them.

The Knicks' organization, all the way up to Checketts, had long been concerned about Ward's obsession with religion. They thought his focus on the Bible took away from his focus on the court. Checketts, a Mormon, had warned Ward not to use the locker room as his pulpit. Even Camby and Sprewell thought Ward and Houston got carried away with religion, but it never became a major issue on the team.

Actually, it had become an issue among the seven beat writers. Chris Broussard of *The Times* often attended the pre-game chapel with Ward,

Houston, Thomas and Jackson. The chapel service occurred after the access period for reporters, but Broussard, a born-again Christian, was permitted to be with the players. The issue was brought up among the network of national basketball writers who corresponded weekly to exchange information.

Some writers on the Knicks beat couldn't care less about Broussard's chapel appearances. Broussard was not a fake about his religion and often engaged others in debates on Bible interpretations. Broussard even went to Christian hip-hop clubs on the road to unwind. Broussard often exchanged Christian hip-hop CDs with Houston and Ward.

But some writers thought Broussard's attendance at chapel was a conflict of interest. They believed it crossed the line of impartiality, just as if a writer went out to strip clubs with the players. A reporter is not supposed to put himself in a compromising position with the people he writes about. When the *New York* magazine story surfaced and the pre-game chapel turned into a issue, Broussard stopped attending.

Ward and Houston seemed genuinely disappointed in Van Gundy.

"I got to pray for Jeff more than I've been praying for him," Houston said. "I can't get mad at Jeff. It's a matter of him just not really understanding. One day he will understand."

When Ward and Houston were asked if they were concerned that Van Gundy would try to limit the pastor's presence and their Bible study, their faces flushed with anger.

"He can't change chapel," Houston insisted.

"When it comes to my faith in Jesus Christ and someone tries to take it away, that's worth fighting for," Ward said. "Other things in life aren't worth fighting for. When it comes to that, I'll fight to the end."

Ward found the notion preposterous that pre-game chapel or bible study was a distraction. "We could do things really distracting, like talking to women before games," Ward said. "It doesn't distract us from our goal of playing for him."

Van Gundy didn't duck the controversy. "I shouldn't have talked about it," he said. "That's certainly what I believe, but I would have been better served by being politically correct. The question is, should I have said it? The answer is no because now I have to answer for it. Honesty always, always creates problems."

Pastor Love, who was not at the game that night against the Wizards, said by phone to *The Post*'s Paul Schwartz that he doubted he'd speak to Van Gundy.

"I probably won't make a point of it because he doesn't sound like he really wants me there that much," Love said.

The Knicks went out and beat Washington, setting up a showdown with Miami for the third seed in the Eastern Conference. Alonzo Mourning, his game coming along slowly but steadily, would man the middle this time.

April 8

Barbara Barker, the basketball columnist for *Newsday,* put it best. "What a week it's been for Jeff Van Gundy," she wrote. "First he takes on God, then Joey Crawford."

With Miami Madness at its height, a wild final minutes played out at crazed American Airlines Arena. The mayhem began when Thomas got called for a technical foul for brutally tackling Jones. Two minutes later, Ward zeroed in on Bruce Bowen like a safety, flying in the air to strip Bowen of the ball with 20.4 seconds remaining in the game and the Knicks down by two. Ward flipped over Bowen's back as the ball popped loose. A flagrant foul was called on Ward.

Van Gundy went ballistic, waving his arms and screaming at referee Joey Crawford. Bowen made two free throws, giving the Heat a 77-74 lead. Instead of the Knicks getting the ball, the Heat kept control because of the flagrant foul. On the inbounds pass, Mason was fouled. As he stepped to the foul line with 19 seconds left, Van Gundy continued to yell at Crawford about "costing us the game." Crawford turned to Van Gundy, made the T sign, then shot his right arm in the air, the basketball signal for an ejection. The Heat crowd cheered joyously. Van Gundy, who had never before been thrown out of an NBA game, stood motionless and speechless before heading for the locker room. Hardaway knocked in the technical foul shot, Mason made his second foul shot and the Heat had a five-point lead and the ballgame.

Van Gundy apologized to his team in the locker room, but was terse with the press. "I didn't say a whole lot," Van Gundy said regarding what triggered his ejection. "It was a mistake on my part to get a technical foul."

The players understood the irony of the situation. "It's kind of rare," Camby said. "Usually, Coach stresses staying in the game and not letting the officials get to you. But the first thing he did was apologize to the team."

Crawford was in no mood to meet the press or come face-to-face with the gaggle of angry Knicks fans in Miami. Dressed in his black and white referee's uniform, Crawford was ushered out of the building by security and into a waiting cab.

Ward defended his dive at the ball to the writers, but not to Crawford. "I don't mess with Joey," Ward said. "He's been known for throwing guys out. I just stayed away. That's called wisdom."

The coach should have acted so wisely.

April 10-12

Johnson had been in the mix for eight games, but hadn't made an impact. He was happy just to be able to suit up again. The day before the Knicks faced Charlotte at the Garden, Johnson, in his first extensive interview since he came back, chatted with his old confidant, John Delong of the *Winston-Salem Journal*.

"You don't feel sick, then all of a sudden you take something and three hours later, you get up and you're bent over and throwing up," Johnson said. "I was worried. The whole time it was happening, I was just wishing I could get that one opportunity to win an NBA championship. I wish everything will be OK and I could struggle through this one more time. I'll take what I have to take, do what I got to do for the back and just struggle through it one more time to try to get us a push in these playoffs and try to win one back."

One day after the interview, Johnson was unable to play against his former team, the Hornets. He had been given Prevacid to protect his stomach lining, but it wasn't having a strong effect. Without missing a beat, Thomas was thrust back into the starting lineup and scored 22 points in the Knicks' easy win. Camby had 18 points and 17 rebounds. The Camby-Thomas duo played with finesse, leading fast-breaks and fulfilling the pre-season prophecy about the club being more athletic and faster without Ewing. With five games remaining, Thomas had proven indisputably he deserved to start over Johnson. In the last six games, Camby had averaged 19.5 points and 14.5 rebounds. Only another injury could stop him now.

■ ■ ■

Before the Knicks played the Pacers at Conseco Field House, Van Gundy talked about the new defensive rules that would legalize zone defenses next season. The league's 12-member executive committee was about to vote them in, but not one coach was on the committee, a fact that appalled Van Gundy. The latest proposal puzzled Van Gundy, who thought the league wanted to increase scoring.

"If they put the new rules in, I'd be disappointed if anyone scored 80 points on us," Van Gundy said.

■ ■ ■

On the Knicks' first possession against the Pacers, Camby drove the left baseline and soared in the air for a dunk. Making slight contact with Perkins as he rose, Camby tilted off-balance as he slammed the ball through the cylinder. He thought about hanging onto the rim to brace his fall, but he had already gotten two technicals this season for doing so. His body went horizontal as he crashed to the floor and slammed his left hip against the hardwood. Excruciating pain flooded through Camby's body.

Camby was helped off the court by the trainers. He shuddered to think that he had fractured his hip. The playoffs were less than two weeks away. Could his breakthrough season end like this?

Playing without Johnson, Camby and Houston, who sat out his second straight game with a bruised thigh, the Knicks lost, 100-93. That result didn't matter nearly as much as the results of Camby's X-rays: He hadn't broken anything. The Knicks listed the injury as a hip contusion.

But as Camby limped out of the locker room that night, the agony on his face made it clear he had played his final game of the regular season. The next morning, he woke up with a bump the size of a grapefruit on his hip. Just as he was playing his best ball of the season, another freak injury had struck him down.

April 13-15
With Houston out of action again, the Knicks beat Atlanta, then braced for Philadelphia for their first meeting since Mutombo joined the Sixers. The Knicks were still battling Miami for the third seed and the right to avoid top-seeded Philly until the conference finals.

Houston played in his first game since missing three with a bruised thigh. In the second quarter, after a timeout, he walked by the press table, glanced at a couple of writers and said, "I'll bet you 20 dollars I hit my next shot." Nobody took him up on the bet. When he drilled a three-pointer from the right wing, he glared at the writers and winked. The byplay was out of character for Houston, who usually doesn't show emotion on the court.

In the end, though, Iverson was too tough. He finished with 27 points and Mutombo had 16 rebounds in the Sixers' 89-82 victory. Undeterred by the loss, Sprewell said, "Even though we didn't win, we let them know that if we're fortunate enough to face them again, it's going to be a battle."

Iverson dismissed the Knicks when asked if they were their toughest challengers in the East.

"Why are they difficult?" Iverson asked. "What's the season series, 3-1? Doesn't sound too difficult."

April 16-18

With Camby sidelined until the playoffs, the Knicks were having trouble sealing down homecourt advantage for the first round. Cleveland, the team the Knicks crushed two weeks earlier at Gund Arena, got revenge at home. In the last seconds, Sprewell had the ball and a chance to blow past the Cavaliers' rookie seven-footer Chris Mihm, who got caught on a switch at the perimeter. Sprewell elected to loft a lazy jump shot that Mihm blocked. Van Gundy was stunned Sprewell didn't drive to the hoop.

The Knicks' third loss in four games put them in danger of losing homecourt advantage. If they lost their regular-season finale to Detroit, their seeding would slip to No. 5, forcing them to start the playoffs on the road, most likely in Toronto. They were out of the running for the third seed. The Sixers loomed in the second round...if they got that far.

■ ■ ■

One more game for Ewing in a Seattle uniform and his stint with the Sonics would probably be over. The Sonics wished to get under the salary cap to sign a free agent, and having Ewing's $14 million shed from the cap would do the trick. Why would Walker want to keep the same team intact after failing to make the playoffs?

Ewing was telling friends he didn't think he'd be able to watch the Knicks in the playoffs. He had followed them on his satellite dish when he was home in Seattle but thought it would be too painful to show up at the Garden after missing the playoffs for the first time in 13 years.

"It would be nice to see him cheering us on," Sprewell said. "At some point, you have to let it go and become a supporter. He's still a Knick at heart."

■ ■ ■

In his last regular-season pre-game meeting with the writers, Van Gundy managed one last dig. Asked how healthy he expected Camby to be for Game 1, he said, "I don't like to speculate on things I know nothing about. If I do that, that would make me, uh, the media."

The Knicks were able to exhale, if not celebrate, after beating the Pistons, 94-88, in the regular-season finale. The Knicks had earned the fourth seed and homecourt advantage in the first round, but their goal in training camp had been loftier. And though they would've rather faced the Hornets in the first round, the Knicks weren't quaking in their boots about playing Toronto. After all, the Knicks had been ravaged by the Raptors in the regular season last year, then swept them in the first round of the playoffs.

The interest level for the Knicks-Raptors series was sky-high. Oakley was sure to mouth off. The Childs-Jackson pairing would prove once and for all who got the better of the trade. And Carter would be out to reverse his image as a playoff softy. Last season, Carter averaged 33 points in the regular season against the Knicks before they shut him down in the playoffs.

"I'm just glad the regular season is over," Sprewell said. "At least we got homecourt. We wanted a little better. We'll take this and go from there. They'll have revenge circling in their minds."

As Camby left the arena, he told the writers he was ready for Game 1 of the playoffs and willing to play in pain if he had to. The game was four days away.

CHAPTER 19

The Christ Debate

April 19-22

Postell and Longley were left off the playoff roster. Van Gundy met with Longley and told the big center they could use his size in the post-season, especially with Johnson injured and Camby returning from an injury. Longley said he couldn't see helping the team in his condition and wasn't willing to go back on the pills.

The Raptors stayed in Washington, D.C., to practice following their regular-season finale. Childs knew to be careful not to goad his former team any more than he already had. "I'm not going to give anyone a chance to misquote me," Childs said.

■ ■ ■

Soon after the media-availability session began at Purchase, the Knicks PR staff walked around the gym handing out copies of an upcoming Sunday New York Times Magazine story by Eric Konigsberg. Some of the reporters barely glanced at the packet, more intent on getting a few minutes with Sprewell about Carter, until Hamamato of the PR staff repeatedly yelled above the din that Ward, in a few moments, would read a statement.

"You're not going to want to miss him," Hamamato warned.

She was right. "This article that's coming out about the Jews persecuting Christians and other things, the writer took it out of context," Ward said. "I didn't mean to offend any one group because that's not what I'm about. I have friends that are Jewish. Actually my best friend is a Jewish guy and his name is Jesus Christ. So, therefore, I have no reason to offend any religion or person of a religion because my best friend is Jewish.

"But my job as a Christian is to let people know what Jesus did and how he lived his life. The context of the article is taken out as if Jews persecute Christians, which biblically is what happened during that time. But if people want to be offended by what happened biblically, that's on them. But I'm not attacking any one group."

In the article, Konigsberg wrote about his bible study sessions with Ward. He wrote:

> In the first class I attended, on the road in Washington in December, everyone asked me about my religious background. They talked about the Old Testament and cultural identity and they had a lot of questions about dietary laws. Now participating in the study-book exercises in Milwaukee, I thought I was doing fine. The players seemed interested in Judaism. They started calling me "E."
>
> I fancied that the seeds of an interfaith fellowship were being planted. Then Ward said, "Jews are stubborn, E., but tell me, why did they persecute Jesus, because he knew something they didn't want to accept?"
>
> "What?"
>
> "They had his blood on their hands." Working quickly, Houston indexed a passage on his Palm Pilot. "Matthew 26, verse 67," he said. "Then they spit in Jesus's face and hit him with their fists."
>
> "It say anything about who wanted Jesus dead?" Ward asked. "There are Christians getting persecuted by Jews every day. There's been books written about this—people who are Jewish and find Christ, and then their parents stop talking to them."

When Houston got off the court, he told me, "Some people don't think the truth is valid. I challenge people to go and read it. Charlie is just speaking from what he's read. It's just the facts."

The Anti-Defamation League, a watchdog for anti-Semitism, had caught wind of the passage earlier in the week and called the Knicks to express their concern. The Knicks' PR staff reacted swiftly. The night before, they convinced Ward to quell the storm before it started. The Knicks were sensitive to playing in a city with more Jews than anywhere else in the country and to a season-ticket base that included many Jews.

But in allowing all the TV cameras and radio stations to hone in on the story before the remarks even appeared in print anywhere, the Knicks PR staff wound up feeding blood to the sharks. Instead of allowing the story to develop at its own pace, the Knicks poured gasoline onto a brushfire. Had a press release with a carefully-worded apology from Ward been distributed to the newspapers, the story might have not developed a life of its own. The TV and radio stations might have ignored it.

With the Anti-Defamation League releasing a statement branding Ward's remarks as anti-Semitic, every media outlet in New York had ammunition to turn the passages into a monumental story two days before the first game of the playoffs. The ADL statement read: "We were shocked to read the comments of New York Knicks players Charlie Ward and Allan Houston blaming the death of Jesus on Jews and accusing Jews of persecuting Christians. We had thought these destructive historic myths, which have been a source of anti-Semitism for centuries, were a thing of the past. Sadly, [Ward] doesn't understand the impact of his comments and that they constitute anti-Semitism and religious bigotry."

Checketts and Layden drove up to Purchase for a private meeting with Ward, Houston and Thomas. The Knicks released a statement from Checketts, who said, "The views expressed by our players in Sunday's *New York Times Magazine* do not reflect the view of the New York Knicks or Madison Square Garden. While we understand from our players that what they said was taken out of context, we find their comments as quoted objectionable."

But Ward wouldn't leave the issue alone. Instead of apologizing again to those he offended and dropping the subject, he continued the debate. After the last practice before the playoffs, the crowd around Ward had doubled in size from the previous day to two dozen journalists. Ward became indignant when a TV reporter wanted to know in what way he was taken out of context.

"If you want to know what the context is, go to the Bible," Ward said. "I give you the opportunity. If you want to read about it, it's in the book of John or any of the gospels. I'm just the messenger. Don't shoot the messenger."

But that's exactly what the columnists did. On the day of Game 1, Vic Ziegel of *The Daily News* wrote that Ward's words were equivalent to an editorial in an Alabama newspaper defending the merits of slavery in the 1800's. "Mazel tov," wrote Ziegel. "You just became the poster boy for dumb, insensitive jocks. You're an anti-Semite. And you can quote me, Bubbeleh."

Columnist Barry Stanton of the Westchester *Journal News* related a story about Ward trying to recruit him to Christianity. Stanton had asked Ward, then a free-agent during the lockout, if he was worried he might leave the Knicks.

"I don't worry about that because I've accepted Jesus in my life," Ward said. "Have you?"

Stanton had thought Ward's remark was a rhetorical question and didn't respond. When another reporter asked Ward about something else, he interrupted the question and turned to Stanton. "I asked you a question," Ward said.

"Well, no, I haven't accepted Jesus," Stanton said.

"Why not?"

"Because I'm Jewish."

"So?"

"Let me put this in a way that you as an athlete will understand," Stanton said to Ward. "The Jews believe we are the chosen people. That means we were recruited. You're just a walk-on."

Steve Jacobsen of *Newsday* wrote, "Charlie Ward shouldn't be playing in New York. And if he says the Jews drove him out of town, that would be fine."

Ian O'Connor of the *Journal News* wrote that Ward was "sounding less like Jesus and more like Pat Buchanan." Alluding to Van Gundy's remarks about being opposed to religion in the workplace a few weeks earlier, O'Connor continued, "The Knicks keep mixing Gatorade with holy water, dragging everyone into the brew. First, Jeff Van Gundy said God and golf had replaced sex and drugs as the league's most serious ills, a teaching not likely to be embraced at the coach's old school, McQuaid Jesuit."

Van Gundy's worst nightmare had unfolded. Religion in the workplace had become a distraction at the worst possible time, though he tried to downplay it.

"I certainly don't have enough historical perspective of the Bible to understand any of what Charlie said," Van Gundy said. "But I do know this: it's going to have nothing to do with the results tomorrow."

On the eve of Game 1, after the Sabbath ended, the American Jewish Congress joined the fray, releasing a statement to *The New York Post* which said, in part, "Ward and Houston should stick to basketball and leave the theology to those who know at least something about it."

April 22

An hour before Game 1 at the Garden, Ward, sitting as his locker, wrote "Eph 6:10-20" on one of his sneakers and "Romans 16:20" on the other, along with the inscription, "Peace of God Rules." Ward felt betrayed by Konigsberg, whom he had graciously invited into his private life when so many of his teammates had not given the writer the time of day. Thomas hoped Konigsberg would come to the game. He didn't.

"The least he could do is show his face," Thomas said in the quiet locker room. "He won't have the guts. The thing I don't understand, it was a short conversation and he made his points. He didn't seem offended. At the end, he complimented us, said it's really great we get together like this and aren't going out, running the streets. Sure we feel betrayed."

■ ■ ■

Johnson suited up, but he was not expected to play. Having missed the last six games of the regular season and 14 of the last 22, finding his rhythm figured to be an impossible task. Van Gundy asked him to dress anyway, just in case, promising he wouldn't put him into a situation in which he would fail.

The game's first play set the tone for the game. Carter dashed to the hole, beating Sprewell by half a step. As Carter leapt for a dunk, Thomas viciously slapped the ball away, getting a piece of Carter's head as well. Carter crashed to the court. No foul was called.

Early in the second quarter, Childs reported to the press table to check into the game for the first time. Van Gundy immediately pointed to Ward, who took off his warmups and waited alongside Childs. When the two entered the game, a torrent of boos rained down. A Knicks official on press row said, "They're booing Childs."

That theory stood to reason until Ward touched the ball for the first time and dribbled downcourt. The crowd booed louder. Every time Ward touched the ball, the boos resounded. When a video of Ward and his wife, Tonja, kissing their baby was shown on the scoreboard, the fans booed again. No Knicks player had ever been treated this harshly at the Garden. In comparison, Childs was treated like a conquering hero.

"Charlie, you're persecuting me," a fan behind the Raptors' bench shouted at Ward after he committed a turnover. When Ward returned to the court for the second half, another fan yelled, "We should've traded you instead of Childs."

In the fourth quarter, with a playoff game on the line, the cheers drowned out the boos when Ward hit a huge three-pointer with 5:58 left, then sank two free throws in the last 30 seconds to seal the Knicks' 92-85 win.

A mob scene ensued in front of Ward's locker .As he twisted his way through the crowd to get to his locker, Ward muttered, "You all have not seen anything like this, Lord, Jesus Christ. No, you have not." Ward linked his fourth-quarter heroics with the power of Jesus, saying, "It's not me. It's only the Holy Spirit that lives in me that I'm able to go out and do these things under all the circumstances, all the scrutiny of what happened. It's great. Believe it or not, it's not the first time I've been booed."

After several questions about Jews, jeers and Jesus, Ward said, "I'm through with the boos and what have you. If you want to talk about the way my teammates played today, then I will address your questions."

Bud Mishkin of the cable station New York 1 then asked, "Charlie, I know you said you don't want to talk about the boos, but—" Supranowitz of the PR department interrupted Mishkin and threw his body in front of Ward.

"Bud, he just said he doesn't want to talk about it anymore. He doesn't want to talk about it anymore."

And that was that. Ward walked out of the Garden a wearing a blue baseball cap with a figure of a man holding a cross.

■ ■ ■

Carter, held to 13 points in another lame display that had fans and the media questioning his heart, was approached by his mother outside the visitors' locker room.

"Mamma told you there'd be days like these," she said to him.

Lost in the religious madness and Carter's performance was Camby's emphatic return. After limping out of the tunnel and looking rusty on the offensive end at the start, Camby filled the Garden with energy all afternoon, ripping down a career playoff high 18 rebounds in his first game in two weeks. He figured to only get better, as did the Knicks, even if the boos for Ward didn't die down. A second straight sweep of the Raptors seemed to be in the offing. Camby went home, had a quiet dinner with his girlfriend Eva and went to sleep. When he woke up, his life would never be the same.

CHAPTER 20

The Hostage Crisis

April 24

The call came at 4:15 a.m. Camby fumbled for the phone. It was "Chooey," his older sister Mia's boyfriend. Camby was told to throw on some clothes immediately and drive to his mother's home in South Windsor, Connecticut. Monica's former boyfriend had broken into the house and was holding the family hostage.

Within minutes, Camby hopped into his Mercedes and tore off for Connecticut in the darkness, sick to his stomach. He had spoken to Monica the night before. She had watched the victory on television and told him "Great game," but poked fun at him for scoring just eight points. Camby was close to both of his sisters. His mother, Janice, had worked two jobs and, as the older brother, he had been the family's primary babysitter. But Camby was unfamiliar with the guy she had been dating, Troy Crooms.

He didn't know that Crooms was a career criminal with a rap sheet that included 16 criminal convictions and a mention on the Connecticut State Police's registry for sex offenders. Monica had been trying to break up with him for a week. Three weeks earlier, Janice Camby had called 911 during a dispute Monica and Troy had in their house.

On this night, Crooms, after climbing through a window, went directly to her bedroom on the second floor. The room was dark.

Brandishing a knife, he choked her and threatened to kill her. From her own bedroom, Mia called 911 and gave the dispatcher the code number to the garage door.

Mia heard the struggle in her sister's bedroom. Each time Monica tried to squirm out of Crooms' menacing grip, she cut herself on the kitchen knife.

The police entered the house through the garage door and heard screams from Monica's bedroom. Officer John Bond, carrying a flashlight, headed for the room. The door was slightly ajar. He took the pistol from his holster and kicked open the door. Crooms stood behind Monica, clutching her tightly and holding a knife to her throat.

Blood dripped from her hands, face and clothes and stained the white sheets. Monica's body completely covered Crooms'.

"Drop the knife and let her go," Bonds said.

"Back off," Crooms threatened. "Go down the stairs."

Bond and Crooms talked back and forth for a minute. Bond repeatedly asked him what he wanted. Finally, Bond retreated downstairs. During the byplay, Officer Andre Rosedale snuck into the bedroom across the hall. Janice Camby was awoken up by another officer and led out of the house. As Bond left the house, he radioed Capital Region Emergency Services Team.

"We have a hostage situation here," he said.

With the police still outside the house, Crooms put Monica on the bed, took her underwear off and forced himself on her. During intercourse, Crooms told Monica he loved her. He said he wished it didn't have to be like this and he was sorry. One hour, forty-five minutes later, he raped Monica again.

Marcus arrived at the house at 7:45 a.m. Helicopters flew overhead and members of a SWAT team surrounded the premises, hiding in trees and bushes. Cops were everywhere. Too petrified to move, Mia, clutching her cell phone, had stayed locked in her bedroom for four hours before police coaxed her out. She finally summoned the nerve to climb down a ladder that had been placed at a second-floor window in the back of the house.

During the standoff, Crooms permitted an officer to enter the bedroom and place a telephone on the floor so law enforcement officials could communicate with him. The officer saw Crooms stretched out on the floor by the bed. Monica, bleeding from the hands and wrists, was lying on top of him, with Crooms' arm wrapped around her chest and a knife up against her throat.

For three hours, Crooms' only demand was for the police to give him back the boots he had left outside the window he had climbed through.

Then he made another demand. "I want to speak to Marcus," Crooms told police.

The police were puzzled. They felt it would be too dangerous to allow Camby to speak to Crooms, who probably would demand ransom and threaten to kill Monica if he didn't get the money. As a compromise, the police briefly positioned Camby in the driveway so that Crooms could see him. Fearing he might get shot at, Crooms sent Monica to the window to make sure Camby was there.

Delaying a rescue attempt, however, was risky. They knew Monica had lost a lot of blood. She was in danger of bleeding to death.

The SWAT team came up with a plan to have Camby act belligerent. Camby walked near the police negotiator who was on a phone with Crooms and shouted, "I'm not talking to that bastard until he lets my sister go."

According to the Hartford *Courant,* Camby said to police "I feel like I'm in the movie *The Negotiator,* but this is real life." It was 10:30 a.m. and Camby thought, "I'll give up basketball forever if only my sister gets out of this alive."

■ ■ ■

News about the Camby crisis was all over the radio. As Houston walked out the front door of his house, his wife Tamara called him back and told him she had just heard on the news that Camby's sister was being held hostage at knifepoint. Most of the other players didn't know about the situation until they got to the gym and Van Gundy informed them of the crisis during a brief meeting.

The players seemed startled when they met with reporters. "At this time of the year, you don't really think about other things," Sprewell said. "Everything else is put on the backburner. But we're human, too. We have families. It makes you want to go home and be with your kids and make sure everything is all right."

Brunson, Camby's closest friend, shook his head and said, "Every time he's ready to play well, something happens."

Van Gundy was watching tape and planning for Game 2 when he found out about the Camby situation. When Van Gundy addressed the team, there was no talk about basketball. He wasn't sure if the team would practice the next day, either. When a reporter asked him about this being another distraction, Van Gundy snapped, "No, this is not a distraction. This is life and death. Let's not trivialize this and put it in anything to do with the game. That's ridiculous." Layden was dispatched to South Windsor to join Camby.

■ ■ ■

At 11:09 a.m., Crooms dropped his knife and told police on the phone he was surrendering. Camby's act of belligerence had apparently flustered Crooms, who saw no way out. Camby hopped into the back of the ambulance with his sister. On the way to the Hartford Hospital, Monica nodded when the ambulance driver asked her if she had been sexually assaulted. Marcus broke down in tears. In the hospital waiting room, family and friends waited silently as Monica was treated for knife wounds. For half an hour, Camby sat by himself with his head in his hands, trembling.

By the time Layden reached Connecticut, the hostage standoff was over. Joining Camby at the hospital, Layden told him that the Knicks family prayed for him and asked him to not think about basketball. Layden had four daughters. By six p.m., a nurse wheeled Monica out to the waiting room and Marcus took Monica and his family home to South Windsor.

■ ■ ■

That night, Stern released a statement admonishing Ward. Ostensibly, the statement was released to quell questions about whether Ward would be fined. But Stern, an observant Jew, wanted to get in his two cents.

"Ward would have been better off not to have uttered his uninformed and ill-founded statements," Stern said. "But I do not wish to enhance his sense of martyrdom by penalizing him for giving them public voice. He will have to accept the reactions and judgments of fans and all fair-minded people who have been offended."

Earlier in the day, Ward said, "I've had Jewish people say to me, 'It's cool, I understand who you are and what you're about,' and I've had other people who said I'm anti-Semitic." On whether he'd get booed again in Game 2, Ward said, "I can't control it. The Lord asked me to go out and play as hard as I possibly can to show his power that lives within me. When that happened, I was overjoyed because I know he's still on his throne. Whatever that article meant to do to me personally, the Lord showed me he's still in control."

After Stern's statement, Ward's supporters believed only a strong apology would lessen the furor. In an interview that day with The Times, Ward said, "If you don't put it in the right context, then it's going to really look bad. If we were just doing an interview one-on-one and I made those statements, or if I was just sitting around talking about Jews like that, I can understand why it would make people angry. If you take it out of context, it looks wrong."

Ward finally was getting it right. If Ward was as clear in his apology that first day, the furor might have lessened. An hour after Stern's statement, the Knicks released Ward's third attempt at an apology. Ward said he would open dialogue with Rabbi Yechiel Eckstein, president and founder of the International Fellowship of Christians and Jews "in an effort to heal the wounds of the last few days. I want to truly apologize to everybody who was offended by the magazine story. I will say again that I would never condemn or criticize any group or religion. I also want to apologize to my teammates, the Knicks, the fans and the NBA for the distraction this has caused."

Late that night, Houston's wife, Tamara, gave birth to a seven-pound, two-ounce baby boy, Allan Wade Houston III. It was the Knicks' only blessing of the day.

April 24

Camby stayed home in Westchester with his girlfriend as the Knicks practiced. He was frazzled and physically exhausted, in no shape to work out. Van Gundy went to his house and met with him for 30 minutes. The coach told him to take care of his family first.

"If you are in a frame of mind to play, we welcome you," he told Camby. "If you aren't, you must be honest, for your good and the good of the team."

The Knicks had sent him food and flowers. He was also receiving calls and flowers from players around the league.

Before practice, Van Gundy advised the players not to refer to the Camby situation as a distraction. "A distraction is me saying something stupid," he told the group. "This is not a distraction. I don't want it talked about it in light terms."

Van Gundy was waiting for the first reporter to call the situation a distraction. The man who had admitted to having no perspective earlier in the season was oozing with it now.

"This has nothing to do with how it affects us," Van Gundy said. "We have a basketball issue that we want to do well with but it is totally inconsequential when you compare it to what he's doing. If this has an impact on the series or he doesn't play as well, then that's just too bad for us. No one cares. This has nothing to do with a distraction. This is as serious an issue as a family could face."

None of the players had spoken to Camby. They wanted to give him time.

■ ■ ■

While the two Jewish organizations, the Anti-Defamation League and the American Jewish Congress had sent out releases accepting Ward's apology, the AJC had not withdrawn its request to Florida Secretary of State Katherine Harris to have Ward removed as the state's spokesman for literacy. Florida Governor Jeb Bush announced he was sticking with Ward. Saying Ward "didn't have meanness in his heart by these comments," Bush rejected the American Jewish Congress' bid.

"I don't necessarily ascribe to the same biblical interpretation, but I do believe we need to have tolerance on both sides," Bush said. "I wouldn't necessarily conclude what he concluded, but he has every right to do that. If we're going to become so rigid a country to be able to disallow speech, even though it may not be politically correct, I think we're in danger."

CHAPTER 21

Picking up the Pieces

April 25

A sullen Camby returned to practice. The players saw right away that he wasn't himself. Nobody saw him smile the entire practice. He was quiet, not the loud quipster he usually was. The players hugged him when they first saw him, but none of them felt comfortable enough to talk to him about the crisis.

The NBA would have understood if Camby had decided not to address the media, but he insisted. In the atrium outside the gym where Van Gundy normally speaks, Camby stood before two dozen television cameras. The story had gone well beyond the sports pages, and all of the local TV stations had sent their news reporters.

"This is where I want to be," Camby said, his face hidden by the gaggle of microphones set up before him as if a head of state was speaking. "It's better than being in the house surrounded by the other stuff. Don't feel sorry for me. My sister is the one who has to go through this for life. I'm just more hurt for her sake and my mom's sake. For the most part, I'll be fine. I just have to be the backbone of the family."

A playoff game against the Raptors faced him, and Camby was honest about his situation. "It will be hard for me to focus and be where I need to be and have my head right," he said, "But I have 24 hours."

April 26

The call came in mid-afternoon to Lori Hamamoto. Patrick Ewing wanted to know if he could get a ticket to the game that night. Only President Bush would have been given higher priority. The day before, Sonics general manager Wally Walker had all but said Ewing was not going to return to the Sonics next season.

"The decision on Patrick is, do we look to re-sign him at age 39 after we didn't make the playoffs," Walker said. "We all love Patrick here. He gave us everything he had. The final decision hasn't been reached yet, but I think you understand what I'm saying."

Ewing arrived at the Garden fashionably late, early in the first quarter. He took his seat on celebrity row, courtside, and shook hands with Keith Richards of the Rolling Stones. Spike Lee came bounding down the row to hug Ewing.

Most of the fans hadn't noticed Ewing's arrival, but a few minutes after he took his seat, Ewing's face flashed on the scoreboard. The fans stood as if it was February 27 all over again and gave Ewing a thundering ovation that lasted 30 seconds. Wearing a big smile, Ewing waved, then finally stood up to acknowledge the cheers.

At halftime, Ewing said, "It's hard not being in the playoffs. I fully expected it. The season didn't turn out the way I'd like, but that's life. You've got to move on. I don't know the future of where I'm going to be playing, but I will be playing."

Ewing was there, but the Knicks weren't in spirit, and neither was Camby. He trotted around the court with a broken heart and a cluttered brain. He was not the same player who had leapt and flown toward the glass throughout the season. He was zombie-like, standing around watching the action go by him. Camby, who had 18 boards in Game 1, had two points and two rebounds in 31 minutes. He didn't grab his first board until the fourth quarter. He missed all four of his free throws. At some point, Van Gundy should've taken him out of the game, but didn't have the heart. The Knicks lost, 94-74.

"It just happened a few days ago," Camby said. "I don't expect miracles. I just didn't have it in me."

Camby had sensed he'd have this kind of night. An hour before the game, he couldn't focus. His mind wandered to South Windsor.

Rice, showing shades of the griping malcontent from the 2000 Finals, campaigned again for more shots and minutes. Van Gundy had said at the morning shootaround, "You can't ask at this time of year for unhealthy players to carry a huge burden." Rice got angry when that sentiment was relayed to him. "If he can't count on me, he shouldn't play me," he seethed.

The best-of-five series was tied at one. The next two games were in Toronto, where the Raptors had a chance to wrap up the series by winning both.

April 27

Camby called Van Gundy first thing in the morning. He wanted to let him know he would not attend practice and wasn't sure he'd be ready for Game 3 in Toronto. Camby told Van Gundy he didn't want to hurt the team. He said he'd be back when he felt he could be effective. He was still having trouble sleeping. The flashbacks were vivid.

"You're the only one who knows when you're ready to come back," Van Gundy told him.

Van Gundy wanted to make sure the players didn't feel Camby was letting the team down. "It's a tragedy," he told them before practice. "Turn the tables and you know you'd be there for your family, too. You'd feel the same way."

Rick Kaplan, Camby's business manager, told reporters there was a 50-50 chance Camby would be ready for Game 3. If he practiced the next day, Kaplan believed he'd be a go.

Knicks management asked Camby if he wanted to speak to a professional counselor. He consented. There was no official diagnosis, but the counselor believed Camby was suffering from post-traumatic stress syndrome, an affliction that beset thousands of Vietnam War veterans when they returned to the U.S.

■ ■ ■

Ward had received a smattering of boos when he checked into Game 2. The wrath against him had lessened considerably. Before the game, Ward, as promised, had spoken to Rabbi Yechiel. They talked about making a trip to Jerusalem over the summer.

April 28

Camby was a no-show for practice again. When practice ended, the Knicks still didn't know if he would join them for their flight to Toronto in a few hours. Van Gundy didn't plan on having him.

Dipping deep into his well of motivational talks, Van Gundy came up with a doozy, sounding as desperate as he had at any time in his career. In an impassioned rant, Van Gundy told both the players and the media, "Certain things we can control and that is to play a great basketball game tomorrow. I don't think there's anything else we can control. All these other things that have been swirling around, those things aren't in our control. Other than support, there's nothing we can do to help him. We have to get our eyes on the prize again, and the prize is advancement.

"Five days from now, we're flying from Toronto. We're flying home either having advanced, heading toward a Game Five or going home for vacation. Our whole year's work is coming down to these five days and what we do with them. That doesn't take away from how badly we feel for Marcus' sister and his family. But our year's work is on the line right now."

Van Gundy had struck all the right chords. He had spent the past few days tip-toeing on eggshells around the Camby situation. Now he was telling his players that they couldn't let Camby's grief bring them down. The talk was by far Van Gundy's most inspirational, heartfelt address of the season.

At 12:15 p.m., an hour before the charter flight was scheduled to leave, the Knicks got the official word from Kaplan. Camby was staying home. Kaplan admitted to confidants that he didn't think Camby would be ready for Game 4, either.

■ ■ ■

Camby's decision to leave the team indefinitely had no effect on Johnson's back woes. He sat out the first two games of the playoffs and knew it was unlikely he'd play again until the second round.

"It was frustrating a long time ago," Johnson said. "Now I'm taking life as it comes."

Sprewell had watched the tape of Game 2 and didn't need the box score to tell him that Camby was in a different world.

"He was there, but he wasn't there," Sprewell said. "He was just kind of gazing out there."

Spree sent an e-mail on his two-way pager to Camby, asking him how he was doing. The response was curt: "I'm all right."

April 29

As Jackson got off the Knicks' bus in the tunnel inside Air Canada Centre, he told his teammates, "When we get back on this bus later tonight, we're going to be up 2-1."

Four hours later, Jackson and his mates pranced into the visitors' locker room with Jackson singing the new gospel hit from Donnie McClurkin, "We Fall Down But We Get Up." The song had been in Jackson's head all day and the lyrics fit. He even sang it on the court a few times during the Knicks' 97-89 win over the Raptors that gave them a two games to one lead in the series.

Houston, who scored a game-high 24 points, had known something special was going to happen. He had seen it in his teammates' eyes on the plane ride to Toronto.

Rice was due for a breakout game. He usually came through after he talked up his lack of shots and minutes. The other day, he had brought a surprise to practice to break up the depressed mood of the club. He showed off his championship ring, sprinkled with diamonds. It was big, fat and beautiful.

"Man, I gotta get me one of those," Sprewell said. After showing off the ring the first day he got it, Rice had kept his treasure away from his teammates, feeling it was out of place to wear the jewel in front of them. He picked the perfect time for his show-and-tell. He scored 18 points and pulled down seven rebounds, showing glimpses of greatness.

"I played on a championship team," Rice said afterwards. "That has to count for something."

Sprewell and Childs verbally sparred late in the game, making the victory even sweeter.

"I think Chris is a little frustrated," Sprewell said.

Before the game, Sprewell had tried to send a message to Camby through his two-way pager. The device that had become the rage among NBA players didn't work in Canada. In the fourth quarter, Sprewell huddled up the players after a timeout. He was about to say, "Let's not forget Marcus," but decided not to. He figured they were all thinking about him anyway, just like he was.

■ ■ ■

Camby watched Game 3 on television from his White Plains house with his girlfriend, Eva, Kaplan, and two friends. He was nervous before the game, fearing he had had let the team down and they were going to lose. He was quiet during the game. Even during the game's most exciting moments, Camby sat stonily. His somberness lifted in the final seconds when the outcome was decided. He smiled for the first time since the ordeal began. He said he was relieved and told Kaplan he would do everything he could to play in Game 4.

■ ■ ■

Ward walked though the tunnel inside Toronto's Air Canada Centre and headed for the bus. A long-haired man who claimed to be a Jew for Jesus intercepted him. The man held a small, red Bible. The bus waited, but Ward was too polite to blow the man off, even though he had slipped past security. For 15 minutes, the man spoke animatedly with Ward, turning pages of his small Bible, pointing to passages, and talking scripture. Ward had always sought attention for his religious convictions. Now he couldn't get away from it.

April 30

With two days off between Games 3 and 4, the Knicks flew back to Westchester and practiced in Purchase rather than lingering in Toronto. That made it easier for Camby to rejoin the team for the first time since Game 2. The last player to arrive, Camby went through the entire practice and joked with his teammates for the first time since his sister was taken hostage.

"You're going to see the old Marcus," Camby told Rice. He tried to laugh, smile and let his teammates know he was his old self again. He appreciated that they did not ask too much about his sister, who was about to undergo wrist surgery. He congratulated the guys on their win in Game 3.

Although he was still having nightmares and waking up covered in sweat, Camby felt he needed to play again. He was tired of being cooped up in his house. He had seen a professional counselor and his mind felt freer, not locked in the horror of the past week. Both of his sisters had told him they wanted him to play. They were tired of reporters coming by the house and asking about their brother's status.

"Go out and play," Monica told him. "We want to watch you on television again."

Van Gundy spoke to Camby before practice and advised him not to rush his decision.

"I don't want you back until you feel you can play effectively," Van Gundy told Camby. "If something changes with you between now and game time, please let me know. I don't want to put you out there in a position to fail."

May 1

For the past two days, Sprewell and Jackson had become increasingly vocal. With Johnson out for the series and Houston not about to raise his voice, Sprewell repeatedly reminded his teammates about the importance of closing out the Raptors in Canada and not facing a decisive game at the Garden. Sprewell knew he'd be running miles in the next series tracking Iverson. He wanted—needed—a few days off to get ready for him.

Van Gundy picked up on his readiness. He knew Sprewell was ready to go for the kill. He remembered his speech the day before Game 5 against Miami in the 1999 playoffs. "They're right down the hall and they're going to be down the hall in 24 hours," Van Gundy had told the team. "You wanted them? Well, they're still going to be there. What about you?"

At that point, Van Gundy had glanced at Sprewell and saw his fierce, menacing eyes glaring back at him. Van Gundy knew Sprewell wanted to beat the Heat badly. Houston's shot would save the Knicks' season and Van Gundy's job, but Sprewell's ferocious play made the biggest impression on Van Gundy.

So, in words he used only for special players like Ewing and Oakley, Van Gundy said on the eve of Game 4, "When we line up tomorrow, I know one guy who's going to be ready to win that game. That's Latrell." He didn't mention Houston, Rice, Camby or even Ward. The implication was clear: He wasn't sure if the rest of the Knicks were ready to bring that killer instinct to the game.

"To me, Latrell embodies what can help you win tight games," Van Gundy told *Bergen Record* columnist Adrian Wojnarowski. "He's unafraid to take big shots and live with the consequences. And he's not scared of competing against other great players. He doesn't shrink. And those are things that you never know about until you get in those situations."

If this was meant as a motivational kick in the pants to Houston, the timing was surprising. Houston had lit up the Raptors, averaging 20.3 points in three games. He had a fresh spring to his step and crispness in his jump shot.

"I'll tell you one thing," Houston said after practice. "I'm not going to go back and watch tapes from three weeks ago. I'm sure a lot of people were worried about me."

Jackson, too, had emerged as a leader. He had found it more difficult than he expected to be a vocal presence early in his second stint with the team. He wanted to fit in and not step on anyone's toes. He didn't want Sprewell and Camby to mistake his orations for arrogance. He wasn't joining a mediocre club where he could say, "This is the way to do it." But now he felt comfortable enough in the locker room to speak up. The Knicks had obtained Jackson with the playoffs in mind.

Camby, meanwhile, seemed in the right state-of-mind. He was anxious to play and see what he could do.

Toronto was the tense team. After the Raptors practiced, Oakley, during an interview with the writers, challenged Carter. He was tired of the team's star not accepting greater responsibility when the team lost and acting as if he was just another role player.

"All the plays go through Vince, so it's not too much focus on Vince," Oakley said. "You can't shy away from it now. This is the time you've got to step up and be a man about it. When they went to play for the Dream Team, he went. All 12 of us didn't go. When they do a commercial, we don't go, he goes. It's one of them things."

On the surface, Oakley was trying to motivate Carter. But deep down, he felt Carter had been coddled by Raptors coach Lenny Wilkens and the entire organization because they feared he was going to leave as a free agent after the 2001-02 season. If anyone in the organization was going to prod Carter, it would have to be him.

May 2

At the morning shootaround before Game 4, Carter answered questions about Oakley's challenge.

"He's always in my ear," Carter said. "I love it. What am I supposed to do? Hide from him now? Not at all. That's his way of telling me, 'We're behind you.'"

Stealing a page from the Hornets, who had donned white head-bands in their stunning first-round sweep of Miami, several Raptors came out for the pre-game warmups wearing purple headbands. Carter wore one, too. It was a sign of unity.

On the first possession of the game, Carter sliced through the heart of the Knicks' defense and through the lane, getting two steps on Sprewell. Carter's eyes bulged as he saw a clear path to the basket and slammed down a wicked windmill slam dunk. The Knicks watched in awe. As surely as the Knicks had set the tone in Game 1 when Thomas rejected Carter's dunk attempt in the opening minute, Carter's rousing jam had created the same aura in Game 4. The power dunk lifted the Raptors' fans out of their seats as pandemonium reigned.

Sprewell was horrified, not merely because Carter had caught him by surprise, but because none of his teammates had moved over to confront the soaring Carter. Houston and Jackson watched Carter's dunk without budging.

Camby started the game aggressively, attacking the basket and soaring for the first rebound of the game. The Raptors' crowd, which still held a grudge against Camby, booed him during introductions and chanted, "Camby sucks" in the first quarter. Camby was no factor in the second half and finished with four points and four rebounds in 32 minutes. Childs, meanwhile, scored 25 points, his career playoff high. After a timeout in the first quarter, he jawed in Jackson's face. At another juncture, Childs walked near the Knicks' bench and toppled over a plastic container of gum.

The Raptors won, 100-93. The Knicks' season would come down to Game 5 at the Garden.

"The bottom line is we didn't want to be in this position, but we are," Sprewell said. "So what are we going to do? Are we going to snap out of it and get the job done? We played all year for homecourt advantage and now is our time to go out and take care of the home court."

The Raptors had played with desperation. The Knicks had played as if they still had one more game to take out the Raptors. Which they did.

May 3

Van Gundy and Knicks officials had warned the Purchase College hierarchy a week ago that they might need the gym for their most important practice of the season, May 3, if they had to play Game 5. The Purchase College circus arts class, nicknamed Clown College, had a performance in the gym scheduled for that day. The college told the Knicks there was nothing it could do. The Knicks would be allowed to practice in a smaller adjacent gym, which didn't have a regulation-sized court.

The Knicks believed this was payback. Purchase College officials were upset over the Knicks' decision to abandon them in two years for a state-of-the-art facility in Greenburgh, 15 minutes away. Unable to scrimmage because of the size of the gym, the players watched film for an hour and shot free throws.

"It's not how you would have drawn it up in your coaching manual," Van Gundy said about practicing in the tiny gym.

The scene was surreal. One loss away from a first-round knockout, Van Gundy addressed the media, drowned out by the music and applause from the circus show next door.

Sprewell stood on the other side of the gym, still ticked off after watching the tape of Game 4, particularly Carter's dunk. Van Gundy pointed out the breakdown during the film session, but there wasn't much for him to say. Any basketball novice could see that the Knicks had fallen asleep at the wheel.

"We had three guys sitting right there that didn't even move," Sprewell said. "Somebody has to take a foul or take a charge, one way or the other. It was ridiculous, guys just sitting there watching him wind up and dunk the ball like that."

Sprewell believed the time for coddling Camby was over. They needed him to have a big game tomorrow night. No more excuses. Sprewell would be in his ear the next 24 hours getting him pumped up for Game 5. He knew better than anyone that the Knicks were nothing more than an average team when Camby was not at his best. But Camby had played only three games in three weeks.

Post columnist Kevin Kernan asked Sprewell where he expected to be Sunday, when Game 1 of the second round was played.

"I expect to be in Philly," he answered. "I think this team has a lot of heart, a lot of character and a lot of pride, and I wouldn't accept anything less than that."

May 4

Jackson's clean-shaven head was more significant than any statement Van Gundy could make at the morning shootaround. He had shaved himself bald the night before. Jackson had gone hairless during most of the Pacers' run to the Finals in 2000, so he decided to break up the tension and get his teammates joking again.

"You look like Charlie Batch," Rice told Jackson.

"More like a bald-headed snake," quipped Camby. Another Knick called him "The Golden Child." Jackson's little daughter's said, "You're a bowling-ball head."

"This isn't a good-looks contest," Jackson said. "This is war. I want the guys to look at me and say, 'Hey, this guy couldn't care less about how he looks. I also want them to loosen up, have fun."

Van Gundy, caught up in his own, tiny basketball world, didn't notice Jackson's bald head during the shootaround. "You guys are kidding, right?" Van Gundy said after being told about Jackson's hairless pate following the morning shootaround.

Van Gundy had given Ward a pep talk before the shootaround. Ward, seemingly diverted because of the religious furor, had just six assists and five turnovers in the first four playoff games. In the fourth quarter of a tight game, Van Gundy was prepared to go with Ward over Jackson for defensive purposes.

"Nobody can have more impact on the game with hustle plays than you," Van Gundy told Ward, envisioning a frantic final minute during which a Ward steal could win the series.

■ ■ ■

In the moments after the pre-game introductions, Johnson was a lively, cheerleading presence. Still unable to play and wearing a gray suit, Johnson hugged Camby and whispered in his ear about winning the game for his sisters. Johnson clapped and screamed at his mates to take the game from the start. If only they could win this one game, Johnson felt he could be back for the second round.

The Raptors wore their purple headbands again. The Garden crowd was as souped up as it had been at any time this season. Wilkens told the Raptors in the locker room, "It's just another place to play. Don't do anything differently. There's no need to be frightened. Just play ball."

Camby got off to an energetic start. He banged home a 12-footer from the right side on the Knicks' first possession. He blocked a shot and drew a charge in the first two minutes. His body and spirit were at the Garden this time, not in South Windsor.

A heckler wearing an orange-and-blue "Cat in the Hat" getup waved his orange towel at the Raptors' bench and screamed, "This is New York, baby. It ain't gonna happen here in the Garden!"

In the second quarter, Oakley chased a loose ball that sailed out of bounds. Van Gundy caught the ball. Oakley playfully dug his elbow into Van Gundy. Oakley's shove landed Van Gundy on the press table. Oakley smiled, but Van Gundy did not.

The Knicks were wracked with foul trouble in the first half. Thomas, Camby and Houston each picked up a quick two. Harrington came in and picked up three fouls in one minute, 20 seconds. With 1:43 left in the half, Houston picked up his third foul on a play away from the ball. He had barely touched the Raptors point-guard-turned-shooting guard Williams as he came off a pick.

Sprewell's 15 points at halftime, mostly on penetrations through two or three Raptors at a time, kept the Knicks close, down 49-43 at half-time. On the opening possession of the third quarter, Childs penetrated the lane, Thomas stepped up to help out, and Childs twirled a perfect bounce pass to a wide-open Antonio Davis underneath for an easy layup.

Houston picked up his fourth foul early in the third quarter after doubling Childs and leaving Williams free at the three-point line. Williams drained the 20-footer as Houston slapped him on the wrist for a continuation foul. Williams then hit the free-throw to give the Raptors a 54-45 lead. The Knicks were completely out of sync.

Late in the third quarter, after a timeout, Van Gundy put Ward into the game. "I want you to take control of the team," Van Gundy barked at him. Layden had obtained Jackson for these playoff moments, but Van Gundy had planned on Ward running the floor for the fourth quarter.

Rice threw up an airball from the right wing with 30 seconds left in the third quarter and the Knicks trailed, 70-59. All the missed practice time was starting to catch up to him. The Knicks rallied to within two, 73-71, in the fourth quarter. Ward took a pass behind the three-point line and was wide open for the shot. The Garden crowd was ready to forgive and forget once and for all. Ward's shot clanged off the rim. On the next possession, Ward made a wild drive through the lane and threw up a runner that bounced off the glass, missing the rim completely. Carter came down and hit a three-pointer, giving the Raptors a 76-71 lead with 6:48 remaining.

Camby fouled out with 6:15 left when he was called for a questionable blocking foul as he helped out on a Carter drive. Although he showed less spirit in the second half than he had in the first, Camby had a respectable game with 11 points and eight rebounds in 32 minutes. But he was far from the dominating presence he had become during the season.

The Knicks were down, 78-76, before Houston, playing with five fouls, again broke down on the defensive end. Williams drilled a three-pointer over his outstretched hand with 4:50 to go, putting Toronto ahead by five points. The Knicks clawed back to 81-80 with Sprewell and Thomas leading the charge. Childs, showing the poise of a point guard who had led the Knicks through many wars, faked a three-point shot, dribbled past Ward, pulled up at the top of the key and nailed a jump shot with 3:30 remaining, giving the Raptors an 83-80 lead. There were no smirks, no taunts, just a cool, professional executioner's look on Childs' face.

Although he was clearly winded from keeping up with Carter, Sprewell would not give up. With 2:29 left, he slithered through three Raptors, first Williams, then Childs, then Oakley, to barrel in for a layup and trim the deficit to 85-83. Sprewell intercepted Childs' pass but, with a chance to tie the game, missed a jumper from the left of the lane.

Carter missed a jump shot, then snuck in behind the defense to retrieve the loose ball and put in a layup as Ward and an exhausted Sprewell watched. The score was 87-83 with 1:19 remaining. The crowd became stone silent. Van Gundy's face twisted in agony at Carter's hustle play and he waved his hand in disgust.

When play resumed after a timeout, Rice butchered a three-point shot from the right corner. At the other end, Williams lost control of the ball. Houston dashed for it, but Carter beat him to it. Houston then mistakenly doubled Carter about 40 feet from the basket. Alertly, Carter flung a pass to a wide-open Williams, who buried a 22-foot jumper with 42 seconds left to put the Raptors ahead by six, 89-83.

Ward rushed up to midcourt and hurriedly delivered the ball to Houston, standing a few feet away. It went right through Houston's hands. Williams snatched the ball and Sprewell intentionally fouled him.

There were 33.9 seconds left and the game was all but over. Sprewell threw up his hands, palms up, face twisted, looking toward Houston. His expression said it all: "Couldn't we have at least gone down fighting?"

Houston had just 10 points, two in the second half, before hitting two meaningless three-pointers in the final few seconds. Rice shot three-for-10 from the field. Exhausted from defending Carter all game, Sprewell wound up with 29 points and a broken heart. The Knicks lost, 98-89. Their season was over in the first round for the first time since 1991.

With five seconds remaining and the issue decided, Childs chatted up Spike Lee on the sidelines. After the buzzer sounded, he high-stepped to midcourt, slapping the ball with his right hand. Carter walked around the court with his right fist thrust into the air. Van Gundy walked through the tunnel with his head down. He had very little to say in a quiet locker room. The players sat by their cubicles in stunned silence. "Thanks for all your hard work" was all Van Gundy could muster.

In the interview room, Van Gundy was asked if this game and Game 6 against Indiana last spring showed that the Knicks couldn't win the big ones unless Houston was at the top of his game.

"I thought Sprewell was really good and I think it takes more than one player playing at his best," Van Gundy said. "Allan was in foul trouble. That's part of the game."

Sprewell walked into the interview room wearing a gray pinstriped suit and sky-blue-tinted Cartier shades. He sat down next to Van Gundy, who got up from his chair and punched Sprewell in the arm, a punch that said, "You did everything you could."

"I don't know what has to happen," Sprewell said when asked about the off-season. "The only thing I know is I left it all on that floor tonight and whoever comes here and plays and puts on the New York uniform, they should do the same thing. I don't know if everybody can really say that. I left it all out there and I'm exhausted right now. I don't know if everybody left it all on the floor."

The remark needed no interpretation. The finger was being pointed, mostly at Houston and partly at Rice. "There were times when I felt I had to carry the load for the team" Sprewell continued. "It was on my shoulders to try to carry us. I definitely needed some help. I was worn down from chasing Vince around and having to do it on the offensive end, too. I needed that one other guy to take the load off me a little bit, especially down the stretch."

Houston walked into the interview room as Sprewell was finishing the last sentence. Quickly changing the topic, Sprewell said, "It just wasn't in the cards for us tonight."

In the Knicks' locker room, Camby said, "We didn't give Latrell any help. He carried us the whole ballgame and no one stepped up to give him the help to get us over the hump. I had a bad two weeks and it just got worse today."

In the Raptors' ;, Childs shouted, "We won Game 5 in the Mecca. We did it in the Mecca."

Lenny Wilkens told his team, "It's good to be excited, but we still have another series to play." Philadelphia and the second round awaited.

Michele Carter, Vince's mother, who had ripped Oakley for criticizing her son, was crying in the hallway, her cell phone ringing with congratulatory phone calls amidst the hubbub. Childs emerged in a flashy white suit.

"I guess this was the reason I was traded," Childs said. "I came into this series and I didn't run off at the mouth because that's not helping the team. That's selfish."

The Raptors had a pillow fight on their charter flight to Philly while the Knicks headed back to their pillows in Westchester. Sleeping was impossible. Van Gundy stayed up watching an *Adam-12* marathon. Instead of giving them a day off to soak in the loss, Van Gundy had the players report the next morning for their breakup meeting and individual talks at Purchase. Van Gundy wanted to get it over with.

Sprewell arrived the earliest and met for 30 minutes with Van Gundy and Layden in the coach's office. Each player would have a post-season interview, with Van Gundy usually stressing to the players the importance of keeping in shape over the summer. The meeting with Sprewell was different, an emotionally-charged session in which the Knicks' superstar was given freedom to vent while Layden and Van Gundy listened carefully. Still wounded, Sprewell talked about the devastation he felt losing in the first round.

"I think we need to make changes because I don't want this to happen again," Sprewell said. "I want a ring."

He expressed his belief that they needed more size and toughness, and that the Raptors had exposed them for the undersized club they were. "I hope we have a shot at getting Chris [Webber]," Sprewell said to them. He said he was most disappointed by the loss because he truly felt the team got outworked by the Raptors in a do-or-die game. Layden explained to Sprewell that making major moves such as acquiring Webber would be difficult because of their salary-cap restrictions.

When he met with the writers, Sprewell held nothing back. He was still in shock and would be for the next two weeks. Again, he lobbied for changes. He had kept his mouth quiet for most of the season because he wanted to see if the perimeter trio of himself, Houston and Rice could work. After the bitter defeat, he now believed it would not work in the playoffs.

"We're a perimeter team," Sprewell said. "We have a bunch of guards on this team. We got away with it to a certain extent during the regular season, but I think at the end, the evil monster reared his head."

Asked about Webber, Sprewell said, "I don't know. I'm just hoping that happens. We need a guy like that. I don't know what the chances are." Asked if he would be willing to give up Houston and Camby for Webber, Sprewell said, "I think I would. I would hate to see it because I'm obviously close to some of the guys, but I'm all about winning. Right now, we have to make changes to get better. Personal feelings have to be set aside. They have to bring in guys who are going to help us get back to the Finals."

Sprewell was asked if the Ewing trade backfired. "Obviously, when you look back, we could've used him in this series," he said. "I don't know if the trade made sense. That situation is difficult. Patrick wanted out." With that, Sprewell walked out to his black Mercedes and rode away with no plans other than to build a recording studio in his basement. He wasn't going to Milwaukee to jet-ski the summer away for another five weeks.

One by one, the players filed out from their meetings and spoke with the writers in the Purchase gym. Johnson and Longley talked about retirement. Rice talked about the possibility of having surgery on his left foot. He thanked the writers for how they had treated him.

"You guys could've been really hard on me considering the kind of year it was," Rice said.

Jackson talked about the difficulty of watching the fourth quarter from the bench. "I believe that's the time I'm most effective," he said. Jackson had long been in Van Gundy's corner and respected him as much as any coach in the league. But this one decision he couldn't rationalize. Hadn't they traded for him just so they could use him in the fourth quarter of a deciding playoff game? Jackson felt using two point guards didn't work. The club had to make a commitment to either him or Ward. "You have to have somebody who's your guy," Jackson said. "If it's not me, so be it."

Houston was not surprised to learn that Sprewell had gone off again about the team needing changes. The two had not talked since the final buzzer. Houston became agitated when asked to comment on Sprewell's blanket accusation that not everybody had given their all.

"Point the finger in someone's direction," Houston said. "We're all frustrated. No one wants to go down like we went down. But if you're going to point fingers, point them. Don't point them in the air. It's a team sport. You win with five people, you lose with five people."

Camby was numb and spoke in clichés, without emotion. His sister would need more surgery on her wrist tendons. "These past two weeks, nobody's been through what I've been through," he said.

Camby then shrugged his shoulders. "I think we're a good basketball team. It just wasn't our year. It wasn't our turn to go all the way."

When Van Gundy finished his last interview, he came down to the gym and defended Sprewell's right to voice his opinion. He felt his bond with Sprewell was equivalent to the one he had with Ewing.

"There is no player I have felt closer to as far as being so committed to the goal of winning," Van Gundy said.

A year ago on Trash Bag Day, Layden had stood outside Purchase College in the sun and talked about needing Ewing for the team to get back to The Finals. The rain was coming down now, so Layden talked to the media horde inside the dank gym, standing against a padded wall. He said losing in the first round "doesn't cut it" and claimed to be set for "a busy summer." And then he walked out into the rain.

Epilogue

"Scott who?" Charlene Johnson asked over phone.

"Scott Layden," I said.

"Let me look at my list," Charlene said. "We've had so many calls."

A half-minute later, Charlene said, "Oh yes, here he is. Yes, he's on our list of phonebacks."

Attorney Charlene Johnson, Chris Webber's aunt and acting agent, was fielding a phone call from *The Post* on July 6, almost a week into the free-agent recruiting period. Webber never hired another agent. After all the talk, Webber planned to re-sign with Sacramento. The Knicks, who showered Webber with gifts, including a glass replica of Madison Square Garden, never had a chance.

By then, Dave Checketts had been fired by James Dolan on May 14. After failing to agree on a new contract, Dolan, incensed that the team did not have a public relations staffer with Ward during his bible-study session with the magazine writer, decided he wanted a tighter grip on the Knicks' daily operations.

With Mutombo a stalwart, the Sixers sailed to the Finals. The Lakers, after losing to the Knicks on April 1, captured 19 straight games en route to winning the NBA championship—without Glen Rice—in five games over the Sixers.

With Houston opting out of his contract to become a free agent and able to reject any trade, the Knicks had no choice but to re-sign him to the maximum six-year, $100 million contract on July 23. In August, the Knicks traded Rice to the Rockets for Shandon Anderson and Howard Eisley, after which Rice nearly flunked his physical.

Management shopped Charlie Ward around the league the entire summer. Ward never made it to Israel. Luc Longley and Larry Johnson retired. On the day Houston re-signed, Lori Hamamoto, who ran the Knicks public relations department, resigned.

The Patrick Ewing era was truly over.